The Mushroom Hunter's Field Guide

ALL COLOR & ENLARGED

Alexander H. Smith
and Nancy Smith Weber

The University of Michigan Press

Thunder Bay Press

Copublished with Thunder Bay Press 1996
Copyright © by the University of Michigan 1958, 1963, 1980
Color plates copyright © by the University of Michigan 1980
All rights reserved
Published in the United States of America by
The University of Michigan Press

1999   1998   1997   1996   5 4 3

Thunder Bay Press ISBN 1-882376-24-2

Library of Congress Cataloging in Publication Data

Smith, Alexander Hanchett, 1904–
    The mushroom hunter's field guide.

    Bibliography: p.
    Includes index.
    1.   Mushrooms—United States—Identification.
2.   Mushrooms—Canada—Identification.   I.   Weber,
Nancy S., joint author.   II.   Title.
QK617.S56   1980   589.2′097   80–10514
ISBN 0–472–85610–3

Printed in Hong Kong

Preface

In the last fifteen years handbooks on the fleshy fungi have appeared at an astounding rate due to an almost explosive public interest in mushrooms. This interest shows no sign of abating and, at the time of this revision, it seems appropriate to discuss the situation and the factors producing it. As we see it, there are four major factors that contribute to this awakened interest in mushrooms. Their use as food is the primary factor. To satisfy public demand, there has been a fantastic increase in the commercial mushroom crop in the last twenty-five years to the degree that mushrooms are an important part of the North American diet. As the price of fresh produce goes higher each year, the idea of being able to use a resource obtainable at low cost becomes even more popular. Our yearly crop of wild mushrooms, though admittedly somewhat unpredictable, is such a resource. Interest in wild mushrooms is also but one facet of the general interest in wild and natural foods.

The second factor is the advances that have been made in the third quarter of the century in man's knowledge of the toxins present in fleshy fungi. Two aspects of this development directly relate to the awakened interest in mushrooms as food: as we learn more about these toxins and their action, there has been a concomitant improvement in the care of those who contract mushroom poisoning; and as our knowledge of the different types of poisonings increases, so does our ability to predict which species are likely to be toxic. The intelligent collector can learn to avoid certain kinds and greatly reduce the risk of serious poisoning. We also now know that even within a species, different populations and even different fruiting bodies within a population may vary in the amounts of toxins present. Some mushroom toxins have become valuable research tools in studying how certain parts of living cells work. An interest has also developed in using some mushrooms as "recreational" drugs.

Third, with the expansion of suburbia has come an increase in the number of cases of mushroom poisoning of an accidental nature. Grassy lawns like parks and golf courses have a special mushroom flora. New residential areas where many of the original forest trees remain will have mycorrhiza-forming fungi as well as lawn fungi. Such a situation has the potential (often realized, as we found in our own yard) of producing a crop of mushrooms that includes some of the most poisonous species. Children in the "grazing stage" are the chief victims of these situations. When this *Guide* was first published, most hospitals lacked access to information on how to handle such cases, but this is no longer true. We have included many of the common lawn species, but it is impossible to include all kinds that *might* be found.

The fourth factor is the worldwide advance in the scientific aspects of man's knowledge of fleshy fungi, particularly in the last fifteen years. The amount of published material is voluminous and expensive. This material is often difficult to obtain even for specialists, since library budgets have not increased to keep up with the increase in volume and cost of publications. There has been a flood of "new" genera and species described, and much has been added to our knowledge of already-described genera and species. There simply has not been time to evaluate this material properly. Systematic mycologists, however, are trying desperately to catalog the world's mushroom resources before the undisturbed habitats are all destroyed. The old cliche "It's later than you think" is, unfortunately, all too true. The amateur's dream of a book "with all the species in it" is unrealistic and it will be years before we realize the goal of one name for each kind of mushroom. In this *Guide* we have maintained many of the older generic names, such as *Cortinarius*, in their classical concepts. This approach has the advantage of allowing many of the larger genera to be recognized at sight in the field.

This edition is an all color one, unlike its predecessors. We hope the exclusive use of color photographs will make it easier for the user to verify identifications and improve the usefulness of the *Guide*.

Acknowledgments

We wish to express our appreciation to the following people for aid in the preparation of this revision of the *Guide*: Dr. George Hatfield of the Department of Pharmacognosy of the University of Michigan read the manuscript and made valuable suggestions. Dr. James A. Weber of the University of Michigan Biological Station contributed the photographs of *Calvatia gigantea*, *Cortinarius armillatus*, *Lycoperdon pyriforme*, *Tricholoma aurantium*, *Scleroderma flavidum*, and *Amanita virosa*. Dr. K. A. Harrison contributed the photograph of *Galiella rufa*. Dr. D. Simons contributed the photograph of *Amanita phalloides*. Dr. Helen V. Smith of the Matthaei Botanical Gardens of the University of Michigan assisted in the preparation of the manuscript.

Contents

Introduction

This edition of *The Mushroom Hunter's Field Guide* should be useful throughout the United States and Canada, but users should remember that each region has certain species peculiar to it, and it is impossible to include all of them here. The coverage is best for the Northeast, Great Lakes region, Rocky Mountains, and the Pacific Northwest. We have tried to include most of the truly fine edible wild mushrooms, whether they are common or rare, as well as the most dangerous ones in order that collectors may recognize them for what they are. Some mediocre edible species are included to emphasize that there is no rigid classification into "bad" and "good" species; these terms represent the extremes. In addition, emphasis has been given to kinds found at seasons of the year not generally regarded as good for collecting fleshy fungi. Finally, a few species are included because they are attractive or are objects of special interest.

Beginners should start their study of mushrooms by becoming familiar with the parts of a mushroom (the fruiting body) and the terminology used to describe them. Look through the photographs and study the introductory materials as a first step. Next, collect some specimens and practice using the keys (see p. 21). Do not expect to identify all the species in this *Guide* with equal ease. Some kinds are easy to identify and others are not. Since the species treated in this *Guide* were selected from over 3,000 kinds of mushrooms known to grow in North America, many species will not be treated here.

It is very important for the beginner to learn to be accurate in his/her interpretation of the characters. The user must be responsible for interpreting the characters and for the identifications made therefrom. Neither the authors nor the publisher accept responsibility for the identifications made by users of this book or for the consequences of eating any of these species.

The Mushroom Plant

Mushrooms belong to the group of organisms known as fungi, and, for our purposes, the fungi are regarded as plants. However, fungi are unlike the common green plants both in form and function. The green plants are initial builders of organic compounds and use the sun as their energy source. These compounds are used by all other organisms including fungi as their energy source and basic building materials. The mushroom plant, called the spawn or mycelium (plural: mycelia), is well adapted for its role. The mycelium consists of a mass of threadlike structures called hyphae (singular: hypha) that are about 2 to 15 μm (micrometer; 1 μm is 0.001 millimeter) in diameter. The hyphae are so fine they can be seen by the naked eye only when they become twisted into strands or aggregated into a fluffy mass (mold). There is very little apparent organization in the mycelium—the hyphae grow out from the spore, branch repeatedly, and finally produce a mass of threads. The edge of the mat is the actively growing area; growth continues as long as the growing tips of the hyphae come in contact with new supplies of suitable food. The hyphae secrete enzymes that digest food material outside the hyphae (unlike humans who secrete most of their digestive enzymes into a stomach and associated organs). Once the digested material is in solution, it can be absorbed by the hyphae and used by the fungus.

After a mycelium has accumulated a supply of food, if conditions are proper, it produces reproductive bodies called spores. The spores of mushroom-producing fungi are formed on the mushrooms (called the fruiting bodies of the fungus). Fruiting bodies are somewhat analogous to the familiar garden fruits, and spores, like seeds, serve to distribute the species and perpetuate it. Mushroom spores are typically small, unicellular, and are produced on special parts of the mushroom such as the gills, teeth, and pores. When the spores are mature they are usually forcibly discharged, and are carried to new locations by air currents. Only a small percentage of spores ever survive to establish new mycelia and subsequently to produce more mushrooms. If a spore lands in a suitable habitat, under the proper conditions it sends out a germ tube (a hypha produced by a germinating spore). The germ tube begins the process of secreting enzymes and absorbing nutrients. Gradually the germ tube elongates into a hypha which branches into a new mycelium. When this new mycelium has grown and produced mushrooms, it has completed one turn of the life cycle (pattern of living and reproducing) of the mushroom organism.

The only evidence that a particular kind of mushroom-producing fungus is present in a particular habitat is the mushrooms themselves. The mycelia of most mushrooms are too similar to be distinctive. Since different kinds, or species, have different requirements for fruiting, all the species in an area do not fruit at the same time. Thus, when studying the mushroom flora of a region, one must collect in all the habitats repeatedly over a number of years and in different seasons when trying to make a reasonably comprehensive survey of the mushrooms of the area. As one collector expressed it: "Hunting mushrooms is a never-ending game of poker."

As far as future crops are concerned, picking mushrooms has no more effect on the mushroom organism than picking apples has on the survival of the tree. It is impossible to strip an area of its established mycelia by simply gathering their fruiting bodies.

When and Where to Find Mushrooms

The problem of when and where to find mushrooms can be considered in terms of the local factors determining fruiting and the general problem of the distribution of a species. On the local level, when and where mushrooms fruit is closely related to the availability of food materials, the presence of suffcient moisture, and the occurrence of favorable temperatures. Airborne spores are the principal means of dispersing fungi and also the major means of colonizing new habitats. As yet, no way is known by which the spores of a given species can "choose" to settle in particular places; however, judging by the production of mushrooms, many fungi are "choosy" about where they will grow. Also, in a given habitat, several kinds of mushrooms may be fruiting at the same time. The phenomena of habitat selectivity for a given species and species diversity within a habitat are both related in part to the interrelationships of the moisture, temperature, and nutrition requirements of the fungi involved.

The mycelium of a mushroom-producing fungus must have sufficient moisture to grow and accumulate food reserves before it can form mushrooms. Once sufficient food is accumulated and fruiting bodies have been initiated, more moisture is needed to trigger their enlargement, which is often rapid. This rapid enlargement of preformed fruiting bodies is one reason that some mushrooms appear very soon after rains. The requirements for moisture in terms of amount and timing differ from species to species and in part determine why different species of mushrooms fruit at different times.

Temperature follows the seasons—cold in winter, warming in spring, warm to hot in summer, and cooling in fall. As for moisture, different fungi have different temperature requirements that must be met before they will fruit; thus some species fruit predominantly in the spring, others in the summer, and so on. Just how temperature and seasonality exert their effect is not known, but by observing the seasonal fruiting patterns in an area a collector can improve his/her chances of making a good harvest.

Fungi can utilize a variety of materials for food; in the case of mushroom-producing species the mode of nutrition is generally inferred from observing where the mushrooms are produced. For example some species, such as the oyster mushroom, produce their fruiting bodies on wood and decay it. Such species are termed lignicolous or wood-inhabiting. Some wood-inhabiting species are evidently restricted to hardwood, others to conifers, and a few occur on both types. Species that first attack a piece of dead wood are said to cause "primary" decay (the first decay); they partially break down some of the compounds in the wood and are followed by other species that cause "secondary" decay, i.e., that utilize the partially decomposed materials for food. Consequently, as the components of the wood are changed through the activities of the organisms on it, new species become established and old ones may die off. This is a type of succession, and the successful mushroom collector knows to watch for the right kinds of logs in the right stages of decay for the mushrooms he/she seeks.

Many fungi live in the duff or humus on the forest floor and utilize fallen twigs, needles, leaves, and the remains of dead plants as their food source; others thrive in lawns and meadows. Species whose mycelium grows in the ground are termed terrestrial species. The difference between lignicolous and terrestrial species is important to the collector, since the lignicolous species may persist on a given log for only a few years until the food reserves are exhausted, whereas the terrestrial species may persist for as long as new food materials are added to the habitat. It has been established from the size of fairy rings and the rate they enlarge each year that some mycelia are as much as 400 years old. Thus the location of good "spots" for such species is of considerable interest to collectors, and knowledge of such spots is often jealously guarded.

Various other types of materials can be utilized by mushroom-producing fungi. For example, *Hypomyces lactifluorum* parasitizes mushrooms. Many other species grow on dung and manure or soils that are heavily manured. The fairy ring mushroom grows in grassy areas and may be partially parasitic on the grass. A few species, e.g., *Laccaria trullisata*, fruit in sandy areas that apparently lack any type of humus, but they have a different source of nutrients, as we shall see.

For the mushroom hunter, perhaps the most important "life style" of mushroom-producing fungi is the mycorrhizal association. In this association, the fungus mycelium lives in the humus but is attached to the rootlets of certain trees and/or other plants. The combination of a plant rootlet and fungus hyphae is called a mycorrhiza. The relationship is evidently beneficial to both parties; however, the pattern of passage of compounds back and forth in a mycorrhizal association is not well understood. A single tree may (on different roots) form mycorrhizae with several species of fungi, and there is increasing evidence that many of the plants in a forest are interconnected through these mycorrhizal networks in the soil. The aforementioned *Laccaria*, apparently growing in pure sand, may have a mycorrhizal relationship with the beach grasses in the area. These associations are important to the mushroom collector because certain mushroom species are regularly associated with certain genera, or even species, of trees. Consequently, one can predict where to find a species of mushroom by studying the distribution of its host tree. Furthermore, since trees are generally more conspicuous than mushrooms, knowing various tree species and their associated fungi can help collectors locate likely habitats for particular species.

The Distribution of Mushroom Species

In terms of the distribution of a species, it has become apparent that just as there are recognizable associations of higher plants which give the countryside much of its character, there are also sets of mushrooms that characteristically occur together in specific regions. Each region, such as the Pacific Northwest, the Great Lakes, or the Gulf Coast, is the focal point for a large and rather characteristic mushroom flora. There are species that, based on our present state of knowledge, are restricted to a single region, whereas others are widely distributed and occur in most parts of North America. The latter group, if they were flowering plants, would probably be dubbed "weeds." The important point to keep in mind is that the known distribution of all species will probably be enlarged as areas not previously studied are investigated. Consequently, collectors should concentrate on finding and becoming familiar with likely habitats for the species that interest them rather than relying on lists of previous sightings to guide their collecting. As one mushroom hunter said: "Mushrooms are where you find them."

Collecting and Identifying Mushrooms

The equipment for efficient mushroom collecting is relatively simple and inexpensive. A large market basket is a good container for carrying collections. A hunting knife with a strong blade that can be used for cutting and prying specimens from logs or digging them out of the ground is useful, but a small trowel can also be used. Wrapping each collection in waxed paper permits some air circulation around the specimens and helps prevent them from "stewing" as they may do in plastic bags on a hot day. A hand lens or pocket magnifier is useful for making observations on small fruiting bodies or checking details on larger ones. Learn to use and always to carry, a pocket compass. A whistle is good optional equipment—if one is lost one can blow a whistle longer than one can yell, and the sound carries better—but it is hoped the whistle will never be needed if the compass is used properly. For comfort, insect repellent is often necessary, and of course anyone planning to spend time in the woods should learn to avoid the poisonous plants and animals of the area. In the Great Lakes region more mushroom hunters collecting in bogs are poisoned by poison sumac than by the mushrooms they find.

Once mushrooms are located, the next step is to gather them in such a way that no important information is lost. Dig up the base of the stalk; do not cut it off at ground level, or important characters may be left behind. Wrap all the specimens that appear to be of the same species in a single package—this is a collection. As more collections are added, place the heavier ones on the bottom of the basket and the lighter, more fragile ones on top. For each collection note how the specimens grew, i.e., clustered or scattered, on wood, duff, mucky soil, manured soil, and so forth. Special considerations on gathering mushrooms for food are discussed in the section on edibility.

Identifying wild mushrooms is perhaps the greatest challenge facing mushroom hunters once specimens have been found. Frustrations will be frequent, since there is no book on all the mushrooms of North America in spite of over 150 years of mycological activity. It is estimated that there are about 3,000 kinds of mushrooms in North America; only a small fraction of them are discussed in any book. Persons beginning the study of mushrooms should use as food only those species they can identify with confidence and that are recommended in this or other reputable books.

Some species, such as *Morchella esculenta* and *Calvatia gigantea*, can usually be identified accurately the first or second time they are encountered, and beginners should start with such species. However, each kind of mushroom is not distinguished from all others with equal ease. It may be necessary to collect some kinds repeatedly before one feels that one "knows" the species. Taking classes or attending field trips led by competent instructors are good ways to start learning mushrooms.

Variation within a species complicates the problem of mushroom identification. For example, how much variation is allowed in the color of the cap of specimens referred to as one species? It depends on the species and the person asked. The "experts" debate such matters at length. According to many mycologists (people who study fungi), the fly agaric, *Amanita muscaria*, can have a white, yellow, orange, or red cap, while in other groups the difference between a red and an orange cap might be sufficient to place the specimens in different species. Such problems are hard to treat in field guides and are refinements in outlook that come with experience.

Size of fruiting bodies is another variable which often causes confusion. To some extent it is affected by the available food supply. Wood-inhabiting species, when growing on sawdust piles, often produce large clusters of large fruiting bodies. When growing on dead trees, the fruiting bodies of the same species may be solitary and much smaller. Consequently, size is not emphasized other than to give a general idea of the dimensions usually encountered.

Sterility can produce some striking changes in fruiting bodies that may make identification difficult and bring grief to the unwary. In the brick cap, *Naematoloma sublateritium*, the gills of normal specimens are dark gray brown at maturity, but in sterile specimens (ones where no spores are produced) they are brilliant yellow. In one case some competent collectors ate *Chlorophyllum molybdites* thinking they were eating *Lepiota rhacodes*. They were aware of the need to determine the color of the spores (for a discussion of spore color see p. 11) and had set up a cap for a spore deposit in the evening. The next day they checked it, decided the deposit was white, and ate the mushrooms. Unfortunately they became ill, and after being released from the hospital they brought some of the specimens into the office to find out how the mistake happened. It took us several hours and many sections of gills to find two basidia, each with four olive green spores attached, which confirmed that the specimens were *Chlorophyllum molybdites* but were essentially sterile.

The process of making an identification is not necessarily a smooth one. If one is collecting mushrooms for food, any specimens that do not conform to the proper pattern for the species in question should be discarded. One acquaintance expressed it succinctly: "When in doubt, throw it out."

The Mushroom Fruiting Body

A glance at the photographs reveals that there are many variations on the basic pattern of a mushroom fruiting body. The pattern—stalk, cap, and gills—is well adapted to producing spores efficiently. The stalk serves to elevate and support the cap. On the underside of the cap are thin, radiating blades of tissue called gills. The surface of the gills is covered with a palisade of microscopic club-shaped cells called basidia (singular: basidium) that typically have four prongs at the apex (fig. 3*). A spore is typically formed on each prong. When the spores are mature they are forcibly ejected from the basidia and are carried away on air currents before eventually settling on the ground or other surface. The palisade of basidia that covers the gill surfaces is called the hymenium, and the part of the fruiting body that bears the hymenium is the hymenophore (in this case the gills). All fungi in which the spores are borne on basidia are called Basidiomycetes, or basidium-bearing fungi.

The variation in size, color, texture, and shape of the cap and stalk are fairly obvious characters of importance when one is identifying mushrooms. Less obvious at first are the gills, but they too can be important. For example, gill color may be indicative of spore color, but not always—as shown for *Hygrophorus kauffmanii*, in which white spores are produced on almost coffee colored gills. A less tricky character is gill spacing. A comparison of the gill spacing of three white species of *Lactarius*, *L. piperatus* (crowded gills), *L. neuhoffii* (close gills), and *L. subvellereus* var. *subdistans* (sub-

---

*References to numbered figures throughout this volume refer to the illustration of microscopic characters on p. 301.

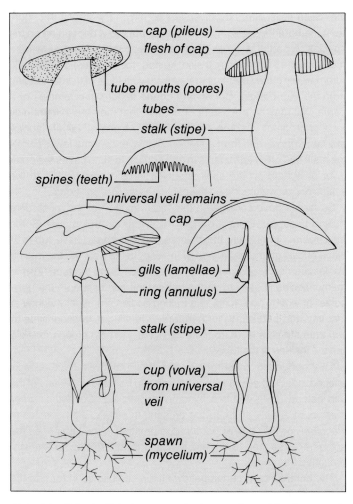

distant to distant gills) shows one instance where this character is very useful in distinguishing species. Finally, the manner in which the gills meet the stalk, called the attachment, may vary. In some genera such as *Amanita*, *Agaricus*, and *Pluteus*, the gills typically are free from the stalk. In others, the gills may be attached to the stalk in some manner; for example, *Phylloporus* and *Chroogomphus* have decurrent gills, *Tricholoma* has notched gills, and *Collybia* has bluntly attached gills.

Some mushrooms have one or more layers of tissue called veils that protect the developing hymenium from drying out and from mechanical injury. There are two major types of veils: the universal or outer veil that covers the entire young fruiting body, and the partial veil that extends from the edge of the cap to the stalk. In species with a universal veil, the veil is broken as the young mushroom expands. The veil may break in a variety of ways. If it is tough, it may break at a single point and the veil remnants will form a cup (the volva) around the base of the stalk as in *Amanita virosa*. If it is brittle, it may break into many small pieces which may persist on the cap and/or around the base of the stalk without forming a cuplike volva, as in *Amanita muscaria*. If it is powdery, the veil remnants may soon wither and be difficult to find on mature specimens.

A partial veil covers only the gill cavity where the gills are developing. Such veils, like the universal veil, may vary greatly in texture from membranous to slimy, fibrillose, or powdery, depending on the species. A partial veil may break at the cap margin and remain attached to the stalk leaving a skirtlike ring (the annulus) on the stalk. Alternatively it may break at the stalk leaving flaps of tissue hanging from the cap margin. Depending on the texture, the remains of a partial veil may be persistent or so faint that they are evident only for a short time. In some species the two types of veil are apparently intergrown and form a stockinglike layer over the lower part of the stalk that often terminates in an annulus. In such cases the outer layer or sheath on the stalk is similar in color and texture to the scales or ornamentation on the cap (see *Pholiota squarrosa*).

So far we have considered the "basic model" of the mushroom fruiting body, but there are many variations on this model. Some mushrooms, principally the boletes and polypores, have tubes in place of gills on the underside of the cap. In the boletes, the fruiting bodies are fleshy and generally decay readily, and the tube layer in many species is easy to separate from the cap tissue. In the polypores, or woody pore fungi, the fruiting bodies are usually woody at maturity and persistent; furthermore, it is difficult to impossible to separate the pore layer from the cap tissue. In both groups, basidia line the insides of the tubes.

The hedgehog mushrooms and their relatives have closely spaced, needlelike spines or teeth hanging from the underside of the cap instead of gills or tubes. In some species, e.g., *Dentinum repandum*, both a stalk and cap are present; in others, e.g., species of *Hericium*, neither a stalk nor a cap is present. In the latter case the spines are attached to a mass of tissue (a tubercle) or to a much-branched framework.

The coral fungi in general show little resemblance in form to the groups discussed so far. In these fungi the fruiting body is basically a simple (cylindrical or clublike) or branched upright structure whose surface is covered with the hymenium. There are no devices in this group to protect the developing hymenium—even a cap is absent.

The puffballs and their allies are perhaps the most diverse and bizarre group of conspicuous Basidiomycetes. In many of the true puffballs the fruiting body itself is modified to project the mature spores into the air currents; in some of the other groups insects or small mammals may be important in dispersing the spores. It is the spore-producing tissue in the interior of the fruiting body that is edible in many immature puffballs. The stinkhorns are often smelled before they are seen; their slimy spore mass attracts flies, beetles, and other organisms interested in rotting meat. The insects carry the spores away on their bodies.

Some mushrooms belong to a second large group of fungi, the Ascomycetes. In these fungi the spores are formed in long sacklike or sausagelike cells called asci (fig. 4). The spores of the species we mention are typically squirted out of the asci at maturity—sometimes in such numbers as to form a visible puff of "smoke." The fruiting bodies of such Ascomycetes are completely different from the basic mushroom model discussed previously. Most of the Ascomycetes we illustrate have fruiting bodies that are basically shaped like a cup or bowl or are apparently modified from this basic form, i.e., a stalk may be present and the cup may be inverted and wrinkled. These fruiting bodies are technically called apothecia (singular: apothecium); the subgroup of Ascomycetes with such fruiting bodies is called Discomycetes or cup fungi. Generally the hymenium is on the upper exposed surface of the apothecium in Discomycetes. Consequently, Discomycetes can generally be distinguished from Basidiomycetes without using a microscope to determine how the spores are formed. For example, if an unknown fungus has distinct gills, teeth, pores, or is branched and coral-like, it is almost certain to be a Basidiomycete. If it is cup- or saucer-shaped with the cup "upright" (not hanging down like a bell without its clapper) it is likely to be a cup fungus, especially if the flesh is fragile. If the unknown is jellylike and more or less flat to cup-shaped and grows on wood, it might be either a Basidiomycete (a jelly fungus) or a Discomycete. If it is stalked and has a distinct upper portion (in place of a cap) that is wrinkled, pitted, lobed, or a combination of these, it is likely to be a Discomycete. Finally, if the fruiting body is unbranched, small (usually less than 5 cm high), and club-shaped, it may be hard to determine whether it is a simple coral fungus, a small *Clavariadelphus*, or a Discomycete such as *Mitrula elegans*. In such cases, all alternatives should be checked and the descriptions and illustrations studied carefully before deciding on an identification.

Spores

Many people have expressed an interest in having information on the microscopic features of mushrooms. A detailed consideration of such characters is outside the scope of this book; however, spores are relatively easy to study with a microscope, and they frequently are useful in confirming or rejecting a tentative identification. The information on spore characters is auxiliary to the field data; in most cases careful attention to the field characters will be sufficient to make an accurate identification if the mushroom in hand is in this book.

Most fungous spores are too small to be seen without the aid of a microscope; for the species we discuss they are mostly in the range of $3-30$ μm in length and consist of a single cell. Both Basidiomycete and Ascomycete spores function in reproduction and dispersal, but there are significant differences between the two types of spore.

In Basidiomycetes that actively discharge their spores from the basidia, the color of the spores in mass, as determined from a spore deposit, is an important character. In mushrooms with a distinct cap, a spore print or deposit is made by cutting off the stalk and placing the cap with the gills, tubes, or spines down on a piece of white paper. For species without a cap, lay the fruiting body on a piece of white paper with the hymenium down. Then wrap the setup in waxed paper or cover it with a cup or bowl to prevent the mushroom from drying out. If the specimen is fertile and mature, spores will be discharged from the basidia and will be deposited on the paper; in a few hours there will be a sufficient accumulation of spores so their color can be judged. If after four to eight hours there are no signs of a white to distinctly colored powder under the specimen, do not assume the spores are white—they may be immature or the specimen might be sterile. Be sure spores are present before deciding on their color! If the spores are likely to be white, place a wedge of dark paper under part of the cap to make it easier to determine whether or not a deposit has been made. The color of the deposit is determined after allowing the paper to dry in the air for about ten minutes after the specimen is removed. Sometimes one can get some idea of spore color in the field by looking for a dusting of color over the apex of the stalk, on the annulus, on a cap which developed under another of the same species (this often happens in clusters), or on the duff around the specimen—especially if the specimen has a short stalk. Spore color can also be guessed at from the color of the mature gills, but as was mentioned for *Hygrophorus kauffmanii*, this method is often unreliable. For the puffballs and their allies, the color of the mass of mature spores is used as a standard for determining spore color.

Tests for the presence of certain chemical compounds can be performed on spores from a deposit. For example, if the spore wall contains starch, it will stain dark blue to violet in iodine solutions and is then said to be amyloid. One way to determine whether spores of a given species are strongly amyloid is to scrape up a small pile of spores from a print, place them on a piece of clear glass such as a glass slide or spot plate, add the iodine (we use Melzer's reagent, p. 306, but tincture of iodine will also work), and check the color after about five minutes. Hold the glass slide over a piece of white paper to check the color; do not test the spores directly on the paper as the paper itself may give a positive reaction.

If a microscope is available, especially one with an oil immersion lens, much more can be learned about the spores. Size can be determined, preferably from spores from a deposit since such spores are presumed to be mature. Shape is also important; several common shapes are shown in figs. 9–15. Basidiomycete spores have a small projection, or apiculus, as it is called in most mushrooms, where the spore was attached to the basidium. In the puffballs, the point of attachment is often a stubby projection called a pedicel. At the apex of some spores (the end opposite the apiculus) there may be a clear spot called the pore. Germination typically occurs through the pore in species that have pores. Many spores are ornamented (figs. 6–9), and the pattern of ornamentation is often important in distinguishing one species from another. In some genera such as *Russula* and *Lactarius* the ornamentation is amyloid and is best studied on spores mounted in iodine solutions. In other groups, such as the Cortinariaceae, the spore ornamentation does not stain selectively and is more difficult to study.

In the Ascomycetes, the spores are produced in asci and typically forcibly discharged from the asci at maturity in the species we illustrate. Unlike basidia, the characters of asci are often important in distinguishing one genus or even one species from another. In the early morel the asci typically contain only two spores at maturity; however, in *Verpa conica* and most other species we include, the asci typically contain eight spores at maturity. The means by which the asci open when spores are released, i.e., by a lid (operculum) that flips back or by a pore, is important in classifying these fungi. Species with an exposed hymenium and operculate asci are grouped together in the operculate Discomycetes; those with an exposed hymenium and whose asci open by a pore are grouped into the inoperculate Discomycetes. Most of the conspicuous species of interest to mushroom hunters belong to the former group. Asci in some groups may stain blue to violet in iodine solutions, and the occurrence and pattern of such reactions is another important character in distinguishing genera.

As in the Basidiomycetes, spore size, shape, and ornamentation are important characters in the Discomycetes. However, since the fruiting bodies of many Discomycetes are small, it is generally difficult to judge the color of the spores in mass; thus, except for species with spores that are highly colored individually, spore color is not emphasized. Ascomycete spores lack both an apiculus and a pedicel and are frequently symmetrical or nearly so. Furthermore, few Discomycete spores will give an amyloid reaction in iodine. Many Discomycete spores contain one or more oil droplets that are visible as bright globular bodies in the spore. When these droplets are present, their arrangement and relative size may be important characters. Finally, the spores of many inoperculate Discomycetes may be divided into two or more cells, in contrast to the Basidiomycete mushrooms, in which the spores are unicellular.

Edible or Poisonous?

Thousands of people in North America have been eating and enjoying wild mushrooms safely for years. It has been said that there are old mycophagists (mushroom eaters), bold mycophagists, but no *old bold* mycophagists. The secret to becoming an old mycophagist is care in collecting, identifying, and preparing the mushrooms, coupled with moderation in eating them. Old mycophagists generally avoid known poisonous species, thus lessening the probability of becoming seriously, even fatally, poisoned. They soon learn that there are *no* empirical tests that will distinguish "good" from "bad" kinds (or "mushrooms" from "toadstools"). After the known poisonous species are eliminated from consideration for eating, there is no practical way to predict which of the remaining species, even those generally rated edible, one can safely eat except by testing them individually. The idea that such empirical tests exist is the worst booby trap into which a mycophagist can fall. Bold mycophagists often rely on such tests, and much of our knowledge of poisonous species is the result of their philosophy.

Our comments on edibility are predicated on having the collector and consumer of wild mushrooms observe certain precautions. These are as follows: (1) Eat only one kind at a time so that if any difficulty should develop, the cause is known. (2) Eat only young or freshly matured specimens free from insect larvae (worms) and decay. The presence of worms should be suspected if there are pinholes in the flesh of the mushroom; often the worms themselves are all too obvious. (3) Cook the specimens well. The edibility ratings may not hold for raw specimens. (4) Eat only small amounts when testing a species for the first time. Do not overindulge under any circumstances. There is always a danger of indigestion from eating too much of any food. (5) Have all members of the family test each new kind for themselves. (6) The most important precaution, however, is to be critical when selecting specimens, making sure they are correctly identified.

Especially when one is collecting mushrooms to eat, it is difficult to overemphasize the need for care in collecting and identifying specimens. Many kinds of mushroom may fruit in a small area, particularly during a good season when many species are fruiting. The late C. H. Kauffman found 100 species of *Cortinarius* in a 160-acre woods in a single day, and Helen Smith once found about 50 species representing several genera under an isolated Douglas fir tree. It is under such conditions that the careless collector is almost sure to make a mistake. Observe each specimen critically to be sure it has the characters of the species to which it is thought to belong. Dig up the base of the stalk to check for the presence of a volva. When collecting puffballs, cut them in half longitudinally (probably at home so the flesh stays clean) and discard any that might be button mushrooms—some *Amanita* buttons and stinkhorn eggs are superficially similar to certain puffballs. When, and only when, the necessary details have been carefully checked should the dirt and unwanted parts of the fruiting body be trimmed away. Mushrooms are difficult to clean once dirt works into a mass of specimens. Keep each kind of mushroom separate. This practice helps build one's critical knowledge of the subject and forces the collector to examine each specimen carefully. When it comes time to sample the harvest, only one species should be tried at a time, and then in small amounts. Not only do people's tastes vary in regard to what species they like, but also their tolerance of different species may vary.

In the section on edibility in each description, a variety of ratings are mentioned. The best species, in our opinion, are those rated "edible and choice." To the best of our knowledge, most people can eat cooked material of these species in moderate amounts safely and with enjoyment. Such species should have a pleasing flavor and consistency and should be easily identified. Obviously, few species meet all of these requirements, and it should not be surprising that out of a mushroom flora of more than 3,000 species in North America it is difficult to find more than a couple of hundred that meet most of these requirements. However, just as certain foods such as eggs or chocolate may upset some people, some people may have adverse reactions even to the edible mushrooms. Ultimately, it is the responsibility of the user of this book to decide which mushrooms to eat and which to avoid, and to accept the consequences.

Low on the edibility scale are the "edible but not recommended" and the "not recommended" species. Many harmless species cannot be recommended for eating because they have an unpleasant flavor or consistency, very small fruiting bodies, or are superficially similar to known poisonous species and often cannot be reliably identified using field characters. (Pairs of similar species where one is edible and the other poisonous are called "look-alikes.") Some species are included in the "not recommended" category because they are poisonous unless processed in a certain manner. Other species have been reported to be edible by some authorities and poisonous by others and thus have a doubtful reputation, while still others cause illness only in some people.

The final category is that of "poisonous." Over the years knowledge of which species are poisonous has been built up through the study of case histories of people who became ill after eating wild mushrooms. There are degrees of poisoning, called intoxications in the technical literature, that range from mild discomfort to severe and even fatal illness. We are often asked why the edibility of all wild mushrooms has not been scientifically evaluated, perhaps using laboratory animals. Unfortunately, several of the common laboratory animals have digestive systems different enough from that of humans that the animals can tolerate species that are poisonous to people. For the same reason, just because a wild mushroom has been gnawed or partially eaten by a wild animal, it does not mean that a person could eat the mushroom with impunity—for all we know, the animal may have become ill and died!

When collecting is good and a favorite species is abundant, many people preserve wild mushrooms for later use by drying, canning, freezing, or pickling. No matter which method is used, start with firm, fresh, insect-free, preferably young fruiting bodies. Since mushrooms are nonacid, canning should be done in a pressure cooker to avoid the danger of botulism. Mushrooms may be frozen either raw or partially cooked. Drying can provide excellent results for many species. A commercial home food drier is satisfactory, or one can be made fairly easily and cheaply. A set of screens arranged one above the other, with a sheet of flame-proofed canvas around the frame (to obtain the effect of a chimney) and a hot plate at the bottom as a source of heat, is all that is needed. Use the lower temperature settings on the hot plate in order not to overheat the material. Overheating causes the tissues to collapse and results in an inferior product. Overheating is often a problem when ovens are used as driers. The specimens should be sliced into reasonably small pieces to allow for good air circulation and rapid drying. Once dried, the mushrooms should be stored in closed jars or sealed plastic bags. Dried mushrooms mold readily and become infested with insects if not properly stored; some people store their dried mushrooms in a freezer to avoid these problems.

We have been emphasizing the positive aspects of eating wild mushrooms; however, it is important for mycophagists and potential mycophagists to have some idea of what is involved with mushroom poisoning. Two books on poisonous mushrooms that go into detail on the subject are listed in the reference section, so this discussion is deliberately generalized. If it is likely that mushroom poisoning has occurred, call a physician, since he/she is best qualified to distinguish true mushroom poisoning from an attack of the flu or other inconvenient ailment. If mushroom poisoning is diagnosed, the physician will almost certainly want to know what species was eaten, since there are about seven commonly encountered types of mushroom poisoning known from North America, and treatments for the different types are different. Thus, when experimenting with new species (to the mycophagist) of wild mushroom, put a few specimens aside as insurance. If problems develop, such specimens will usually make identification more rapid and hasten the start of correct treatment, thus improving the victim's chances for a rapid recovery. If no physician or poison control center can be reached and the symptoms appear within about six hours after eating mushrooms, first aid methods to empty the victim's stomach are generally advised, but they should be followed up with a consultation with a physician as soon as possible. Never place yourself in the position of practicing medicine unless you have a license to do so.

The types of poisoning discussed below are roughly in order of decreasing severity, and the classification is based on the symptoms and the poison. As more data is accumulated, the list of poisonous species becomes longer and longer.

Cyclopeptide poisoning. The first symptoms of this type of poisoning appear from about ten to fourteen hours after the mushrooms were eaten, but they may be delayed as many as forty-eight hours. The symptoms include nausea, vomiting, and bloody diarrhea. Usually these symptoms abate, and the victim may feel so much better that he/she may even be discharged from the hospital. On the second to fourth day signs of liver, and sometimes kidney, failure appear. These are manifested by severe abdominal pain, jaundice, convulsions, coma, and sometimes death. Laboratory studies have shown that the toxin attacks the liver tissue within a few minutes of ingestion. This effect can be detected by studies of blood chemistry very soon after the mushroom is eaten, although the results of this attack may not be evident for a few days. This group of compounds is the cause of most fatal mushroom poisonings. At present there is no certain antidote for this type of poisoning, although with proper medical care most victims recover. If mushroom poisoning is likely, and the onset of symptoms is more than about six hours after ingestion, it has been recommended that the case be treated as if it might be this type of poisoning. Unfortunately for mushroom hunters, several common and attractive species contain the cyclopeptide toxins, i.e., *Amanita phalloides*, *A. bisporigera*, *A. virosa*, the *Galerina autumnalis* group, and *Conocybe filaris*. By learning these species and assiduously avoiding them, a lot of the danger from eating wild mushrooms will be eliminated.

Monomethylhydrazine poisoning. Monomethylhydrazine is a decomposition product of certain constituents of some false morels. The onset of symptoms is usually delayed from six to twelve (occasionally up to twenty-four) hours. The victim first experiences fatigue, headache, a feeling of fullness or abdominal pain, sometimes accompanied by watery diarrhea and cramps. In serious cases there are obvious signs of liver damage, loss of consciousness, delirium, and occasionally death. In our experience, children, possibly because of their relatively lower body weight and the consequent higher dose of toxin from eating a given quantity of mushrooms, often suffer the most severely. Proper medical care will generally prevent fatalities. However, there is no specific antidote as yet. Furthermore, there is mounting evidence, based on laboratory studies, that monomethylhydrazine is carcinogenic in laboratory animals. The principal species that are definitely linked with this type of poisoning are false morels: *Gyromitra esculenta* (in spite of its name), *G. ambigua*, and *G. infula*. Most of the species we place in *Gyromitra* have been suspected at one time or another of causing this type of poisoning, but we have not seen comparative studies on the chemistry of the other species based on well-documented, well-described, accurately identified material, and we hesitate to implicate other species. In addition, it should also be mentioned that the toxicity of *G. esculenta* appears to be quite variable. That is, in some areas the mushroom is evidently nontoxic, while in others it is definitely poisonous. Until this situation is clarified, we recommend that Gyromitras be avoided. Many accounts indicate that members of this group are edible after parboiling and discarding the cooking water; we believe it is safer simply to avoid these species, since there is no easy way to determine whether all the poison has been removed.

Muscarine poisoning. We come now to types of poisoning in which the symptoms appear relatively soon after the mushrooms are eaten. In this type, symptoms appear in thirty minutes to two hours; they include excessive perspiration, salivation, and tear formation, often accompanied by vision disturbances and abdominal cramps. The pupils of the eyes also become constricted. In addition to getting the remainder of the undigested mushroom out of the victim's digestive system and providing suitable supportive care, the physician may cautiously use atropine as an antidote. This is the only type of mushroom poisoning for which atropine should be used. In initially healthy adults who receive proper care, this type of poisoning is seldom, if ever, fatal. Muscarine is the principal toxin in several species of *Inocybe* and *Clitocybe dealbata*, and is present in small amounts in *Amanita muscaria* and *A. pantherina*. (In the last two species, muscarine *is not the primary toxin* involved in most poisonings; see below.) Muscarine is also suspected to be responsible for some poisonings by boletes and some species of *Hebeloma*. Poisoning by *Omphalotus illudens* is sometimes attributed to muscarine, but the symptoms are not typical, and further study is needed to clarify the situation.

Ibotenic acid and muscimol poisonings. Symptoms of this type of poisoning appear in thirty minutes to two hours and may include dizziness, lack of coordination, visual disturbances, muscle cramps, and deep sleep. Some people use mushrooms in this group "recreationally." However, the concentration of active compounds apparently varies widely in wild populations, and the effects of these mushrooms are difficult to predict. In addition, the personality and expectations of the individual eating the mushroom are factors in determining the effects of these compounds. We have had reports of people who ate *Amanita muscaria* and experienced "good trips" with no bad side effects, but others of "bad trips" that caused the users to seek medical treatment, and even one report from northern Michigan where a pale variant was eaten in considerable quantity with no effect at all! The toxins are seldom, if ever, fatal in basically healthy humans, although we have heard of one cat who apparently died as a result of eating a dried cap of *Amanita muscaria*. Treatment consists of ridding the system of the undigested mushroom and providing suitable supportive care. Commonly encountered species in this category include *Amanita muscaria* and *A. pantherina* (reportedly the cause of more cases of mushroom poisoning in the Pacific Northwest than any other species), and possibly *A. cothurnata* and *A. gemmata*.

Psilocybin and psilocin poisonings. This is perhaps the most controversial type of poisoning in that many people consider these species to be edible and seek them out deliberately for "recreational" use as hallucinogens, while other collectors shun them. The symptoms usually appear within an hour after ingestion and consist of alterations in mood and hallucinations followed by sleep, but characteristically not "deep sleep" like that following muscimol poisonings. In healthy adults the experience is seldom, if ever, fatal, but there are indications that children may experience more severe effects, including convulsions. At least one fatality has been attributed to this group. Again, ridding the victim's system of undigested mushrooms and providing supportive care is the usual course of treatment. It should be noted that possession of any material containing psilocin and/or psilocybin is illegal; permits for possession must be obtained from the federal Drug Enforcement Administration. Some states have additional laws further regulating the possession and transport of such mushrooms. Even unwary collectors intent on learning the local mushroom flora and not interested in hallucinogens run the risk of breaking the law in some areas, so check local regulations on the subject. Many books are available on the hallucinogenic mushrooms. Some species in this group are *Psathyrella foenisecii*, many species of *Psilocybe*, *Panaeolus subbalteatus*, *Gymnopilus validipes*, and *G. aeruginosa*.

Coprine poisoning. This type is easily avoided if one does not eat mushrooms and then drink alcoholic beverages for the next several days. If alcohol is consumed, flushing (especially of the head and neck), a metallic taste in the mouth, nausea, vomiting, and sweating may result. Recovery is typically spontaneous and occurs in two to four hours. This type of reaction closely parallels that of people on antabuse programs to treat alcoholism. Both coprine and disulfiram (or antabuse) interfere with the body's ability to break down acetaldehyde, a product of the metabolism of alcohol. Acetaldehyde is toxic, and the poisoning in both cases is from the accumulation of acetaldehyde. The prime culprit in this type of poisoning is *Coprinus atramentarius*, which contains high levels of coprine. Recently *Clitocybe clavipes* has also been shown to cause this general type of reaction. However, the active constituent of *C. clavipes* is unknown. Adverse reactions following a meal of wild mushrooms and one or more alcoholic drinks have been reported for many species, but most of these reports are not consistent with coprine poisoning and as yet are not well explained.

Gastrointestinal disturbances. This is a catchall for poisonings of the digestive tract in which the chemistry is not well known. A variety of situations are lumped into this category. Generally, symptoms appear within two hours of ingestion and may include nausea, vomiting, and/or diarrhea. In healthy adults recovery is often spontaneous, but in severe cases or where children, elderly persons, or persons in poor health are involved, supportive care may be necessary; let a physician decide. In any case, getting the undigested material out of the victim is usually the first step in treatment. Individual idiosyncracies such as allergies or metabolic peculiarities enter into this type of poisoning, and it is not unusual for one member of a family to be sickened by a mushroom that the rest eat without incident. It seems that almost every major group of fleshy Basidiomycetes that one might consider eating is represented in this category, and a listing of these species would include almost a quarter of the species in this book. However, a few notorious genera and species in this respect are: *Chlorophyllum molybdites*, *Cantharellus floccosus*, *Paxillus involutus*, *Laetiporus sulphureus*, *Lepiota naucina*, *Ramaria formosa*, and *R. gelatinosa*; several species of *Agaricus*, *Entoloma*, *Lactarius*, and *Tricholoma*; some blue-staining boletes; and even the morels.

In conclusion, it is emphasized throughout this guide that deadly poisonous and excellent edible species are the two extremes in wild mushrooms. Not many kinds are deadly, and not many stand out as excellent edible species. The danger is largely that some of the very poisonous species produce great numbers of fruiting bodies, are attractive, and are encountered frequently by collectors. The collector is gambling the price of a dish of mushrooms against the possibility of doctor and hospital bills. With such odds in mind, it is up to the collector to be critical of what he/she collects, and he/she must accept the ultimate responsibility for deciding whether or not to eat a given mushroom.

Mushroom Names

Many mushrooms are so little known to the general public that they do not have common names. Hence it seems best to emphasize the scientific names (given in Latin) in this *Field Guide*. Those who learn the scientific names at the beginning of their study will find them a great help in using the more technical literature as well as when using other popular books.

The scientific name for a species is composed of two words, for example, *Agaricus campestris*. *Agaricus*, as a name, applies to a group of species with certain features in common, i.e., free gills, purple brown spores, a ring on the stalk, and a readily separable cap and stalk. Such a group is called a genus (plural: genera). The word *campestris* designates the species of *Agaricus* under consideration, and is called the specific epithet. The name of the species, then, is composed of the generic name and the specific epithet—in this instance *Agaricus campestris*. When we mention the name of a man or woman we say John Smith or Ruth Smith. The generic name of a plant corresponds to the name Smith, and John and Ruth to specific epithets—they tell us which of the numerous Smiths are under consideration. When discussing a number of kinds of *Agaricus*, it is customary to abbreviate that generic name to the first letter (as *A. campestris*) if this will not cause confusion. However, if one were discussing species of *Agaricus* growing under species of *Acer* (maple trees), one would have to write out both generic names.

Species are grouped into genera; a group of similar genera is called a family. Family names typically end in -aceae, for example, Agaricaceae or Morchellaceae. A group of families constitutes an order, and the name of an order typically ends in -ales: Agaricales, Cantharellales.

While the scientific names often appear formidable, in most cases they are descriptive. For example, *Lactarius aquifluus*, when analyzed and translated, means "the milk mushroom with the waterlike fluid." Many specific epithets are adjectives, such as *albus* or white, *crassipes* or thick-footed. The meaning of many of the specific epithets is given with the species. You will see that many "common names" are actually translations of the scientific names. A specific epithet that ends in *-i*, *-ii*, or *-ae*, such as *Hygrophorous kauffmanii*, is named for the person who found the species.

How to Use the Keys

A key is merely a system of contrasting choices, usually arranged in pairs, which should enable the user to identify an object—assuming the object is included in the key. The keys in this book are designed to help the user identify mushrooms; they also emphasize important characters of the fungi of which the user should be aware.

Using the example of *Dentinum repandum*, we will demonstrate how to use the keys in this book. First look at the illustrations of that species (number 40): the specimens have a stalk, cap, and spines on the underside of the cap. Now turn to the first key—the one to "Major Groups of Fungi Illustrated." It begins with two statements numbered "1." Such a pair of statements is called a couplet. Read both choices of the couplet completely; they are contrasting statements. Decide which choice best fits the sample mushrooms; in this case it is the first of the two: "Fruiting bodies with distinct gills, pores, or pendant spines on the underside of the cap." Reading across to the right you are directed to proceed to couplet 2. Again read both choices and decide which is most appropriate. In this couplet it is the second choice that reads: "Fruiting body with pores or spines." Reading to the right, you are directed to the fourth couplet. Read both choices of the fourth couplet and decide which one best describes the specimen. In this case it is the one that reads: "Spines hanging down from underside of cap" and directs the user to the Hydnaceae. Turn to the key to the species of the Hydnaceae and continue in the same manner until the name of a species is at the right side of the best choice you make. Turn to the description of that species and compare the specimens with the description and illustration. If all the characters fit, the material should be correctly identified. The process is the same when you are working with fresh material, the only exception being that you begin not knowing the answer.

By now you have noticed that the second choice in many couplets reads "not as above." This is a time- and space-saving device. It simply means that if the specimens do not fit the first choice, the user should take the "not as above" choice. Do not guess at key characters. If your collection does not key out convincingly you should assume the species is not treated in this book. Some mushrooms will key out clearly to a species name, but may differ in some respect from the description and/or illustration. Such a situation usually indicates that several species have the same characters as presented in the key, but yours is not the one described and illustrated.

The technical terms used in the keys and elsewhere in the book are defined in the Glossary.

How to Read
the Species Descriptions

One problem that faces a beginner in the study of mushrooms is how to interpret the descriptions of the various species. In technical monographs of all the species in a genus, detailed descriptions of all parts of the fruiting bodies of each species are given. In this book we discuss only the diagnostic field characters that are important in making an accurate field identification. Many additional characters can be seen in the photographs.

Certain conventions have been followed in the descriptions. For example, we give the color of a fruiting body for the typical condition rather than including all known variations. Much the same policy is followed in discussions of size and shape of the fruiting bodies. Size is often given as a range, e.g., cap (9) 11–15 (17) cm broad. This statement means that most specimens have caps 11 to 15 cm broad at maturity, but mature individuals with a cap as small as 9 cm or as large as 17 cm may be encountered. Numbers in parentheses represent extremes, not the normal range. Dimensions are given in the metric system—μm or micrometers, mm or millimeters, cm or centimeters—because it is the system used in scientific work. When describing the shape of the cap or any other part, we start with the shape of the young cap and end with that of a mature cap, thus following the developmental changes of the fruiting body.

Various chemicals are mentioned in the descriptions (potassium hydroxide or KOH, Melzer's reagent, ammonia or NH_4OH). All of these are potentially dangerous—some may cause burns, holes in clothing, or poisoning if ingested. Consequently, all of these solutions should be kept in properly closed containers away from children and pets, and should be used sparingly and with care at all times. Since it may be difficult for the beginner to obtain some of the chemicals or to make up the solutions, chemical characters are not given as much emphasis in this work as they are currently in technical works.

Key to Major Groups
of Fungi Illustrated

1. Fruiting bodies with distinct gills, pores, or pendant spines on the underside of a cap 2
1. Not as above 6
   2. Fruiting body with gills 3
   2. Fruiting body with pores or spines 4
3. Gills sharp-edged, typically somewhat brittle ... (p. 114) Gilled Agaricales
3. Gills blunt-edged, narrow, often veinlike or resembling radial wrinkles .... (p. 72) Cantharellales
   4. Spines hanging down from underside of cap .... (p. 66) Hydnaceae
   4. Pores present on underside of cap 5
5. Fruiting body fleshy, soon decaying, stalked .... (p. 87) Boletaceae
5. Fruiting bodies typically tough to woody, typically persistent, stalked or shelving .... (p. 60) Polyporaceae & Fistulinaceae
   6. Fruiting body coral-like or club-shaped and broad at apex; spore-bearing surface smooth and exposed (see also *Mitrula elegans*) .... (p. 72) Cantharellales
   6. Not as above 7
7. Fruiting body a system of pendant spines arising from a framework of branches or a lump of fungous tissue .... (p. 66) Hydnaceae
7. Not as above 8
   8. Fruiting body more or less mushroomlike but with a layer of "pimples" (use a hand lens) known as perithecia present where the gills should be .... (p. 53) Hypocreales (*Hypomyces*)
   8. Not as above 9
9. Fruiting body cup- or saucer-shaped, fragile to firm, occasionally gelatinous .... (p. 26) Discomycetes (Cup Fungi)
9. Not as above 10
   10. Fruiting bodies soft and gelatinous when fresh or somewhat rubbery .... (p. 56) Auriculariales and Tremellales (Jelly Fungi)
   10. Not as above 11
11. Spore mass elevated on a delicate, somewhat alveolate stalk or stalks, slimy and foul smelling; immature stage an egg (the remains of the "egg shell" forming a volva when the stalk elongates) ....
.... (p. 294) Phallales
11. Not as above 12
   12. Fruiting body more or less stalked and hymenium borne on the upper surface (which is smooth to wrinkled or folded) of a head (or an inverted cup with sides hanging down); spores borne in asci (see also *Leotia lubrica*) ....
.... (p. 35) Morchellaceae & Helvellaceae
   12. Not as above (spores borne on basidia) 13
13. Fruiting body of many flattened upright branches in a large cluster; white to yellowish .... (p. 59) Aphyllophorales (*Sparassis*)
13. Not as above 14
   14. Fruiting body dark violet, usually compound; spore-bearing surface veined near the cap margin ....
.... (p. 60) Aphyllophorales (*Polyozellus*)
   14. Not as above 15

15. Fruiting body agaric- or bolete-like, but gills or tubes not oriented properly for spore discharge (hymenophore mostly folded and contorted to form chambers) .... (p. 277) Secotiaceae
15. Spores borne *in the fruiting body* or fruiting body resembling a small nest or vase with "eggs" (peridioles) in it which contain spores ....
.... (p. 281) Selected Gasteromycetes

Ascomycetes

Discomycetes (Cup Fungi)

This is a large and taxonomically difficult group of Ascomycetes characterized by having an exposed hymenium on a somewhat fleshy fruiting body. The fruiting body is essentially disc-, saucer-, or cup-shaped or a modification of one of these basic types. It ranges in size from only a few millimeters broad to 15–20 cm broad. The true morels and false morels are Discomycetes; however, they are treated in separate keys except for a few species with cup- or saucer-shaped fruiting bodies. Only some of the Discomycetes that might interest the field mycologist are included here. Aside from a few of the large species, a microscope and technical literature are needed for making identifications, and even then the task is difficult.

Key to Species

1. Fruiting body with an expanded caplike portion and a distinct stalk (mushroomlike but without gills); dull ochraceous to tan or tinted with green or olive .... 1. *Leotia lubrica*
1. Not as above 2
    2. Fruiting body with a bright salmon orange to orange or yellow club-shaped fertile portion and a white to whitish stalk .... 2. *Mitrula elegans*
    2. Fruiting body cup-, urn-, or saucer-shaped varying to somewhat flattened 3
3. Lining of the cup brightly colored (yellow, orange, or red) 4
3. Lining of the cup duller in color (reddish brown, tan, brown, purple brown, or nearly black) 6
    4. Lining of the cup scarlet; exterior whitish; cup 1–4 cm broad; typically on decaying hardwood debris such as half-buried branches .... 3. *Sarcoscypha coccinea*
    4. Lining of the cup orange to yellow orange or orange yellow; fruiting bodies typically not associated with decaying wood 5
5. Fruiting on conifer duff; lining of the cup yellow to orange yellow; exterior dull to bright green .... 4. *Caloscypha fulgens*
5. Typically fruiting on disturbed soil; lining of the cup orange to reddish orange; exterior white to orange .... 5. *Aleuria aurantia*
    6. Lining of the cup nearly white to pale tan; flesh staining yellow where injured; typically fruiting in basements or cellars, on ashes, plaster, coal debris, or similar material .... 6. *Peziza domicilina*
    6. Not as above 7
7. Fruiting body urn-shaped; lining of the cup dark brown to nearly black; exterior paler at first .... 7. *Urnula craterium*
7. Not as above 8
    8. Fruiting body rubbery; flesh gelatinous; exterior dark brown to nearly black .... 8. *Galiella rufa*
    8. Not as above 9
9. Base of fruiting body often prolonged to form an off-white to pale cream color stalk with distinct ribs which extend onto the exterior of the cup .... 17. *Helvella acetabulum*
9. Base of fruiting body lacking sharp-edged ribs, sometimes appearing gathered or folded 10

Leotia lubrica   1

Identification marks   The tough, gelatinous fruiting body may be mistaken for a basidiomycete at first glance, but the lower surface of the "cap" does not bear the spore-producing layer. Actually, the hymenium covers the upper surface. The color varies from dull dingy ochraceous to tan or at times has a green to olive tone. The fruiting body is 4–10 cm tall, and the fertile portion is 1.5–3 (5) cm broad.

Edibility   Not recommended. It has been said to be palatable, but this is hardly high praise.

When and where   Scattered to clustered on soil or decaying wood, fruiting from summer to late fall, widely distributed. We frequently find a very robust dark olive strain that fruits in dense clusters in sandy soil or almost pure sand in the late summer and fall in Michigan. These clusters often develop buried in the sand.

Spores   16–23 x 4–6 μm, long and narrow, somewhat fusoid to slightly curved, smooth, containing several oil droplets.

Asci   8-spored, inoperculate.

Observations   The rubbery to gelatinous consistency and relatively small size, as well as color differences, serve to distinguish this fungus from the morels and lorchels. *Lubrica* means smooth or slippery.

1   *Leotia lubrica*   About one-half natural size

2   Mitrula elegans

Identification marks   The fruiting bodies are 2.5–8 (10) cm high, and at first glance remind one of some coral fungi. However, the sharp distinction between the fertile and sterile portions, the texture, and the manner in which the spores are formed show it to be unrelated to the coral fungi. In this species the fertile portion is bright orange to yellow or pinkish orange. The white or pinkish white stalk is often half in and half out of the water.

Edibility   Of no consequence.

When and where   It fruits on dead plant material, such as leaves and twigs, at the bottom of shallow pools as well as on mud or mosses, from spring to early summer in the southeastern United States and from early spring to as late as September farther north. It is widely distributed in eastern North America and in the Pacific Northwest. One frequently collects it to the accompaniment of the hum of mosquitoes.

Spores   11–17.5 x (1.5) 2–3 μm, narrowly cylindric to clavate, more or less straight, one- or two-celled.

Asci   8-spored, inoperculate.

Observations   This is one of three North American species which have been lumped under the name *M. paludosa*. Current opinion is that the "true" *M. paludosa* does not occur in North America. *M. elegans* and *M. lunulatospora* (with spores 11–19 x 2–4 μm and somewhat curved) are the two common North American species. *M. elegans* characteristically has its "feet" in the water and may form large colorful patches in transient woodland pools and on wet areas in early spring. The genus name means small miter; the specific epithet, as expected, means elegant.

3   Sarcoscypha coccinea
(Scarlet Cup)

Identification marks   The fruiting body is saucer-shaped to shallowly cup-shaped, the size of a quarter to a silver dollar. The exterior is whitish, and there may be a short stalk. The consistency is firm to tough rather than brittle.

Edibility   Not recommended. It is thin and tough, and one seldom finds enough to make a meal. The taste has been recorded as pleasant.

When and where   Like the skunk cabbage among the flowering plants, the scarlet cup is one of the harbingers of spring. In Michigan it starts fruiting in early April in the southern tier of counties, and in the Upper Peninsula, during late seasons, it can still be found near the end of May. We have not seen it during the summer, but have seen it in Tennessee in March. It is widely distributed in the hardwood areas east of the Great Plains and is usually found attached to fallen branches partly buried in the humus.

Spores   28–34 x 10–13 μm, oblong to ellipsoid, often blunt (truncate) at the ends, smooth, content homogeneous.

Asci   8-spored, inamyloid, operculate.

Observations   The fruiting period begins long before the trees leaf out, usually about the time the first wild flowers start to bloom. The fruiting bodies are quite persistent and may last several weeks if the weather remains cool. *Sarcoscypha* means fleshy cup; *coccinea* means a deep bright red.

2 *Mitrula elegans*   About one-third natural size

3 *Sarcoscypha coccinea*   About one-half natural size

Caloscypha fulgens   4

Identification marks   The bright to pale orange to orange yellow lining of the cup and the greenish tones that usually develop on the exterior, especially near the margin, are characteristic. The cups vary from symmetric to asymmetric and may even be slit down one side.

Edibility   Not recommended.

When and where   This is typically an early spring species which fruits about the time the morels fruit. It occurs in coniferous forests on damp soil across the continent, but is sporadic in its fruiting habits. It favors northern and montane conifer forests, but in Michigan we have found it a few times in great abundance in cedar swamps.

Spores   5–7 μm in diameter, globose, smooth, content homogeneous.

Asci 8-spored, inamyloid, operculate.

Observations The generic name means beautiful cup; the specific epithet means bright colored.

4   *Caloscypha fulgens*   About one-half natural size

---

5   Aleuria aurantia
(Orange Peel Fungus)

Identification marks The striking bright orange color of the fruiting bodies is usually the first feature noted. The fruiting bodies are shallowly cup- or saucer-shaped, and are often split around the margins in age. They may be up to 7 cm broad. The exteriors vary from orange to almost white.

Edibility Edible and reported to have a pleasant flavor; when dried and revived it tends to be tough.

5   *Aleuria aurantia*   About one-half natural size

When and where   Scattered to clustered, sometimes in large quantities, on bare earth along paths, old roads, and other recently disturbed soil. It may occasionally be found in the spring and summer but, in our experience, it is most abundant in the late summer and fall. It occurs across the continent and is particularly common in the more northern and montane forested regions.

Spores   16–18 (25) x (8) 10–12 μm, bluntly fusoid to somewhat ellipsoid, distinctly reticulate with the reticulum 1.5–3 μm high and forming prominent projections at the ends.

Asci   8-spored, operculate, inamyloid.

Observations   This is both one of our most common cup fungi and one abundant enough to be of interest to the casual collector. Its bright color and tendency to fruit on exposed mineral soil are distinctive. *Aleuria* is derived from a word meaning flour, possibly a reference to flourlike granules present on the exterior of the cup in some species; the specific epithet means orange.

Peziza domicilina   6

Identification marks   The ghostly white or off-white fruiting bodies stain yellow when broken. There is a short stalk, and the cup itself is saucer-shaped or more flattened in age. At times the lining of the cup may be pale tan, especially in age. The fruiting bodies are rather fragile. The habitat on very alkaline materials such as ashes or plaster is also characteristic.

Edibility   We have no data on its edibility.

When and where   It occurs in houses in basements and cellars; occasionally in greenhouses on damp cement, plaster, or gravel; or around coal bins —it favors strongly alkaline (basic) habitats. We had a spectacular fruiting of this species on a bucket of fireplace ashes that overwintered under our porch. The following spring the area for three feet around the bucket was covered with the fruiting bodies; the bucket and the ashes in it also had fruiting bodies on them. The fruiting lasted several weeks.

Spores   13–15 x 8–9 μm, oval to ellipsoid, essentially smooth, at times containing two small oil droplets.

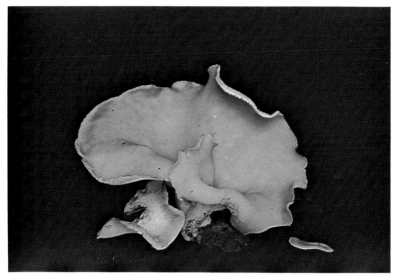

6   *Peziza domicilina*   About one-half natural size

Asci 8-spored, operculate, with a distinctly amyloid ring around the apex; walls in mass also slightly amyloid.

Observations The presence of this species often surprises householders since they are not expecting large fleshy fungi this close to home. *Peziza* is an ancient term which refers to a mushroom without a root or stalk; *domicilina* means of a dwelling or domicile.

---

7   Urnula craterium
(Urn Fungus)

Identification marks At first glance these fungi look like holes in the ground, but on further investigation each is found to be distinctly urn-shaped and to have a nearly black interior. The exterior is paler, usually dull pinkish gray when young, and becomes grayer to nearly black in age. It may have small flakelike patches over the surface. The stalk is darkest near the base, where there is a patch of dark brown to nearly black, soft to wiry mycelium.

Edibility Not recommended; the very tough consistency renders it unfit.

When and where In early spring in hardwood forests, solitary to clustered. It is usually associated with dead wood, either buried or exposed. It is one of the characteristic early spring cup fungi found east of the Great Plains and is often encountered by morel hunters.

Spores 22–37 x 10–15 μm, elongate-ellipsoid to sausagelike, smooth, content homogeneous.

Asci 8-spored, operculate, inamyloid.

Observations As indicated, the fruiting bodies are relatively tough and persistent. In southern Michigan it may appear in late April and often continues to fruit to mid- or late May. The generic name means a little urn; *craterium* refers to the shape, i.e., like a crater, a vessel used in antiquity in which wine and water were mixed.

---

8   Galiella rufa

Identification marks In contrast to many cup-fungi, this fruiting body is rubbery and gelatinous because of a jellylike interior. In a young fruiting body, the hymenium is enclosed, but by maturity it is exposed and brown to reddish brown. The exterior of the cup is densely felted with blackish brown hairs. The short stalk is often inconspicuous.

Edibility We have no data on its edibility; its rubbery-gelatinous consistency renders it unappetizing.

When and where On buried to partially exposed wood, especially small branches or slash from hardwood trees. The fruiting bodies are typically clustered and appear during the summer in the Great Lakes region as well as both eastward and southward.

Spores 19–21 x 9–12 μm, elliptic to oval, minutely roughened, content more or less homogeneous.

Asci 8-spored, operculate, inamyloid.

Observations This is a common but easily overlooked species, since it blends well with its surroundings. It was described from material collected in Pennsylvania. The masses of the fruiting bodies are often quite large. The genus honors Mme. Marcelle Le Gal of France; *rufa* means reddish in reference to the color of the hymenium.

7 *Urnula craterium*   About one-fourth natural size

8 *Galiella rufa*   About one-half natural size

Jafnea semitosta   9

Identification marks   These medium to large fruiting bodies have a firm
texture and long retain their cuplike shapes. The tan to pale brown interior
blends with the surroundings and is about the color of dead leaves. The exterior has sparse, short, brown hairs on it. The base appears "gathered"
rather than distinctly stalked.

Edibility   We have no information on it.

When and where   Scattered or in small groups on soil, usually under hardwoods; we usually find it on damp, relatively rich soil under aspen, jewelweed, or along small streams. It is common in the midwest, where it fruits
in the late summer on into fall, but is reportedly rare in New England.

Spores   25–33 x 10–12 μm, fusoid to fusoid-ellipsoid, distinctly warted, lacking prominent oil droplets.

Asci   8-spored, operculate, inamyloid.

Observations   This is one of the largest late summer and fall cup-fungi east of the Great Plains. It is easily overlooked, and consequently may be more common and more widely distributed than is currently known. It has a tougher consistency than most species of *Peziza*, the most common genus of large cup-fungi. *Jafnea* is a cryptonym based on the initials of Professor J. A. F. Nannfeldt of Sweden; *semitosta* means partially toasted, possibly a reference to its colors.

9   *Jafnea semitosta*   About natural size

Morchellaceae (True Morels) and Helvellaceae (False Morels)

As a group, these two families are more familiar to collectors than any other Ascomycetes. Both families include species with large conspicuous fruiting bodies that are readily recognized as members of these groups. However, some of the species are not so readily recognized as belonging in either family. Some of our best edible mushrooms as well as some poisonous species belong to these families.

Although the larger members of the two families can be separated into their respective families on field characters, spore characters are more reliable. In the true morels, the spores are essentially smooth, lack warts or projections at their ends, have a homogeneous content, and, depending on the species, have fifteen to sixty nuclei per spore. In the false morels the spores may be smooth but are ornamented in many species; projections may be absent or present; typically at least one distinct oil droplet (a shiny globule in the spore) is present; and the spores contain only four nuclei.

Both families include species such as *Disciotis venosa*, *Discina macrospora*, and *Helvella acetabulum* which are basically cup- or saucer-shaped and link up with the cuplike Discomycetes in form but have spores and anatomical features typical of these families. In both families the number of spores produced per fruiting body has been increased over that produced by simple cups by the apparent inversion of the cup and subsequent folding and pitting to increase the potential spore-bearing surface. The development of a prominent stalk completes the transition to the familiar morel or lorchel fruiting body.

We have keyed out the cup- to saucer-shaped species with the cup fungi based on their field characters. The larger morels and lorchels or false morels with a distinct stalk can be placed into the respective families as follows:

Key to Families

1. Having one or more of the following sets of characters: a) a distinct pitted to ridged fertile portion which is white to brown or black but not reddish brown to liver color; b) a thimblelike fertile portion attached to the stalk apex or ingrown with it part way with the remainder hanging free .... Morchellaceae
1. Having one or more of the following sets of characters: a) a lobed, often saddle-shaped fertile portion that is never truly pitted; b) a smooth to bumpy fertile portion, or, if pitted, then deep red brown; c) fertile portion yellowish tan to yellow brown, reddish tan to red brown, cream color, gray, or black; if dull brown then distinctly lobed and not pitted .... Helvellaceae

Morchellaceae (True Morels)

The true morels, or sponge-mushrooms, have a fruiting body consisting of a stalk and an enlarged apical part which is the fertile portion. The expanded fertile portion (which is covered with the hymenium) is often called a head or cap; however, we reserve the term cap for the basidium-bearing mushrooms.

The all-important point to remember about morels is that the fertile portion is pitted in most species. The nature and arrangement of the pits differs from species to species. Morels fruit in the spring, or, rarely, in the fall; in the mountains where "spring" comes late in the summer at high elevations they have been found as late as the middle or end of August. Because of the varied habitats in which morels are found, it does not seem likely that they form mycorrhizae with any of our trees or shrubs. Some species fruit in recent burns, others in cultivated soil, and the diverse habitats of *Morchella esculenta*, in particular, all argue against a mycorrhizal relationship with higher plants, or at most a generalized one.

Although morels are among the easiest mushrooms to identify to genus, deciding how many species occur in North America and what the correct names for them are is difficult at the technical level. Over fifty names have been proposed; however, it has been estimated that only about five "good" species of *Morchella* occur in North America.

Key to Species

1. Fertile portion with the lower third or more free of the stalk, i.e., skirt-like 2
1. Fertile portion and stalk continuous as seen in a longitudinal section; margin of fertile part not free 4
  2. Fertile portion attached only at apex of stalk 3
  2. Upper third to half of the fertile portion attached to stalk ......
  .... 13. *Morchella semilibera*
3. Fertile portion longitudinally ribbed or wrinkled ..... 11. *Verpa bohemica*
3. Fertile portion relatively smooth to merely undulating ...... 12. *V. conica*
  4. Fertile portion not black to blackish by maturity 5
  4. Fertile portion all or in part black by maturity or in age ....
  .... 14. *M. conica* & *M. angusticeps*
5. Fertile portion large, 6–12 cm or more high, usually more or less conic .... 16. *M. crassipes*
5. Fertile portion smaller than above and usually rounded rather than conic .... 15. *M. esculenta*

---

10 Disciotis venosa

Identification marks   The cuplike to saucerlike fruiting bodies may be up to 21 cm broad. The fertile surface is a rich chestnut brown or duller; the lower surface is often radially fluted or wrinkled and "gathered" at the center to form at most a short, ribbed stalk. The fertile surface by maturity typically has wrinkles radiating from the center; it may also appear pebbled or have a network of wrinkles or veins.

Edibility   Edible and choice; the flavor of cooked specimens is much like that of the true morels. The fresh fruiting bodies may have a slightly alkaline odor and taste. We have found that it does not take up as much butter when fried as do the morels.

When and where   Solitary to gregarious on damp soil in low hardwood forests during morel season, usually in May in the Great Lakes region. It is to be expected east of the Great Plains but is sporadic in its occurrence.

Spores   22–25 x 12–15 μm, oval, smooth, content homogeneous.

Asci   8-spored, operculate, inamyloid.

Observations   This species is recommended for table use only for collectors with the equipment to check the microscopic characters. There are a number of large brown cup fungi that might be confused with this one in the field. The specific epithet means conspicuously veined, a reference to the configuration of the hymenium.

10a   *Disciotis venosa*   About natural size

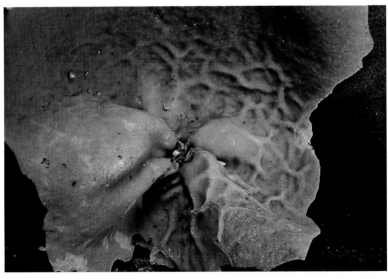

10b   *Disciotis venosa*   About natural size

11   Verpa bohemica
(Early Morel)

Identification marks   The fertile portion resembles a thimble on a finger with the two touching only at the tip of the finger. The surface of the fertile portion is folded or wrinkled with wrinkles that extend from the top down the sides; at times the wrinkles and cross veins may form elongated pits.

Edibility   CAUTION. For most people this is an edible and well-flavored fungus, but do not eat it in large quantities or every day for periods of several days. We have eaten it in both large and small quantities. When eaten in large amounts (two of us consumed a quart of cooked mushrooms at one meal), a definite lack of muscular coordination was noticed four to five hours later. When small amounts were consumed no symptoms of any kind were experienced. However, it would be dangerous for one who reacted to fairly small amounts of the early morel to drive a car three to six hours later. We have heard of a case in the Upper Peninsula of Michigan where a person became quite ill after eating mushrooms—apparently this species—for three consecutive days. So many people eat and enjoy this species, however, that it cannot fairly be labeled poisonous. It is often collected during morel festivals in Michigan.

When and where   It is the first morel to appear in the spring and usually fruits before the trees and shrubs in the area have leafed out. It favors rich wet soil along streams and on swampy ground but not in bogs. Its appearance varies with the season and the latitude. In the Great Lakes region it fruits from about April 9 to the first week in May. In the West it fruits in the stream valleys where hardwoods such as maple and cottonwood occur.

Spores   50–80 x 14–17 (22) μm, resembling long, slightly curved sausages, smooth, content homogeneous.

Asci   2-spored (rarely 4-spored), operculate, inamyloid.

Observations   Fruiting begins before the leaves are out on the trees and shrubs in the area, hence the common name. There appear to be two races of the species: one, often found under cottonwood on wet soil or in cedar swamps, of very large fruiting bodies 10–15 cm tall; and the "normal" (smaller) race usually encountered under brush at the edges of wet areas in southern Michigan. Some authors place this species in a separate genus, *Ptychoverpa*, because of the 2-spored asci. *Verpa* means a rod; *bohemica* refers to Bohemia.

11 *Verpa bohemica*   About two-thirds natural size

Verpa conica
(Conic Verpa)

12

Identification marks   The surface of the fertile portion is relatively smooth compared to that of the early morel. If it is wrinkled, there is little or no pattern to the irregularities of the surface. As in the early morel, the fertile portion is attached to the stalk only at the apex of the latter, and the sides hang free. The stalk is quite fragile, particularly in age.

Edibility   Edible. We know of no reports of problems with muscular coordination from eating this species, in contrast to the early morel. Also, during most seasons it is difficult to find enough for a meal.

When and where   It is found scattered to abundant under hardwoods, in stands of mixed hardwoods and conifers, and at times in plantations of conifers with broad-leaved shrubs as an understory. It usually appears a week or two later than the early morel, but one should expect considerable variation in this pattern. In the Great Lakes region it usually fruits just before the apple trees are in full bloom. We have found large fruitings under wild cherry trees, and, in particular, under old apple trees.

Spores   20–24 x 12–14 μm, oval, smooth, with homogeneous content.

Asci   8-spored, operculate, inamyloid.

Observations   If one has doubts as to which species of *Verpa* one has collected, a quick check of the number of spores per ascus and of the spore size will settle the matter. *Conica* means conic or pointed, somewhat of a misnomer in this instance.

12   *Verpa conica*   About natural size

Morchella semilibera
(Half-free Morel)

13

Identification marks   The fertile portion is attached to the stalk for about half the length of the fertile portion instead of at the extreme apex, as in the early morel, or for its entire length, as in the black morel. The surface is ridged and pitted in about the same way as the early morel, though as the ridges on *M. semilibera* dry out they tend to blacken somewhat and the fertile portion shrinks markedly. When young the half-free morel may have a relatively large fertile portion and only a short stalk, but as the specimen matures, the stalk enlarges and the fertile portion shrinks, thus reversing the "head"-to-stalk size ratio.

Edibility   Edible and of good flavor, but the stalks tend to be stringy when cooked. If one is sensitive to the early morel, one should not eat *M. semilibera* without checking to see that the asci are 8-spored.

When and where   *M. semilibera* fruits ten to fifteen days later than the early morel, usually after the leaves are out on such trees as the small-toothed aspen. It usually occurs on better-drained soil than the early morel. We have found it mostly in oak-hickory and beech-maple forests. Its range is about the same as that of the early morel.

Spores   20–30 x 14–18 µm, oval, smooth, content homogeneous.

Asci   8-spored, operculate, inamyloid.

Observations   In about one season in three, in southern Michigan, one can collect this species in sufficient quantity for table use. This species is sometimes placed in a genus of its own, *Mitrophora. Morchella* is an ancient name meaning morel; *semilibera* means half-free, referring to the way the cap is attached to the stalk.

13   *Morchella semilibera*   About natural size

14   Morchella conica & M. angusticeps
(Black Morel)

Identification marks   There is no appreciable free margin as a skirt on the fertile portion of the fruiting body, and the fertile portion is distinctly pitted with prominent, elongated pits delimited by vertical ribs and transverse ridges. When young, the entire fertile portion is grayish, but the ridges and ribs blacken by the time the spores mature, and by old age the entire fertile portion is often black.

Edibility   Edible but, as with all common edible fungi, some cases of gastrointestinal disturbances have been recorded, especially when alcohol has been consumed along with this species. We recommend against eating large quantities of it for several consecutive days.

14 *Morchella angusticeps*   About two-thirds natural size

When and where   The black morel is the common morel of the conifer as well as the aspen areas of North America. It is very abundant in the upper Great Lakes region and also occurs in the Pacific Northwest. It fruits early in the spring soon after, or at the same time as, *Verpa bohemica*. In central Michigan it is one of the important species sought during the morel festivals. There, it is scattered in the aspen-birch-balsam stands as well as under red pine, and is usually out when the serviceberry bushes are in full bloom.

Spores   20–25 (27) x 12–15 μm, oval, smooth, content homogeneous.

Asci   8-spored, operculate, inamyloid.

Observations   Both the names given above have been applied to the black morel. Which of these is the "correct" name will remain in doubt until types (standards of reference) have been established for the European species. *M. angusticeps* was described from North America, but the specimens may have been old ones in which the stalk had enlarged considerably and the fertile portion had begun to shrink. *Angusticeps* means narrow-headed; *conica* means conic.

   A second black morel occurs in western North America. The fruiting bodies are superficially similar to large specimens of the common black morel; however, the spores are (22) 25–30 x (15) 17–20 μm. This may be the *M. elata* of some European authors. At the present time, we are not sure which of the black morels are responsible for the reported poisonings, or whether both are.

Morchella esculenta   15
(Sponge Mushroom or Morel)

Identification marks   The fertile portion (the "head") varies from globose to elongate, and the distribution of pits over the surface is such as to break up the longitudinal ridges into a distinctly irregular pattern. The ridges themselves remain pallid to grayish or become pale cinnamon but do not blacken. As can be seen in a longitudinal section of a specimen, there is a continuous hollow from base to apex of the fruiting body. The stalk is pallid to cream color.

Edibility   Edible and choice; one of our most popular wild mushrooms, and one of the easiest to recognize at sight.

When and where   The habitats are diverse. It may fruit in old orchards; beech-maple and oak forests; lightly burned areas such as old grassland; lawns (rarely); and swampy ground under elm where there is a cover of jewelweed. May is the month for it in the central and eastern states. Many people look for it when the oak leaves are in the "mouse ear" stage of expansion. We have found this to be a good indication of the progress of the morel season.

Spores   21–25 x 13–16 μm, oval, smooth, content homogeneous.

Asci   8-spored, operculate, inamyloid.

Observations   This species is sometimes called the white morel, but the name is inappropriate. Fruitings often occur in the same area for several years, and the location of morel "spots" are often jealously guarded secrets. Appropriately, the specific epithet means edible.

15   *Morchella esculenta*   About natural size

16   Morchella crassipes
(Thick-footed Morel)

Identification marks   The fertile portion is conic and typically 6 cm or more high, the pits are very wide and irregular, and the whole fruiting body often assumes relatively gigantic proportions. Young stages are easily confused with those of *M. esculenta*. The opinion that *M. crassipes* is nothing more than a variant of *M. esculenta* is rather reasonable when one recalls the presence of giant variants in other species such as *Verpa bohemica*. We continue to recognize *M. crassipes* in the *Guide* because in the Ohio River drainage and adjacent areas it is a striking and easily recognized "species."

Edibility   The best of the morels! Prepare it as you would *M. esculenta*.

When and where   The fruiting period of this species is later than that of *M. esculenta* by about ten days, with the result that in Michigan we look for it around the 20th of May. It occurs in oak and beech-maple forests as well as under elm and ash on low ground or in rich garden soil. Its distribution is typically more southern than that of *M. esculenta*, but the latter has such a wide range that this pattern may be more apparent than real.

Spores   20–25 (28) x 13–15 (16) μm, oval, smooth, content homogeneous.

Asci   8-spored, operculate, inamyloid.

Observations The most impressive fruiting we have seen was under a large elm tree that had died from dutch elm disease within the past two to three years. *Crassipes* means thick- or large-footed.

16   *Morchella crassipes*   About natural size (young specimens)

Helvellaceae
(False Morels or Lorchels)

Since some of the false morels are very good to eat and some are poisonous, people collecting them should be careful to identify their finds correctly. Unlike most true morels, the false morels have a wrinkled rather than a pitted fertile portion ("head"), and the fertile portion has the sides free from the stalk or, in only a few localized areas, intergrown with it; but the fertile portion is not thimblelike as in *Verpa*.

The false morels present a difficult problem to one trying to write a field guide. In recent years various schemes for classifying them have been proposed and are being debated. For convenience, we take a conservative position and place the species we treat into *Discina*, *Gyromitra*, or *Helvella*. *Helvella* is construed to include a range of species including some with a cuplike fruiting body as well as those with a distinct stalk and saddle-shaped fertile portion. *Discina* is reserved here for species with a cup- to saucerlike fruiting body and ornamented spores. The stalked species with a yellow tan to reddish brown fertile portion are placed in *Gyromitra*; many of these also have ornamented spores. Species of *Gyromitra* and *Discina* are often very slow to develop mature spores. If the specimens are wrapped in wax paper and left in a cool place for several days, the spores usually mature and an identification can be confirmed. Usually, the worse a specimen looks, the more likely it will be mature. In *Helvella* spore maturation is usually sequential, not simultaneous, and it is relatively easy to find mature spores.

Many mushroom hunters collect false morels, especially *Gyromitra esculenta*, for food and even preserve them for winter use. However, the more we learn about these fungi, the more we advise caution, since *G. esculenta*, if not properly prepared, can produce serious to fatal cases of poisoning. The line between safety and death can be a very thin one in this case, and parboiling or soaking the specimens first may not always make them safe to eat.

Key to Species

17 *Helvella acetabulum*   About one-half natural size

4. Typically fruiting on decaying wood or soil rich in woody material, fruiting in the fall; fertile portion usually saddle-shaped ... . 22. *G. infula*
4. Typically terrestrial, fruiting in the spring; fertile portion distinctly folded to convoluted or saddle-shaped 5
5. Stalk chalky white, stout; edge of fertile portion usually curved away from stalk in young specimens; fruiting under hardwoods .... 23. *G. fastigiata*
5. Stalk pale pinkish tan or toned with colors of the fertile portion, not remarkably stout; edge of fertile portion usually curved toward the stalk; fruiting under conifers or mixed conifers and aspen early in the spring .... 21. *G. esculenta*

Helvella acetabulum 17

Identification marks The interior of the cup is typically brown, but when developing under leaves it may be a creamy white. The exterior near the margin is usually about the same color as the interior and becomes paler toward the stalk. The stalk varies from very short to prominent, and is creamy white and heavily ribbed with sharp-edged ribs which continue onto the exterior of the cup.

Edibility We have no reliable data.

When and where Solitary or in groups, usually on sandy soil under hardwoods. It is not infrequent east of the Great Plains and also occurs in the Rocky Mountains and Pacific Northwest. It fruits in the spring to midsummer, often along paths and old roads in the woods. It is rarely collected in abundance.

Spores 16–18 (20) x 11–14 μm, broadly ellipsoid, smooth, with one large oil droplet.

Asci 8-spored, operculate, inamyloid.

Observations This species is placed in *Helvella* because of similarities in spore and anatomical features with the main group of Helvellas. *Helvella* refers to a kind of small pot herb; *acetabulum* means a cup.

Helvella crispa 18

Identification marks The pale overall colors; the usually cream to pale buff, saddle-shaped to 3-lobed fertile portion; and the fluted and pitted stalk form a distinctive package of features. In addition, the margin of the fertile portion is curved over the hymenium at first, and the underside of the fertile portion is covered with fine hairs which can be seen with the aid of a hand lens.

Edibility Edible, but we know of few people who have tried it. Its generally small size and scattered pattern of fruiting do not attract the mycophagist.

When and where Late summer on into fall is the prime fruiting period; it often fruits on well-decayed wood, but is more frequently found on the ground. Usually one encounters only a few specimens at a time, but we have seen it almost carpeting a pine plantation in southern Michigan. It is widely distributed in the forested regions of Canada and the United States, where it occurs as far south as Florida and New Mexico.

Spores 17–21 x 10–13 μm, oval to elliptic, smooth, containing one large central oil droplet and zero to four smaller ones at each end.

Asci 8-spored, operculate, inamyloid.

Observations As the fruiting bodies emerge from the ground, the hymenium is protected by the inrolled margin. The margin gradually unrolls and is almost flaring in age so that specimens in different stages of development may appear quite different. *Crispa* means irregularly curled or wavy.

18 *Helvella crispa*   About one-half natural size

19   Discina macrospora

Identification marks The fruiting bodies are typically saucer-shaped to more or less flat rather than distinctly cuplike. They are thick and fleshy but still moderately brittle. They often become slightly umbilicate. Tones of brown, especially dull purple brown to reddish brown, predominate on the upper surface; the lower surface is paler when moist but varies to dull cream color as moisture is lost. A short stalk may be present, but it usually does not elevate the expanded saucer much above the surface of the ground.

Edibility Not recommended.

When and were This species fruits in the early spring from late April to mid or late May in southern Michigan, usually under pine, and is common in pine plantations as well as under native pines. It first appears during the early part of the morel season but is slow to mature spores. It is widely distributed in North America, primarily in northern and montane conifer forests.

Spores 30–36 x 13–15 μm, ellipsoid, with a sharp conic projection 4–6 μm long at each end, surface more or less reticulate to roughened, containing three distinct oil droplets.

Asci 8-spored, operculate, inamyloid.

Observations The Discinas (fewer than a dozen are reported from North America) are closely related to *Gyromitra*, especially those species having projections on their spores. The two groups are combined into a single genus by some authors. Because of problems associated with eating some Gyromitras, we do not recommend experimenting with species of *Discina*. *D. perlata* is not easily distinguished in the field from *D. macrospora*. In the Great Lakes region both are associated with conifers. Of the two, *D. perlata* has broader spores with shorter projections.

19 *Discina macrospora*   About one-half natural size

Gyromitra californica & G. sphaerospora   20

Identification marks Superficially these two species are very similar. In both, the fertile portion appears "puffed up" and is typically a gray brown to umber brown or dull yellow brown on the upper surface, and paler on the lower surface. The stalk is distinctly fluted; the wings and ridges extend out

20 *Gyromitra californica*   About one-half natural size

to support the lobes of the fertile portion. Typically the stalk has no internal chambers and is cream colored with a flush of purple at the base.

Edibility   We have no reliable information on either species; however, in view of what is now known about some species of *Gyromitra*, we do not recommend them.

When and where   *G. californica* is western and found under conifers both on the ground and on rotting wood. *G. sphaerospora* occurs east of the Great Plains on hardwood slash and debris or on humus near rotting wood. Both species fruit in the spring to early summer. *G. californica* may also fruit in the fall or winter, depending on the weather, but such fruitings are regarded as most unusual.

Spores of *G. californica* are 15–18 x 7–9 μm, ellipsoid, smooth, and contain two small oil droplets. Those of *G. sphaerospora* are 8–12 μm, globose, smooth, and homogeneous.

Asci of both are 8-spored, operculate, inamyloid.

Observations   Both species have been placed in the genus *Helvella* and the genus *Pseudorhizina* at different times in the past. *Gyromitra* apparently means a curved or twisted turban or miter. *Californica* refers to the state from which the species was described; *sphaerospora* means spherical-spored.

---

21   Gyromitra esculenta
(Beefsteak Morel, Brain Mushroom)

Identification marks   The surface of the fertile portion progresses from smooth at first to undulating, wrinkled, and finally very folded and convoluted. It is never truly pitted in the manner of a morel, nor is it typically strongly lobed. The color varies from dull yellow to bay brown or dark purplish brown. The pigment appears to be at least somewhat soluble in water and often leaches out as the fruiting bodies age. In cross section, the stalk is either "stuffed" as if with cotton or more typically has a simple cavity (if the stalk is flattened, the cavity may be almost divided into two parts). This species fruits at the time the serviceberry bushes are in full bloom or a few days later.

21   *Gyromitra esculenta*   About one-half natural size

Edibility POISONOUS. This species, we now know, contains a compound which breaks down during cooking and releases a poison. Parboiling and discarding the water apparently cannot be relied upon to remove *all* the poison (see p. 16 for details). Although many people eat this species, we do not recommend it under any circumstances.

When and where It occurs throughout northern regions under conifers, in particular balsam, pine, and spruce; and at times in open aspen stands with scattered pines included. The cutover lands of the upper Great Lakes region produce quantities of it almost every spring. It also occurs in the forested areas of the Rocky Mountains. In central Michigan it fruits from about April 20 to May 15, depending on the season. In Idaho we have collected it in late June near melting snowbanks.

Spores 17–23 x (7) 10–11 μm, narrowly ellipsoid, smooth, containing a small oil droplet at each end.

Asci 8-spored, operculate, inamyloid.

Observations *G. infula* occasionally may fruit in the spring, but is predominantly a summer and fall species. It has a smoother, more saddle-shaped fertile portion than *G. esculenta*, but is also poisonous. The fruiting bodies of *G. esculenta* may persist for five to ten days in the woods. The specific epithet *esculenta* means edible—a misnomer in the light of recent experience with the species.

Gyromitra infula   22
(Saddle-shaped False Morel)

Identification marks The saddle-shaped to 3-lobed dull yellow to reddish brown fertile portion, the simple hollow in the stalk, and the habitat on rotting wood or soil rich in woody debris, are to be noted. The hymenial (upper) surface is relatively even to uneven but not folded as in *G. esculenta*.

Edibility POISONOUS, or at least should be so regarded. The closely related *G. ambigua* has been associated with cases of poisoning of the monomethylhydrazine type. The two species are almost indistinguishable in the field.

22 *Gyromitra infula*   About one-half natural size

When and where   It is rare in the spring, infrequent in the summer, and often common and abundant during the fall on into cold weather. It is generally found on rotting wood, but we have also seen it flourishing along unpaved woodland roads and on burned over areas. It may fruit on either the wood of conifers or that of hardwoods and is common in the Pacific Northwest and from the Great Lakes region eastward.

Spores   (15) 17–23 (26) x (6) 7–10 μm, elongate ellipsoid, smooth, containing two small oil droplets.

Asci   8-spored, operculate, inamyloid.

Observations   *G. ambigua* has spores 22–33 (37) x 7–12 μm with a distinct blunt projection at each end, and the fruiting bodies often have more pronounced purple tints in the stalks than do those of *G. infula*. Both species are primarily montane, but *G. ambigua* appears to be restricted to higher latitudes. Evidently both North American versions are poisonous. The fall fruiting time and the less wrinkled fertile portion distinguish each from *G. esculenta*. We have seen very young fruiting bodies of *G. infula* each consisting of a small shallow cup on a short stalk. Such specimens illustrate the continuity in fruiting body morphology in the Discomycetes and make it harder to establish rigid limits for the species. *Infula* means a band, or bandage.

23   Gyromitra fastigiata
(in the sense of European authors)

Identification marks   Among the large lorchels the deep brownish red to reddish tan color of the fertile portion which contrasts to the typically stark white of the stalk is unusual. An additional important character is the fertile portion, which is typically saddle-shaped to 3-lobed and only slightly wrinkled. The stalk, in cross section, usually has only a single irregular cavity. This combination of characters readily distinguishes this species from the other species of *Gyromitra* that fruit in the spring.

Edibility   This species was reported to be poisonous in previous editions of the *Guide*; however, we have had one report that it is edible, at least in small amounts. A former student, recalling she had heard it discussed in class, collected and ate some specimens and enjoyed them. When recounting her experience, she was chagrined when told that in class it had been discussed as a poisonous species. Because at least some species in the genus are known to be poisonous, we still do not recommend experimenting with this species until more is known about its chemical constituents.

When and where   In southern Michigan it fruits in May, near the end of the *G. esculenta* season. It is characteristically found in hardwood forests on low ground, east of the Great Plains. It usually fruits in or at the edges of damp areas and is sporadic in its appearance. The fruiting bodies are quite slow to mature.

Spores   24–30 (32) x (12) 13–15 μm, fusoid-ellipsoid, reticulate, with one to several short (1–1.5 μm) projections at each end; content granular with one large and two smaller prominent oil droplets.

Asci   8-spored, operculate, inamyloid.

Observations   This fungus is better known in North America as *Gyromitra brunnea* or *Helvella underwoodii* (as in the previous edition of the *Guide*). *G. fastigiata* was described from Europe, and recent studies in Czechoslovakia have provided rather convincing evidence that it is the species shown here. At one time (see *A Field Guide to Western Mushrooms*) the name *G. fastigiata* was applied to a species in the *G. gigas* group. *Fastigiata* means erect and having the sides nearly parallel but narrowing toward the top, resembling a gable.

23 *Gyromitra fastigiata*   About one-half natural size

Gyromitra gigas & G. korfii   **24**
(Snow Mushroom, Bull Nose)

Identification marks   The stout, massive, irregular stalk with its conspicuous internal folding as seen in a cross section, the dull yellow to crust brown fertile portion which is more wrinkled than distinctly lobed, and the early fruiting time should all be noted.

Edibility   Both species are edible and choice in our experience and are collected in quantity in western North America and the Great Lakes region. However, at least one recent European guide lists *G. gigas* as poisonous unless parboiled.

When and where   *G. gigas* is primarily a species of our western mountains, where it grows in conifer forests and is a member of the "snow bank flora"

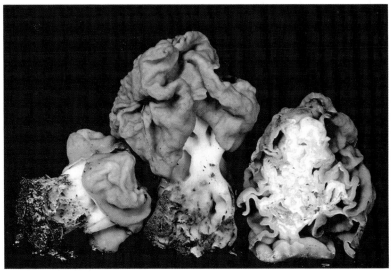

24 *Gyromitra gigas*   Less than one-half natural size

(species regularly fruiting near melting snow banks). *G. korfii* is more common in eastern North America, where it fruits in both deciduous and coniferous woods. In the Great Lakes region it typically fruits in April and May.

Spores of *G. gigas* are 26–34 x (12) 13–15 μm, oval to broadly elliptic, with a finely wrinkled surface and no projections (or only a small pad) at the ends. In contrast, the spores of *G. korfii* resemble long lemons 27–34 x (9) 11–13.5 μm which have a finely wrinkled surface and a distinct blunt projection at each end up to 1.5 μm long.

Asci of both are 8-spored, operculate, and inamyloid.

Observations   Since first including *G. gigas* (as *Helvella gigas*) in this *Guide*, the names applied to species of *Gyromitra* have multiplied, and several additional species have been described. Consequently the nomenclature has become more complex and less stabilized. We are using a concept of *G. gigas* in the sense of the earlier editions, and it is, we think, consistent with the original description. However, this species in North America has received the name *G. montana* from one European author. Following the principle of emphasizing the original description, the name *G. fastigiata* is used here for a species outside the *G. gigas* group (see species 23). *G. korfii* is the species that has been called *G. fastigiata* in some guides. The fungi are constant; the people keep changing their minds! *Gigas* means large; *G. korfii* is named for Dr. R. P. Korf of Cornell University.

Hypocreales

Identification marks   This picture shows a curious anomaly—a fruiting body of a gilled mushroom infected by an Ascomycete parasite. The overall shape is that of the host mushroom. The fruiting structures of the parasite are the small orange pimples over the area where the gills of the mushroom should be. The parasite somehow inhibits the development of worms or bacteria in the host, thus preserving the host tissue for longer periods than it would normally persist. In the field the large fleshy masses of fungous tissue, with obscure gill formation on the underside of the cap and covered with orange pimples, identify the host-parasite combination. In age or when exposed to basic substances such as ammonia or potassium hydroxide, the orange color changes to a bright magenta.

Edibility   Edible, but not recommended. Its edibility rests largely on the identity of the host, and this can not be ascertained because the host is malformed. The host is most likely a member of the Russulaceae.

When and where   It is a widely distributed species common in late summer and fall in open oak, aspen, and beech-maple woods east of the Great Plains. It also occurs in the southwestern United States and along the Pacific Coast.

Spores   35–40 x 6–8 μm including projections, approximately fusoid but often slightly flattened on one side, 2-celled, ornamented with low rounded warts.

Asci   8-spored, inoperculate.

Observations   The generic name *Hypomyces* means living on a fungus; *lactifluorum* means with white or milklike juice; possibly the describer thought a *Lactarius* was the host. The asci are embedded in minute flask-shaped structures called perithecia instead of exposed in a hymenial layer as in the other Ascomycetes we have discussed.

25   *Hypomyces lactifluorum*   About one-half natural size

Basidiomycetes

Auriculariales and Tremellales (Jelly Fungi)

The members of these two orders are not likely to be distinguished accurately in the field by the casual collector. In both orders the fruiting body is more or less jellylike in consistency when fresh. They are distinguished by the features of the basidia. In the Auriculariales, the basidium is basically hyphal-like (tubular) but soon is divided into four cells by the formation of cross walls. Each cell then develops a sterigma on which a spore is finally produced. In the Tremellales the basidia are more or less globose to clavate. Two walls, one at right angles to the other, then divide the basidium lengthwise into four cells of approximately the same diameter (see fig. 1).

Key to Species

1. Fruiting body somewhat cup-shaped to saucer-shaped; dark brown and rubbery-tough in consistency .... 26. *Auricularia auricula*
1. Not as above; fruiting body very jellylike in consistency 2
    2. Fruiting body somewhat resembling a bunch of leaf lettuce; color reddish brown .... 27. *Tremella foliacea*
    2. Fruiting body whitish to pallid; shape extremely variable; consistency very gelatinous and fruiting body soon collapsing ....
    .... 28. *T. reticulata*

---

26   Auricularia auricula

Identification marks   The gelatinous (rubbery) consistency of the fruiting bodies, the very dark brown (not reddish cinnamon) color, the habit of growing on wood, the cup-shaped to ear-shaped or pancakelike form, and the

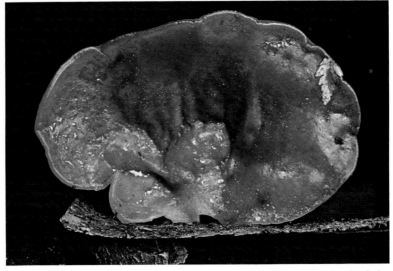

26a   *Auricularia auricula*   About natural size

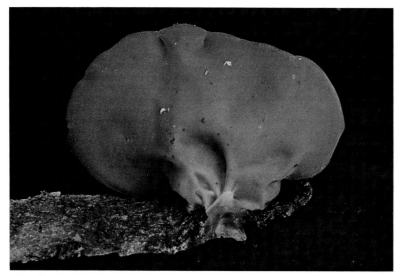

26b *Auricularia auricula*   About natural size

very hard consistency when dried are important. Specimens may be ribbed on the underside. Usually the fruiting bodies are 2–7 (9) cm broad.

Edibility   In the last fifteen years it has become quite popular in North America. For years it has been harvested commercially in the Orient, and some of this material finds its way into our specialty food stores. We have no reports of anyone suffering ill effects from eating it.

When and where   It is found on the wood of both hardwoods and conifers. In the mountains it is often abundant on fallen trunks of conifers having the bark still on them. It is widely distributed in North America, but abundant in some localities and rare in others.

Spores   12–15 (16) x 4–5 (6) μm, smooth, hyaline in KOH, sausage-shaped.

Observations   Fruiting bodies of some cup-fungi are gelatinous, but none of those growing on wood resemble *A. auricula* in their field characters. *Auricularia* and *auricula* both refer to the earlike form of many of the fruiting bodies.

Tremella foliacea   27

Identification marks   Fruiting body 5–15 cm broad, rather rubbery to more or less like gelatin in consistency, shape somewhat resembling a bunch of leaf lettuce and consisting of folds and branches becoming flattened to spathulate, color dull reddish vinaceous to reddish brown or cinnamon (the color variable within the above range).

Edibility   Not recommended. It is practically all water.

When and where   The reddish form shown here is fairly common on hardwood remains east of the Great Plains. It favors oak in particular, and fruits after heavy rain in late August or early September.

Spores   8–9 (13) x 7–9 μm, ellipsoid to ovoid, smooth.

Observations   It is a marvel how so few hyphae can bind so much water into the temporarily "solid" fruiting body. *Tremella* means trembling, and *foliacea* means leaflike.

27   *Tremella foliacea*   About one-half natural size

28   Tremella reticulata

Identification marks   The fruiting bodies are pallid to whitish or finally brownish especially near the base. The shape varies greatly: some resemble the *Sparassis* type of fruiting body but are very watery, and some resemble malformed coral fungi.

Edibility   Not worth trying. It starts to lose water soon after it has been collected.

When and where   It is rare to infrequent, but during wet seasons it may be quite abundant. It is found on humus in stands of hardwood east of the Great Plains.

Spores   9–11 x 5–6 μm, white in deposit, hyaline, mostly ovoid, smooth, often depressed on one side.

Observations   The lobes of the fruiting body are hollow. *Reticulata* means in the form of a network.

28   *Tremella reticulata*   About natural size

Aphyllophorales

This order is larger than the Agaricales and is defined differently by different authors. The Aphyllophorales are generally said to include a seemingly endless series of fungi with membranous to tough or woody fruiting bodies or whose fruiting bodies resemble splashes of paint on decaying wood. The hymenium is smooth to bumpy to more or less poroid or obscurely gill-like. The Polyporaceae, Fistulinaceae, and Hydnaceae belong to this order. In the first two families, the hymenium is poroid; in the Hydnaceae it covers teeth. Two odd genera, *Sparassis* and *Polyozellus*, were formerly placed in the Cantharellales because their fruiting bodies superficially resemble members of the Cantharellales.

Sparassis radicata   29
(Cauliflower Mushroom)

Identification marks   The flattened, crisped ends of the branch system, which forms the framework of the cluster, are distinctive. The color is whitish to pallid to buff, or grayish when young. The spores are produced on the flattened ultimate branches. It is one of our largest edible fungi, the massive clusters weighing as much as fifty pounds.

Edibility   Edible and choice. It is considered a prize by connoisseurs. Its keeping qualities are good and it does not discolor much from handling. Slow cooking is recommended.

When and where   It is a feature of the virgin conifer forests of the Pacific Northwest, and is often found at the base of a tree—where it may fruit year after year. It is a parasite on the tree. Like so many species in the Northwest, it fruits during the rainy season.

Spores   5–6.5 x 3–3.5 (4) μm, ellipsoid, smooth, hyaline in KOH, inamyloid.

Observations   *Sparassis crispa*, a European species, occurs in the area east of the Great Plains, and is fairly abundant in the Southeast. Some workers consider these as forms of a single species. *Sparassis* means torn to pieces; *radicata* means rooting.

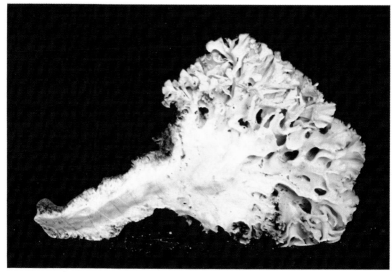

29   *Sparassis radicata*   About one-fourth natural size

Identification marks The fruiting bodies occur in large clusters; they are a frosted (glaucous) blue to deep blue throughout, and the consistency is fleshy. The spore deposit is white and the gills are veinlike, very crowded at times, and most easily seen near the margin of the cap.

Edibility Acquaintances of ours from McCall, Idaho, where this species is often fairly abundant, report it as edible and choice.

When and where It is generally regarded as rare, but in the spruce-fir zone of the Rocky Mountains it is often abundant during wet seasons. It fruits during the summer and fall. It was described from the state of Maine.

Spores 4–6 x 4–6 μm, white in deposit, angular-tuberculate, broadly elliptic to spheric in outline, inamyloid, hyaline under microscope.

Observations It has been shown that this species is not closely related to the species of *Cantharellus*. *Multiplex* means in many pieces (in this case, a compound fruiting body).

30 *Polyozellus multiplex*   About one-third natural size

Polyporaceae and Fistulinaceae (True Polypores)

The true polypores as a group can be distinguished from the Boletaceae by their firmer, even woody, texture. The fruiting bodies are much longer-lived than those of the boletes, in which the basidiocarp discharges spores in terms of a week or less. In the true polypores the process can span several weeks, and many species have perennial fruiting bodies. If, in a mature specimen, a hand lens is needed as an aid to see the pores, it belongs in either the Polyporaceae or Fistulinaceae.

There are many types of pore fungi, and the first fungi one encounters will be those with a woody fruiting body, since they are there the year around, though not always sporulating. The average mushroom hunter, however, is interested chiefly in those tender enough to be eaten. Since even these get rather tough in age, emphasis must be placed on collecting immature specimens. The fleshier species of true pore fungi grow on humus or from buried wood, but some, like the woody species, grow out directly from rotting logs and stumps. Many of the fungi which rot forest trees belong in this group.

Key to Species

1. Fruiting body obviously on wood 2
1. Fruiting body terrestrial or appearing so 4
    2. Tubes on underside of cap separate from each other (use a hand lens) .... 31. *Fistulina hepatica*
    2. Pores present as pinholes or broader in a solid matrix (not separate as individual pipes) 3
3. Cap brown and scaly, the scales finally black; often growing on willow wood .... 32. *Polyporus squamosus*
3. Fruiting bodies shelving; upper surface more or less salmon color; lower surface bright yellow ... 33. *Laetiporus sulphureus* var. *sulphureus*
    4. Caps 4–15 cm broad, white becoming yellow at least on the disc; often in confluent masses, but with many stalks .... 34. *Albatrellus ovinus*
    4. Caps small, borne on a framework of branches 5
5. Individual caps (ends of branches) spathulate ...... 35. *Grifola frondosa*
5. Individual caps centrally stalked .... 36. *Grifola umbellata*

Fistulina hepatica   31
(Beefsteak Fungus)

Identification marks   The surface of the cap is about the color of liver or a paler red, the consistency is fleshy-pliant, and the taste raw is somewhat acid. If one examines the undersurface with a hand lens, it will be noted that the tubes are separate from each other. This last feature places the fungus in a different family from the Polyporaceae—the Fistulinaceae.

Edibility   Edible and popular. Its common name refers to the color of the cap—about like that of raw meat. Some people dry it, powder the dried specimens, and sprinkle the powder over a roast as a tenderizer and flavor enhancer.

When and where   On decaying wood of hardwoods across the continent, but most abundant in the southeastern states, summer and fall.

Spores   4–5.5 x 3–4 μm, brown in deposit, ovoid, smooth, inamyloid.

Observations   Thin spore deposits look yellowish. *Fistulina* means a little pipe; *hepatica* means pertaining to liver. The common name beefsteak morel is often applied to *Gyromitra esculenta*.

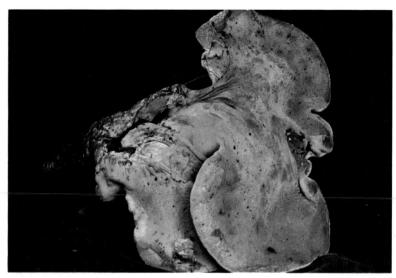

31a   *Fistulina hepatica*   About one-half natural size

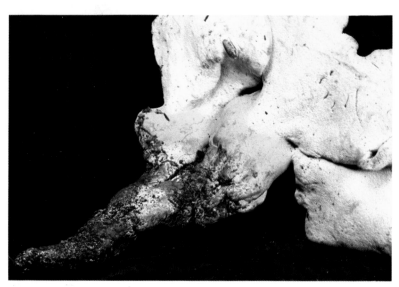

31b   *Fistulina hepatica*   About one-half natural size

32   Polyporus squamosus
(Scaly Polyporus)

Identification marks   The stalk, when there is one, is usually lateral to eccentric, the cap soon becomes conspicuously scaly as shown, and the scales become darker to nearly black by old age. The pores are large (1–3 mm wide), and the context is only semifleshy.

Edibility   Not poisonous, but none of our friends who have tried it ever accused it of being good.

When and where   Very widely distributed over the northern hemisphere.

We find it most often on the wood of *Salix* (willow trees). It fruits during late spring and early summer.

Spores   10–15 (18) x 4–6 μm, elongate, smooth, hyaline, inamyloid.

Observations   *Polyporus* means with many pores; *squamosus* means scaly.

32   *Polyporus squamosus*   About one-half natural size

Laetiporus sulphureus var. sulphureus   33
(Sulphur Shelf)

Identification marks   The pore layer is a bright sulphur yellow. The upper surface varies from about salmon to yellow or in age yellowish tan. The flesh is soft at first but becomes punky as the specimens mature and age. A variety, *L. sulphureus* var. *semialbinus*, with the pore layer white when young,

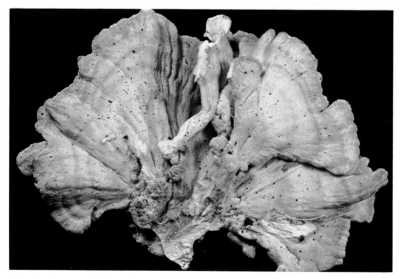

33   *Laetiporus sulphureus*   About one-half natural size

is also fairly common—more common in North America than the technical literature on polypores indicates.

Edibility   Edible and popular, but do not eat it raw. In recent times gastro-intestinal upsets from eating it cooked have also been reported. The tender growing margins of the caps are all that should be used. If the consistency is punky, the material is too old and likely to be of poor flavor.

When and where   It occurs in large masses on the wood of both hardwoods and conifers. Typically it is a fall species, but we have found it in June in Michigan. It is widely distributed. Var. *semialbinus* is known from Oregon, but is most abundant on the hardwoods of the Great Lakes region.

Spores   4–5 x 3–4 μm, hyaline in KOH, ellipsoid to ovoid, inamyloid.

Observations   *Laetiporus* means with bright pores; *sulphureus* means the color of sulphur.

---

34   Albatrellus ovinus

Identification marks   The fruiting bodies are white at first but yellow con-siderably by maturity and in age may be buff to clay color. They are often very contorted and lobed and fused into confluent masses by old age. The tubes are very short, about 3 mm deep, and the pores are minute. The flesh is firm, dry, and brittle.

Edibility   Edible, according to reports, but apparently not popular. Cases of disturbances from eating it are known. Also, little is known about a number of North American populations closely related to *A. ovinus*.

When and where   It fruits solitarily, gregariously, or in the confluent masses mentioned above, under conifers in the summer and fall, often during dry seasons. It is abundant in the Rocky Mountains of Colorado and Idaho, but is also known in the conifer forests east of the Great Plains.

Spores   3.5–4.5 x 2.5–4 μm, ellipsoid to subglobose, smooth, hyaline, inamyloid.

Observations   *Ovinus* means pertaining to sheep.

---

35   Grifola frondosa
(Hen of the Woods)

Identification marks   In addition to the key characters, *G. frondosa* differs from *G. umbellata* in the fleshier framework, more compact branching, and darker upper surface of the spathulate caps. Microscopically, it has smaller spores.

Edibility   Edible and choice—when it is young and fresh. The best stage is that at which the caps are beginning to form. Slice up the whole fruit body if it is still soft and free of worms. If tough, use only the caps. Slow cooking is recommended.

When and where   It occurs on or around hardwood trees, generally in the area east of the Great Plains in North America. It was described from Europe. Look for it in woods containing large mature trees, especially oak. This spe-cies will likely become rare in the next quarter century as the few remaining stands of large hardwood trees are cut down.

Spores   5–7 x 3.5–5 μm, ovoid to ellipsoid, hyaline, smooth, inamyloid.

Observations Both species of *Grifola* are reported to freeze well. *Grifola* is an Italian name for a fungus; *frondosa* means leafy. These species were previously treated under *Polypilus*.

34 *Albatrellus ovinus*　　　　　　　　　　　　　　　About one-half natural size

35 *Grifola frondosa*　　　　　　　　　　　　　　　About one-fourth natural size

Grifola umbellata　　　　　　　　　　　　　　　36

Identification marks The small, centrally stalked, depressed caps arise at the tips of the branches of the basic, compound framework of the fruiting body. In *G. frondosa* the caps are the flattened ends of branches. The overall width of the compound fruiting bodies of *G. umbellata* rarely reaches 40 cm.

Edibility   Edible. The young clusters are definitely preferable. As far as quality is concerned, it is about like *G. frondosa*, only the stalks are tougher.

When and where   In southern Michigan it is generally found during late June and early July in low forests of hardwoods containing beech. Look for it after periods of heavy rainfall. It is widely distributed, but in our experience is less frequently collected than *G. frondosa*.

Spores   7–9.5 x 3–4 μm, more or less cylindric, hyaline, smooth, inamyloid.

Observations   *Umbellata* means pertaining to umbrellas.

36   *Grifola umbellata*   About one-half natural size

Hydnaceae
(Hedgehog Mushrooms)

All members of this group are characterized by needlelike or icicle-like prolongations called teeth, which hang from a cap or from a fleshy mass of tissue that lacks definite shape, or from a compound framework of branches. The spores are produced on the surface of these pendant teeth. Two types of fruiting bodies are included here. In one there is a cap and a stalk, just as in a gilled fungus, but instead of gills the underside of the cap is furnished with teeth. In the second type there is no clearly defined cap and stalk, and the teeth hang from the tubercle or from a branched framework. In some species the teeth are so large they remind one of small icicles.

Key to Species

1. Fruiting body a lump of fungous tissue or a framework of branches; spores amyloid 2
1. Fruiting body with a cap and stalk and with pendant spines on the underside of the cap; spores not amyloid 3
    2. Fruiting body a lump of tissue bearing a dense mass of icicle-like spines . . . . 37. *Hericium erinaceus*

2. Fruiting body a framework of branches, the spines arranged along the branches somewhat like the teeth of a comb . . . .
. . . . 38. *Hericium ramosum*
3. Consistency of fruiting body woody, tints of blue present variously; odor not distinctive . . . . 39. *Hydnellum caeruleum*
3. Consistency of fruiting body fleshy 4
    4. Cap typically glabrous; spore deposit white; context usually staining yellowish where injured . . . . 40. *Dentinum repandum*
    4. Cap distinctly scaly; spore deposit brown; context not staining yellow . . . . 41. *Hydnum imbricatum*

Hericium erinaceus   37

Identification marks A closely packed mass of large spines hang from an essentially unbranched basal mass of tissue. The whole structure is white at first but becomes yellowish to tan in age. The consistency typically is pliant and fairly tough rather than fleshy and brittle.

37   *Hericium erinaceus*   About one-half natural size

Edibility   Edible. Slow cooking to tenderize it is important. If the flavor is strong, it is likely that the specimens have aged considerably before being collected.

When and where   It grows on hardwood trees, most often from scars on living trees, in the summer and fall. Formerly it was fairly common east of the Great Plains, but, with continued cutting of stands of mature trees, this fungus is becoming rare. It has been found in southern Oregon in the Pacific Northwest.

Spores   5–6.5 x 4–5.5 μm, subglobose, hyaline, amyloid, finely ornamented.

Observations   *Erinaceus* means hedgehog.

---

38   Hericium ramosum

Identification marks   The fruiting body is nothing more than a many-branched framework with the spines or teeth distributed along the branchlets, much like the teeth on a comb. The fruiting body is white if perfectly fresh; if yellowish, the specimen is old.

Edibility   Edible and popular, as are also *H. coralloides* and *H. abietis*. Species of *Hericium* are recommended for beginners, since it would be difficult for anyone to mistake them for any known poisonous species.

When and where   It occurs on wood of either hardwoods or conifers during the summer and fall. The fruiting bodies often attain a width of about 30 cm. *H. ramosum* is to be expected in the forested areas of North America north of Mexico.

Spores   4–5.5 (7) x 4.5–6 μm, hyaline in KOH, more or less globose, finely ornamented, amyloid.

Observations   In *H. coralloides* the teeth are located mostly near or at the ends of branches to form tufts. In *H. abietis* the young fruiting body is tinted salmon buff to more or less ochraceous, and becomes paler as it matures. It is found in the Pacific Northwest and was treated in this *Guide* previously under the name *H. weirii*. *H. caput-ursi* is now considered a synonym of *H. coralloides*. *Ramosum* means branched.

---

39   Hydnellum caeruleum

Identification marks   The growing margin of the cap, or the entire surface when young, is often pale bright to dull blue or whitish. In aging, the surface tomentum becomes matted down, and the surface is then a dull brown. Sections through the fruiting body show zones which are blue to some extent, and the teeth are bluish at first. They finally become brown from the spores. There is no pronounced odor.

Edibility   Inedible because of the woody context.

When and where   It is often abundant in the fall, especially under 2-needle pines (lodgepole or jack pine), after heavy rains. It occurs across the continent in the above habitats.

Spores   4.5–6 x 4.5–5 μm, brown in deposit, angular-irregular.

Observations   *H. suaveolens* features blue colors also, but has a strong, heavy, sweetish, persistent odor. *Caeruleum* means blue.

38 *Hericium ramosum*   About one-third natural size

39 *Hydnellum caeruleum*   About one-half natural size

Dentinum repandum   40

Identification marks   The white spore deposit, the fleshy-brittle consistency of the context, and the yellowish stains when bruised are important. The caps vary in size from 3 to 30 cm, and in color from nearly white to pale orange tan to reddish cinnamon, and are convex to nearly flat at maturity. Typically, the surface of the cap is smooth.

Edibility   Edible and choice, and often found in quantity. Also, it is readily identified. Some rate it the equal of *Boletus edulis*.

When and where   It fruits during the late summer and fall on into the winter if conditions are favorable. We have seen the reddish cinnamon material (known as the species *D. rufescens*) most abundant in oak woods, whereas the giant pallid form was found under Sitka spruce on the Pacific Coast. In one form or another it is common in conifer as well as hardwood forests after periods of heavy rain.

Spores   6–8 x 5–6 μm, white in deposit, subglobose, smooth, inamyloid.

Observations *D. umbilicatum*, with a slender stalk and depressed disc of the cap, is likely to be mistaken for some specimens of *D. repandum*. It has larger spores. *Dentinum* means pertaining to teeth.

40 *Dentinum repandum*   About one-half natural size

---

41   Hydnum imbricatum

Identification marks   The cap is very large (up to 20 cm), is covered with broad conspicuous scales, and is dull vinaceous brown. The flesh is grayish and brittle, and the spore deposit is dark brown.

Edibility   Edible, but not recommended. Some collections are not well flavored, and some closely related species have a very disagreeable taste.

41 *Hydnum imbricatum*   About one-third natural size

In Colorado, where it is abundant at times, several of our acquaintances tried it but rated it low-grade. Mild cases of poisoning have been attributed to it.

When and where   In the Rocky Mountains the typical form of *H. imbricatum* occurs under conifers. Variations of this species are frequently found during hot wet summer weather in sandy oak woods east of the Great Plains.

Spores   6–7.5 x 5–7 μm, dark brown in deposit, nearly globose, warty.

Observations   *Hydnum*, in the days before formal rules of nomenclature were first formulated, was the name for truffles. *Imbricatum* refers to the pattern of overlapping shingles on a roof.

Cantharellales (Coral-like Mushrooms and Chanterelles)

These mushrooms, if the term can be applied to them, are characterized by upright growth of the fruiting body. They may take the form of a simple club or of an elaborate system of upright branches, and all gradations between these two can be found among the numerous species. Coral fungi occur on humus, soil, and decaying wood. They fruit during the spring, summer, and fall (depending on the species), though mostly in the late summer and fall. Among the larger branched species, color is a very important character.

Sparassis (see the Aphyllophorales) formerly was classified in the Cantharellales, but it is not closely related to the members of this order. The same is true for *Polyozellus*, which formerly was placed close to *Cantharellus*.

Key to Genera and Species

1. Fruiting body many-branched 2
1. Fruiting body not branched or not repeatedly so; often with a cap and stalk 4
2. Spores amyloid; growing on wood .... 42. *Clavicorona pyxidata*
2. Spores not amyloid; habitat various 3
3. Fruiting body large (5–15 cm broad or more), distinctly colored (in species included here), colors yellow, pink, red, or ochraceous; spore deposit buff to ochraceous .... *Ramaria*
3. Fruiting body small (rarely 10 cm broad), dull white to dark gray; spore deposit white .... 43. *Clavulina cinerea*
4. Fruiting body more or less cylindric to club-shaped, or top of club flattened to form a rudimentary cap; hymenophore smooth to uneven .... *Clavariadelphus*
4. Fruiting body funnel-shaped to pileate, often with the hymenophore veined or somewhat gill-like 5
5. Fruiting body black to gray when fresh .... 53. *Craterellus fallax*
5. Fruiting body brightly colored in some part (cap, stalk, or gills) .... *Cantharellus*

---

42   Clavicorona pyxidata

Identification marks   The fruiting bodies grow out from dead wood, not just from the ground beside it. The ultimate branches are enlarged upward and end in a crown of small projections. The taste raw is slightly peppery. The color varies from white to pale yellow and in age often becomes dingy brown at least over the basal area.

Edibility   Edible and popular with many people. When old (discolored) it is rather stringy and the flavor is inferior to unpleasant.

When and where It is common on the wood of aspen and willow in the spring and early summer in the Rocky Mountains, the area east of the Great Plains, and the Pacific Northwest. In the Northwest a closely related species, *C. avellanea*, occurs on wood of conifers.

Spores 4–6 x 2–3 μm, white in deposit, ellipsoid, hyaline, smooth, amyloid.

Observations *Pyxidata* means boxlike.

42 *Clavicorona pyxidata*   Nearly natural size

Clavulina cinerea   43

Identification marks The fruiting bodies are many-branched and range from pallid to pale smoke gray, bluish gray, or darker. Some become quite dark in age. The taste and odor are mild. The spore deposit is white, and in most specimens the branches present a rather tangled arrangement. The size varies considerably; some specimens grow up to 10 x 10 cm.

43 *Clavulina cinerea*   About natural size

Edibility Edible, and a species collectors will find in abundance in jack pine country.

When and where In the area east of the Great Plains it is common on the duff in low moist conifer woods, especially in jack pine stands. The best areas appear to be old burns with a ground cover of moss. We have not observed it in sphagnum bogs, i.e., on the floating mat.

Spores 6.5–11 x 6–8 (10) μm, white in deposit, smooth, subglobose to broadly ellipsoid, inamyloid.

Observations *Clavulina cristata* is a white, sparsely branched species otherwise quite similar to *C. cinerea*. *Cinerea* means pale gray.

Ramaria

These species were included in the genus *Clavaria* in previous editions of this *Guide*. In dividing up the latter genus into smaller genera, the name *Ramaria* has been applied to the many-branched coral fungi that have nonamyloid spores which are slightly colored in deposits. The surface of the branches stains green to olive when iron salts (such as ferric or ferrous sulphate) are applied to them. Our large many-branched corals are mostly terrestrial, but a few, such as *R. stricta*, occur on rotting wood. *Ramaria* means branched.

Key to Species

1. Growing on wood of hardwoods or conifers; consistency pliant; taste disagreeable .... 44. *Ramaria stricta*
1. Terrestrial and taste bland (not distinctive) 2
    2. When sectioned, flesh of the main branches showing watery streaks and pockets of translucent (gelatinized) tissue .... 45. *R. gelatinosa* var. *oregonensis*
    2. Context of fruiting body not as above 3
3. When truly fresh, tips of the branches yellow and supporting branches flushed pinkish .... 46. *R. formosa*
3. Color pattern not as above 4
    4. Fruiting body more or less pale golden yellow over all except white at base; not staining where injured .... 47. *R. aurea*
    4. Fruiting body brilliant to dingy red when fresh 5
5. Fruiting body a brilliant coral pink on exposed parts when young and fresh .... 48. *R. subbotrytis*
5. Fruiting body dingy vinaceous red at first .... 49. *R. botrytis*

---

44   Ramaria stricta

Identification marks It grows on wood, preferably that of hardwood trees, and typically has a strict upright aspect. The consistency is pliant to tough, and the taste raw is rather metallic and disagreeable. The tips of the branches are yellow at first. In aging, the fruiting body becomes dingy vinaceous brown from the base upward.

Edibility   Inedible because of the disagreeable taste.

When and where   It is found both on the wood of hardwoods and that of conifers, but is rare on the latter substrate. It is frequent in slashings and where blowdowns have occurred. East of the Great Plains it is almost certain to be found during late summer and early fall if the woods are moist. It is also abundant in the Pacific Northwest.

Spores   7–10 x 3.5–4 (5) μm, ochraceous in deposit, more or less ellipsoid, minutely ornamented, inamyloid.

Observations   *Stricta* means straight and strictly upright.

44   *Ramaria stricta*   About one-half natural size

Ramaria gelatinosa var. oregonensis   45

Identification marks   This medium to large coral is pinkish orange to orange buff or yellowish orange except for the whitish main stalk or fleshy base. There is no significant color change on bruising. The sectioned main

45   *Ramaria gelatinosa* var. *oregonensis*   Nearly natural size

stalk or base shows streaks and pockets of gelatinized hyphae (the areas appear watery in contrast to the rest of the tissue).

Edibility   Not recommended. We have had both favorable and unfavorable reports on it, and in view of the taxonomic difficulties with species of *Ramaria*, one wonders if the specimens eaten were actually correctly identified.

When and where   It is found in (and was described from) the rain forests of the Pacific Northwest. Its distribution beyond this area has not yet been determined.

Spores   7–10 x 4.5–6 μm, yellow in deposit, ovoid to cylindric, coarsely ornamented with warts, inamyloid.

Observations   *Gelatinosa* means gelatinous; *oregonensis* means of Oregon.

---

46   Ramaria formosa

Identification marks   That part of the cluster's base below the groundline is whitish, the tips of the branches pale yellow, and the intermediate branches are flushed pink in truly fresh material (but never as dark as in *R. botrytis*). There are no pronounced stains in young material, but in age the context becomes brownish to wood brown, according to modern authorities (these colors are not noted on our material, and are not indicated in the descriptions of Fries and Persoon we consulted). The taste of raw context is mild; when cooked it leaves a rasping aftertaste. The chalky, fragile context of dried specimens is distinctive.

Edibility   POISONOUS according to some (who describe the context as blackening). The small amounts we ate produced no significant symptoms other than the aftertaste.

When and where   In hardwood and mixed forests, widely distributed. It is typically a late summer and fall species, but in the Rocky Mountains it fruits during July and August. The best fruiting the senior author has seen was in a mixed forest near Grants Pass, Oregon, in November.

Spores   9–12 x 4.5–6 μm, ochraceous buff in deposit, more or less oblong, ornamented with small warts, inamyloid.

Observations   *Formosa* means beautiful.

46   *Ramaria formosa* (old fruiting bodies)   Nearly natural size

Ramaria aurea
(Golden Coral)

47

Identification marks   This, in the sense peculiar to a field guide, is a "collective" species (a collection of closely related species and/or varieties). The large yellow coral fungi which do not stain when bruised are common but difficult to identify. In *R. aurea* the fruiting bodies measure up to 15 cm or more wide and high, and do not stain where injured. The tips and upper branches are ochre to egg yellow, and the flesh is even-textured.

Edibility   The group of species related closely to *R. aurea* is edible; at least they are eaten by many collectors in North America. Care to avoid *R. formosa* should be observed, since it is mildly poisonous. It has yellow tips and pinkish branches below, which, unfortunately, fade and soon lose the pink tint.

When and where   During wet seasons in late summer and early fall it is not uncommon in the open oak forests of the area east of the Great Plains. Also, it apparently is not rare in our western area.

Spores   9–13 x 4–5 μm, ochraceous in deposit, in face view more or less oblong, ornamented (finely warted), inamyloid.

Observations   *Aurea* means golden; thus, the golden *Ramaria*.

47   *Ramaria aurea*   Slightly less than natural size

Ramaria subbotrytis
(Rose Coral)

48

Identification marks   When found in perfect condition, this is our most brilliantly colored coral fungus. The fruiting bodies are 5–10 cm high and 4–8 cm wide. When young and fresh they are coral pink or slightly redder all over, and soon become yellowish to orange ochraceous at the base. Eventually the entire fruiting body fades. The base, where embedded in the substrate, is typically white. There are no color changes on bruised areas.

Edibility   Edible, but not usually found in any quantity.

When and where   We have found it mostly in northern California, but it was described from our southeastern states.

Spores 7–10 x 3–4 μm, pinkish in deposit, ellipsoid, minutely warted, inamyloid.

Observations *Subbotrytis* means close to *R. botrytis*.

48 *Ramaria subbotrytis*   About one-half natural size

49 Ramaria botrytis

Identification marks The fruiting body is formed of a large fleshy base from which branches develop. The branches and the upper part of the base are a vinaceous red, and the ultimate tips are even darker. The entire fruiting body becomes paler as it develops. Eventually the fleshy base becomes smaller as the secondary branches develop.

Edibility Edible and often collected in our western area, but bitter specimens do occur. It is not rated highly, possibly on this account.

When and where It is abundant in the spruce-fir zone of the mountains of

49 *Ramaria botrytis* (faded)   About one-half natural size

central Colorado, and not infrequent in the Pacific Northwest. Apparently it is also fairly frequent in our southeastern states.

Spores   11–17 x 4–6 μm, about ochraceous buff in deposit, in face view narrowly elliptic to oblong, faintly longitudinally striate (under an oil immersion lens), inamyloid.

Observations   The specimens illustrated were from near Aspen, Colorado, where the species is often abundant. In areas of higher rainfall the shape of the clusters is as illustrated in the previous edition of this *Guide*. The large fleshy base requires longer cooking than the thinner branches. *Botrytis* pertains to a bunch of grapes. It may refer to the shape of the fruiting body.

Clavariadelphus

These fruiting bodies are cylindric to club-shaped, upright, with the apex flattened and somewhat capitate in some species. The spore-bearing surface is smooth to wrinkled or somewhat veined. If the apex of the club is flattened, no (or very few) basidia are present on it. When a drop of iron salts (FeSO₄) is dropped on the spore-bearing surface, it soon shows a green to olive stain on and around the spot. The species often fruit in groups of hundreds of fruiting bodies, closely gregarious, some under hardwoods and some under conifers.

Key to Species

1. Fruiting body with a flattened apex or a rudimentary cap . . . .
. . . . 50. *Clavariadelphus truncatus*
1. Fruiting body with a rounded to pointed apex 2
    2. Fruiting under hardwoods gregarious to scattered; fruiting bodies 1–3 cm thick or more at maturity . . . .
. . . . 51. *C. pistillaris* var. *americanus*
    2. Fruiting under conifers and densely gregarious; fruiting bodies 3–7 mm thick at widest portion . . . . . 52. *C. ligula* & *C. sachalinensis*

Clavariadelphus truncatus   50

Identification marks   This is one of the largest of the unbranched coral fungi. The wrinkled to smooth surface of the club and the tendency for the top to be flattened are distinctive. The flattened top does not bear basidia, and reminds one of the cap seen in some of the chanterelles. The color is variable: the cap is more or less ochraceous to orange, but the sides (the hymenium) are more often vinaceous brown. The stalk portion is short and pallid to yellow.

Edibility   Edible, but old specimens are inclined to be spongy and soft inside.

When and where   In the Great Lakes area its favorite habitat is in cold, wet cedar and hemlock stands often containing yew (*Taxus*) as undergrowth.

Such locations often contain much sphagnum. *C. truncatus* appears during late summer and fall and is widely distributed.

Spores 9–13 x 5–7 μm, ochraceous buff in deposit, smooth, oblong to ellipsoid, inamyloid.

Observations *Truncatus* means cut or sawed off.

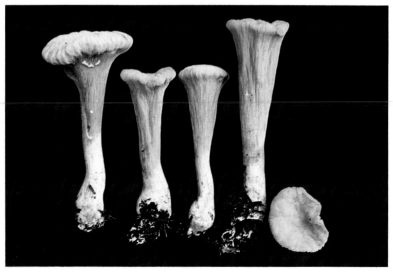

50 *Clavariadelphus truncatus*   Nearly natural size

---

51   Clavariadelphus pistillaris var. americanus

Identification marks The fruiting body is often large—6–20 cm tall and 8–40 mm thick at widest part. The apex is rounded and yellowish to yellowish brown or reddish brown, and stains vinaceous brown where injured. The stalk is pallid and not sharply delimited from the hymenial area above it. The hymenium is slightly wrinkled in age. The context has a mild to bitter taste and stains brown where cut.

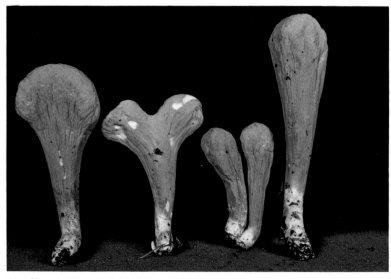

51 *Clavariadelphus pistillaris* var. *americanus*   About natural size

Edibility   Not poisonous as far as we are aware, but not recommended, particularly the variety with the bitter taste.

When and where   Under hardwoods east of the Great Plains after heavy rains in late August and September. When it fruits, it is usually in great abundance.

Spores   9–14 (16) x 4.5–7.5 µm, white in deposit, ellipsoid to oblong, smooth, inamyloid.

Observations   *Pistillaris* means shaped like a pestle.

Clavariadelphus ligula & C. sachalinensis   52

Identification marks   Both have small unbranched fruiting bodies (2–7 (10) cm high) that occur scattered or in small clusters. The stalk is not sharply distinct from the hymenial area above it, and the color of the entire fruiting body is pale buff to more or less pale dull vinaceous brown. The somewhat pithy interior is white. Most collectors will doubtless find it difficult to distinguish between these two here in North America. Intergrading collections are numerous, especially in the Pacific Northwest.

Edibility   Apparently not poisonous, but some collections at least are bitter. Not recommended.

When and where   Both are widely distributed in the conifer forests of the United States and Canada, on well drained situations after heavy rains, clustered to gregarious or scattered, often in patches of several hundred fruiting bodies.

Spores of *C. ligula* are white to very pale yellowish in deposit, 8–15 x 5–6 µm. *C. sachalinensis* has spores 17.5–22 x 4–6 µm, buff colored in deposits.

Observations   *Ligula* means little tongue; *sachalinensis* refers to a group of islands north of Japan.

52   *Clavariadelphus sachalinensis*   About natural size

53   Craterellus fallax
(Horn of Plenty, or Trumpet of Death)

Identification marks   The pale salmon color of the spore deposit is diagnostic, along with the generally gray to blackish color overall and a smooth to uneven hymenium (rather than one of radiating folds or wrinkles). If the spore deposit is white to creamy white, the specimen is most likely *Craterellus cornucopioides*, a European species rare in North America. For years both were included under the latter name in the United States and Canada.

Edibility   Edible and choice in spite of its appearance—it is as black when cooked as it is when fresh.

When and where   This common woodland fungus grows mostly in hardwood forests along old roads, trails, and in open places covered by mosses. It occurs east of the Great Plains, and fruits during the summer and fall.

Spores   11–14 x 7–9 μm, pale salmon color in deposit, approximately ellipsoid, smooth, inamyloid, practically hyaline in KOH.

Observations   *Craterellus* means a large bowl; *fallax* means deceptive.

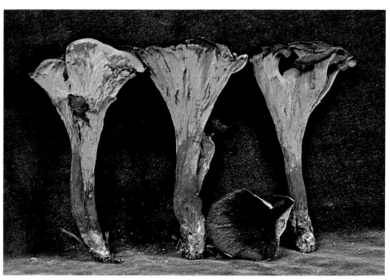

53 *Craterellus fallax*   About natural size

Cantharellus

This well-known genus has basically funnel-shaped fruiting bodies. The spore deposit is white to ochraceous buff. The spore-bearing surface may be smooth, wrinkled, veined, or with narrow blunt-edged gills that may have sharp edges by the time they are mature. The fruiting bodies may be solid or hollow. *Craterellus* consistently has dark gray to blackish fruiting bodies, in contrast to those of *Cantharellus*, which are white to yellow, orange, or red in part at least. Species with solid fruiting bodies with bright colors and smooth or nearly smooth hymenial surfaces approach *Clavariadelphus* closely. *Cantharellus* refers to a vase or cup.

Key to Species

1. Fruiting body hollow or soon becoming so; stalk not sharply differentiated from cap; hymenophore veined to shallowly poroid . . . .
. . . . 54. *Cantharellus floccosus*
1. Not as above 2
   2. Hymenophore veined to shallowly poroid; when young with a
      purple drab tone . . . . 55. *C. clavatus*
   2. Hymenophore lamellate; gills with obtuse edges at first 3
3. Cap egg yellow or paler, often large (3–15 cm broad) . . . . 56. *C. cibarius*
3. Cap vermillion red at first, 2–5 cm broad . . . . 57. *C. cinnabarinus*

Cantharellus floccosus   54
(Floccose Chanterelle)

Identification marks The fruiting body is shaped like a trumpet, and is hollow from early stages of development on to maturity. The hollow is at first lined with fairly delicate soft scales which soon disappear. The hymenophore is in the form of wrinkles and shallow pores resulting from cross veins between the wrinkles. The inner surface of the trumpet is red at first, becoming orange, and in age somewhat ochraceous. The spore deposit is ochraceous.

Edibility Mildly poisonous. Not recommended. Some people can eat it and suffer no ill effects, but others cannot. It is possible that tolerance levels may be involved here.

When and where During late summer and fall in northern regions such as the Northeast, Great Lakes region, and the Pacific Northwest. We have always found it under conifers.

Spores 12–15 x 6–7.5 μm, elongate-ellipsoid, surface slightly wrinkled, weakly dextrinoid.

Observations The species included under the name *C. floccosus* in the previous edition of this *Guide* is actually *C. bonari*. The latter was originally described from incompletely developed fruiting bodies. *C. floccosus* is placed in the genus *Gomphus* by some authors. *Floccosus* means woolly.

54   *Cantharellus floccosus*   About one-third natural size

55 Cantharellus clavatus
(Pig's Ears)

Identification marks There is a purple tinge or cast to the brown of the veinlike gills, and an olive tinge to the cap in age. When young, specimens usually have a much more pronounced purple drab cast on the cap margin. The fruiting bodies are often compound, and the underside of the cap is wrinkled to almost poroid. The spore deposit is pale ochraceous.

Edibility Edible and choice. Use the whole fruiting body—unless damaged by insect larvae. Insects are not a problem very often if the weather is cool.

When and where It is a late summer and fall species found scattered or in arcs in mossy conifer forests. It is widely distributed in the Northern Hemisphere. It is common in the Great Lakes area, New England, and in the Pacific Northwest.

Spores 10–12 x 5–6 μm, pale ochraceous in deposit, narrowly ellipsoid, inamyloid, surface uneven to slightly wrinkled.

Observations Some authors place this species in the genus *Gomphus*. *Clavatus* means club-shaped.

55 *Cantharellus clavatus* About one-half natural size

56 Cantharellus cibarius
(Chanterelle)

Identification marks The typical form has egg yellow colors overall, a fragrant odor both when fresh and when dried, a smooth cap with a wavy to lobed margin, and long-decurrent gills which at first have obtuse edges. The development of cross veins between gills is often rather pronounced. There are numerous variations of this species in North America.

Edibility Edible, and one of the best. We know of a few people who tried it and thought it peppery. However, it is generally highly regarded.

When and where In one or another of its variations, it is found throughout the forested areas of the United States and Canada. In southern Michigan it fruits in the summer in hardwood forests. In the Pacific Northwest it fruits in the fall on into the winter.

Spores   7–9 x 4–5 µm, yellowish in deposit, ellipsoid, smooth, inamyloid.

Observations   *C. subalbidus*, a native of the Pacific Northwest, is white overall at first, much fleshier than *C. cibarius*, and the best of all the Chanterelles for the table. *Cibarius* means food.

56   *Cantharellus cibarius*   About natural size

Cantharellus cinnabarinus   57
(Cinnabar Chanterelle)

Identification marks   The beautiful vermillion (cinnabar red) to pinkish red of the entire young fruiting body is distinctive. Aside from its color it is very similar to a small *C. cibarius*. However, it usually has a flatter cap and

57   *Cantharellus cinnabarinus*   Natural size

a more wavy margin; also, the gills are more inclined to retain their obtuse edges and to be more strongly intervenose. The red pigment fades rapidly in the sunlight.

Edibility   Edible and choice. There is no good reason why the poisonous *Omphalotus illudens* should be mistaken for either this species or *C. cibarius*, but this mistake has occurred many times.

When and where   It is a summer species in the eastern half of North America, where it is found scattered to gregarious along paths under hardwoods and in mixed stands. It is also abundant in the southeastern states. It frequents the borders of grassy oak woods after heavy rains.

Spores   7–9 x 4.5–5 μm, pinkish in deposit, ellipsoid, smooth, inamyloid.

Observations   Reportedly, the pigment in this species is the same as that in the pink flamingo. *Cinnabarinus* refers to the color of the juice of the dragon's blood tree, which is similar in color to cinnabar ore.

Fleshy Poroid Agaricales

Boletaceae (Fleshy Pore Fungi)

The boletes, as these fungi are often called, are fleshy, rapidly decaying, and often worm-riddled. In prime condition they are among our finest edible mushrooms. Relatively few poisonous species are known. Boletes can be collected during the late spring, summer, or fall, but are most abundant during hot wet weather in the summer or very rainy periods later. Many occur under conifers in the fall, and it is this group, now known under the genus name *Suillus*, which we wish to continue to emphasize.

In Michigan during the late summer and fall—when the rainy weather sets in and the heat of the summer is past—the pine and other conifer plantations in the southern part of the state, and the conifer forests in the northern part, literally burst with great quantities of relatively few species. At this time of year in the Michigan state parks and recreation areas, many people collect these boletes for immediate consumption and for preservation by various methods, such as drying, canning, or deep-freezing.

The most dangerous species in the Boletaceae are in the genus *Boletus*, but they are in rather well-marked groups, such as those with red tube-mouths. In the Great Lakes region these fruit mostly during hot wet summer weather. On the Pacific Coast, where the majority of the mushrooms occur in the fall-winter season, one may expect to find the undesirable species along with the "good" ones.

Key to Genera and Species

1. Cap covered with coarse dry gray to blackish scales; spore deposit blackish brown .... 87. *Strobilomyces floccopus*
1. Not as above 2
    2. Stalk shaggy-reticulate .... 86. *Boletellus russellii*
    2. Not as above 3
3. With any two of the following characters: a) Hymenophore somewhat gill-like; b) stalk glandular dotted; c) veil leaving a ring on the stalk; d) cap viscid 4
3. Not as above 5
    4. Spore deposit gray brown to chocolate brown, dark reddish brown to purple drab .... 61. *Fuscoboletinus spectabilis*
    4. Spore deposit dingy yellow to yellow brown, pale cinnamon, olive brown or greenish .... *Suillus*
5. Stalk lateral to eccentric; hymenophore somewhat gill-like .... 60. *Boletinellus merulioides*
5. Not as above 6
    6. Spore deposit pale yellow; cap dry; stalk soon becoming hollow .... *Gyroporus*
    6. Not as above 7
7. Spore deposit gray brown, red brown, vinaceous to purplish brown .... *Tylopilus*
7. Spore deposit olive brown, yellow brown, or amber brown 8

8. Stalk roughened with points, dots, squamules or streaks, and these dark brown to blackish or soon becoming so ...... *Leccinum*

8. Not as above (ornamentation not darkening) .... *Boletus*

Gyroporus

The two important characters of this genus are the yellow spore deposit and the stalk that soon grows hollow, at least at the base. In addition the spores are typically ellipsoid, and the tubes are yellow rather than olivaceous. The North American species apparently form mycorrhiza with hardwoods. The generic name means round pore.

Key to Species

1. Not staining violet or blue when injured .... 58. *Gyroporus castaneus*
1. Bruised or broken areas instantly changing to violet ....
   .... 59. *G. cyanescens* var. *violaceotinctus*

---

58   Gyroporus castaneus

Identification marks   The cap is slightly velvety to unpolished and glabrous, rusty reddish brown, dark yellow brown to pale alutaceous or whitish. The tubes are white becoming yellow by maturity, and do not stain blue when bruised. The spore deposit is yellow. The stalk is soon hollow and is pallid to about concolorous with the cap.

Edibility   Edible and choice, according to most reports.

58 *Gyroporus castaneus*   About natural size

When and where   In forests, generally of hardwoods, east of the Great Plains during rainy periods in the summer and early fall.

Spores   8–12 x 5–6 μm, yellow in deposit, ellipsoid, smooth, very pale in KOH under the microscope, inamyloid.

Observations   In North America we often find a form with a slender stalk growing gregariously in considerable quantity. It is more frequently encountered in the Great Lakes region than the type form which has a stalk up to 3 cm thick. *Castaneus* means chestnut brown.

Gyroporus cyanescens var. violaceotinctus   59

Identification marks   The caps are yellowish, and their surfaces are rough but not viscid. The tubes are white becoming yellow and, when bruised, stain indigo blue so quickly that one can write on the pore surface with a toothpick or needle. The stalk grows hollow rather soon, is colored about as the cap, is fibrillose, and at times has a more or less medial constriction or zone.

Edibility   Edible and choice, but when found in sandy soil it is very difficult to clean.

When and where   In our experience this fungus is most frequent on sandy soil under second growth hardwoods or in mixed woods, especially along roads through such regions. It fruits from midsummer to fall. Its area appears to be that east of the Great Plains.

Spores   8–10 x 5–6 μm, yellow in deposit, ellipsoid, smooth, greenish hyaline in KOH, inamyloid.

Observations   The blueing reaction is not confined to the tubes, and in the course of cleaning specimens for cooking, we found our hands, the kitchen counter, and anything else it touched stained blue. We had to use a chlorine bleach to remove the stains. *Cyanescens* means changing to blue; *violaceotinctus* means having a violet tinge. As the photograph indicates, this species was placed in *Boletus* previously.

59 *Gyroporus cyanescens* var. *violaceotinctus*   About one-half natural size

60　Boletinellus merulioides

Identification marks　The cap is colored olive to olive brown or yellowish olive, but in age it may become more or less date brown. The surface is dry and unpolished at first. The tubes are short, the pores broad and dingy to olive brown and staining slightly bluish where bruised. The radiating lines of the pores cause them to appear more or less lamellate (gill-like) in age. The stalk is short and yellow, often becoming nearly black. It is typically laterally attached but may be eccentric. There is no veil.

Edibility　Edible, but unattractive. It has a peculiar consistency.

When and where　Common under ash trees during late summer and fall east of the Great Plains. It is often found around shade trees in lawns and is a common "urban" bolete.

Spores　7–10 x 6–7.5 μm, olive brown in deposit, ellipsoid to subglobose, smooth, hyaline to yellowish brown in KOH, inamyloid.

Observations　*Merulioides* means somewhat like Merulius, i.e., the hymenophore is intermediate between gill-like and porelike. This species was placed in *Gyrodon* previously.

61　Fuscoboletinus spectabilis

Identification marks　This is a bolete of sphagnum bogs, having spores which are a dark vinaceous brown, yellow tubes, and wide pores (giving the impression of gills with numerous cross walls between them). The young button is grayish and dry, but becomes redder in age, and the surface layer beneath the veil remnants slowly gelatinizes. The veil also finally gelatinizes, becoming a thin translucent layer. When it breaks, it leaves a slimy annulus which becomes dark colored from the spores which fall on it.

Edibility　Edible, but apparently not popular—possibly because of its short fruiting season and relatively inaccessible habitat.

When and where　It is found under eastern larch in bogs east of the Great Plains in southern Canada and the northern United States from late August into September. We find it most abundant in the larch–poison sumac bogs as contrasted to spruce bogs.

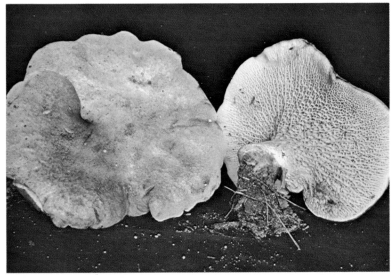

60　*Boletinellus merulioides*　　　　　　　　　　　　　　　About natural size

Spores 9–15 x 4.5–6 μm, deep vinaceous brown in deposit, smooth, inequilateral in profile, pale yellow to tawny in KOH, and strongly dextrinoid.

Observations Any one seeking to collect this species should learn to recognize poison sumac first. *Spectabilis* means distinguished.

61 *Fuscoboletinus spectabilis*   About two-thirds natural size

Tylopilus

The color of the spore deposit is the chief distinguishing character of these species in relation to *Boletus*. In *Tylopilus* it is reddish (flesh color) or vinaceous brown to more or less chocolate brown, whereas in *Boletus* it is mostly in the yellow brown to olive or olive brown range. If the bolete in hand has dark brown to blackish ornamentation on the stalk, and dark brown spore deposits, see *Leccinum*. In *Tylopilus* the young tubes are white to pallid more often than not. *Tylopilus* means having a lumpy cap.

Key to Species

1. Taste mild; base of stalk yellow . . . . 62. *Tylopilus chromapes*
1. Taste bitter; stalk brownish . . . . 63. *T. rubrobrunneus*

Tylopilus chromapes   62

Identification marks The base of the stalk is chrome yellow, the surface of the stalk over the upper half is covered by a pinkish scurfiness, and the cap when young and fresh is a beautiful pink. There is no change to blue on any injured part. This species was placed in *Boletus* previously.

Edibility Edible and, according to some, rather good.

When and where It is not uncommon in the aspen-birch areas in the Great

Lakes area, especially during wet weather in June and early July. It is widely distributed east of the Great Plains in the northern United States and southern Canada.

Spores 11–17 x 4–5.5 μm, vinaceous brown to avellaneous in deposit, somewhat inequilateral in profile view, smooth, nearly hyaline in KOH, inamyloid to slightly dextrinoid.

Observations *Chromapes* means chrome colored stalk.

62 *Tylopilus chromapes*   About one-half natural size

63   Tylopilus rubrobrunneus

Identification marks The distinctly bitter taste (to most people), the pinkish to vinaceous tubes at maturity, the almost complete absence of reticulation on the stalk, and the dull deep vinaceous brown cap are the diagnostic field characters. The caps may reach 30 cm broad.

63 *Tylopilus rubrobrunneus*   About one-third natural size

Edibility   We have no data on it. The bitter taste is about like that in *T. felleus*, and enough to discourage the pot-hunter.

When and where   This is a mid- to late summer species occurring generally east of the Great Plains on poor soil under scrub oak. It has been confused in times past with *T. felleus*, which has a distinctly reticulate stalk.

Spores   10–14 x 3–4.5 μm, vinaceous red in deposit, somewhat inequilateral in profile view, smooth, nearly hyaline in KOH, a small number strongly dextrinoid.

Observations   In the cutover scrub oak lands of Michigan, during wet weather late in the summer, this species produces large fruiting bodies by the hundreds and is a most conspicuous sight on the forest floor. It is often parasitized by a white mold. *Rubrobrunneus* means a dark red brown.

Suillus

This genus is characterized by the pale cinnamon to dark yellow brown spore deposit, by the stalk often being covered by glandular dots and smears, by the cap being typically viscid to slimy, and by many of the species having a veil that grows out from the margin of the cap. There are also a number of important microscopic features, such as the small spores and the bundles of cystidia distributed over the hymenium lining the walls of the tubes. The group is a large one, and nearly all the species form mycorrhiza with conifers. The species known from North America are all supposed to be edible or at the most to cause only minor digestive upsets, and some are highly regarded by mycophagists. A poisonous species has been reported from the island of Majorca. *Suillus* means of or belonging to swine.

Key to Species

1. Cap dry and fibrillose to scaly 2
1. Cap viscid (but may be more or less covered with patches of appressed tomentum) 4
   2. Stalk soon hollow in basal area .... 64. *Suillus cavipes*
   2. Stalk remaining solid 3
3. Stalk with a boot of red veil remnants similar to those on cap; associated with eastern white pine .... 66. *S. pictus*
3. Stalk not booted as above; associated with Douglas fir ...... 65. *S. lakei*
   4. Stalk annulate, 1–2 cm thick; annulus with purple brown zone on under side; associated with pine .... 67. *S. luteus*
   4. Stalk not annulate 5
5. Tubes and/or context staining blue where injured .... 68. *S. tomentosus*
5. Not as above 6
   6. Stalk white when young and lacking glandular dots and smears .... 69. *S. brevipes*
   6. Stalk soon showing brownish dots and smears 7
7. Margin of cap at first with cottony to fibrillose-floccose patches of veil material; stalk 4–8 (10) mm thick .... 70. *S. americanus*

7. Not as above, margin of cap naked when young (lacking any tendency to produce a marginal veil) 8
   8. Cap white to orange cinnamon; associated with conifers, especially pine .... 71. *S. granulatus*
   8. Cap yellow at first; in age often with red stains on cap; associated with aspen .... 72. *S. subaureus*

---

64   Suillus cavipes

Identification marks   The cap is dry and fibrillose to squamulose, and the color ranges from dark rusty brown to yellow. The tubes and flesh are yellow; the pores are large and somewhat radially arranged (sublamellate). The stalk is often annulate, or the ring is present as a slight fibrillose zone. The base of the stalk soon becomes hollow.

Edibility   Edible and choice, but one must be careful not to become poisoned by poison sumac while collecting it. *S. cavipes* cooks up drier than most other species of the genus.

When and where   It is to be expected in North America where larch is found (either eastern or western larch). It fruits during late summer and fall and can be collected almost every year.

Spores   7–10 x 3.5–4 μm, dark yellow brown in deposit, obscurely inequilateral in profile, smooth, greenish hyaline in KOH, inamyloid.

Observations   In the previous edition of this *Guide* it was included as *Boletinus cavipes*. *Cavipes* means hollow stalk.

64   *Suillus cavipes*   About one-half natural size

---

65   Suillus lakei

Identification marks   The cap is distinctly fibrillose to fibrillose-squamulose, dull red to reddish gray in color, and in age at times gray with scarcely a tint of red. This species forms mycorrhiza with Douglas fir; hence one finds it near these trees. The stalk is annulate and when injured stains greenish in the basal area. The ring is dry, not gelatinous as in a number of species in this genus.

Edibility   Edible and choice, according to a number of collectors. It is not as slimy as many species of *Suillus* and so cooks up drier.

When and where   It is a late summer to fall species, often very abundant after the first fall rains. It is found throughout the range of Douglas fir in western North America.

Spores   7–10 (11) x 3–4 μm, dull cinnamon in deposit, in face view approximately oblong, smooth, inamyloid.

Observations   The cap is persistently squamulose, but there is considerable variation in its color. The species was named in honor of Professor E. R. Lake of Oregon Agricultural College (now Oregon State University).

65   *Suillus lakei*   About two-thirds natural size

Suillus pictus   66

Identification marks   The deep red fibrillose to fibrillose-squamulose cap and the floccose remains of the veil on the stalk are conspicuous. The stalk is solid, and the fruiting bodies are always associated with eastern white pine. Both the tubes and flesh are yellow, there is no change to blue on injury, and the pores, by maturity, have become large and radially elongate.

Edibility   Edible and choice; if one lives in the eastern white pine belt it is a species to be learned.

When and where   As we have already indicated, it occurs under eastern white pine. It fruits in the summer on into the fall, depending on the weather. It usually is scattered, but finding enough for a meal is not particularly difficult. However, we have not had good luck finding it in plantations of eastern white pine of pole size or under.

Spores   8–11 (12) x 3.5–5 μm, in deposit olive brown when moist or clay color when faded, inequilateral in profile, smooth, inamyloid.

Observations   The red fibrils on cap and stalk become gray in old fruiting bodies. This species was previously placed in *Boletinus*. *Pictus* means colored or painted.

66 *Suillus pictus*   About one-half natural size

---

67   Suillus luteus
(Slippery Jack)

Identification marks   The cap is very slimy and dull dark reddish brown at first. It becomes paler to yellow (at times) in age. There are no fibrils on the young cap. The tubes are yellow, including the pores. The stalk is glandular dotted above and below the ring. The tissue of the ring is not intergrown with that of the stalk. The veil has an outer, dull purplish brown layer over the exterior which gelatinizes into a purple brown line or zone.

Edibility   Edible and popular. Wipe the slime from the cap when you collect it, and remove the tubes before cooking. For best results use immature fruiting bodies. In older specimens the flesh is often mushy when cooked.

When and where   It is a fall-fruiting species usually available from Septem-

67 *Suillus luteus*   About one-third natural size

ber into November, depending on the weather. We find it most abundant in pine plantations, but it also occurs in natural stands and is known across the continent. It is not common in the Northwest, but there it is replaced by *Suillus borealis*, which is like it in almost every respect except that it does not have a ring on the stalk.

Spores 7–9 x 2.5–3 μm, pale cinnamon color in deposit, duller when moisture has escaped, oblong in face view, slightly inequilateral in profile, smooth, inamyloid.

Observations *Luteus* means yellow.

Suillus tomentosus   68

Identification marks The stalk at maturity is conspicuously covered with dark glandular smears and dots. The cap is yellow to pale orange and is decorated with tufts of grayish to brownish tomentum (rarely reddish). The tubes stain dingy blue when bruised. There are no veil remnants on the stalk.

Edibility Not poisonous, but a number of cases of so-called indigestion have been reported to us. Those who do eat it usually prefer other species if they are available, but it has also been reported as good. Since there are a number of variations of this species, it is possible that the edible qualities vary with the variety eaten.

When and where It is associated with 2- and 3-needle pines, and is common in the Rocky Mountains, the Northwest, and the Great Lakes area. It was described from New York as *Boletus hirtellus* var. *mutans*.

Spores 7–10 x 3–4 μm, in deposit dark olive brown when moist, fading in air-drying to a dull cinnamon, in profile view narrowly inequilateral, inamyloid.

Observations Most collections from the Great Lakes area have had pale yellow caps; those from the mountains of Idaho had a more orange tone; and in the Pacific Northwest var. *discolor*, with a generally dingy brownish tone shading to yellow, is often common. *Tomentosus* means covered with soft hairs.

68 *Suillus tomentosus*   About one-half natural size

69 Suillus brevipes

Identification marks When young the cap is very dark vinaceous brown and slimy. It becomes paler and yellower in age. The pores are pale yellow, and the thick short stalk is white at first and lacks glandular smears. In age a few dots may become evident. The margin of the young cap is naked; no indications of a false (marginal) veil of any kind are evident.

Edibility Edible and widely collected. Wipe off the slime and peel off the tubes. In young specimens the flesh is thick and firm, and the stalks are tender as well. On very young caps the tubes need not be removed.

When and where This is the common *Suillus* found under lodgepole pine in the west, and is common under 2- and 3-needle pines from the Great Lakes area eastward. It is also found in the pine lands of the South in the winter. In northern regions it fruits in August and September.

Spores 7–9 (10) x 2.8–3.5 μm, cinnamon colored in deposit, smooth, obscurely inequilateral, inamyloid.

Observations *Brevipes* means with a short stalk.

69 *Suillus brevipes*   About two-thirds natural size

70 Suillus americanus

Identification marks The bright yellow cap with scattered flattened patches of tomentum, the copious dry cottony material of the false veil along the cap margin of young specimens, the narrow stalk typically less than 1 cm thick, the stalk surface covered with glandular smears, and the association with white pine make it an easily recognized species.

Edibility Of little consequence because of the thin flesh, but not poisonous as far as we are aware. We did learn of a case of severe allergy to this species. The victim could not even handle the fruiting bodies without developing a reaction.

When and where It is a common species associated with eastern white pine, and it fruits during the late summer and early fall. It is to be expected throughout the range of eastern white pine.

Spores 8–11 x 4–5 μm, dull cinnamon in deposit, narrowly inequilateral in profile, smooth, yellow brown in KOH, very weakly dextrinoid.

Observations *Suillus sibiricus*, the most closely related species, is common in the Pacific Northwest. *Americanus* means of America.

70 *Suillus americanus*   About one-half natural size

Suillus granulatus   71

Identification marks The cap is sticky and ranges from whitish when young to orange cinnamon in age; intermediate stages are vinaceous buff to vinaceous brown. The margin of the young cap is naked. The stalk is white

71 *Suillus granulatus*   About one-half natural size

at first but soon shows brownish glandular smears. It becomes yellow in age. There is no veil.

Edibility   Edible and popular. Young specimens are preferred.

When and where   It is common in the northern and western conifer areas of North America. It apparently forms mycorrhiza with various pines and is often abundant in plantations. It fruits following wet weather during late summer and fall.

Spores   7–9 (10) x 2.5–3.5 μm, dingy cinnamon in deposit, in profile somewhat inequilateral, smooth, inamyloid.

Observations   *Granulatus* means pertaining to granules, but the name is misleading for this species, since there is nothing granular about it.

---

72   Suillus subaureus

Identification marks   This pale yellow species has only faint traces or patches of matted-down tomentum on the cap. The tubes are yellow and do not stain blue. The stalk is not conspicuously glandular dotted but when truly fresh is somewhat sticky to the touch. It is regularly 1 cm thick or more. At times the cap shows bright red spots or patches of matted tomentum.

Edibility   Presumably edible. It is reported as edible, but there are problems as to the species actually tested. Not recommended.

When and where   As we know this species, it will occur in stands of aspen and oak with no conifers in the vicinity, and, of course, it occurs in mixed stands. It fruits during summer and early fall and is one of the first species of the genus to fruit in Michigan, often appearing around the middle of June. Its range appears to be in the region of the Great Lakes and eastward.

Spores   7–10 x 2.7–3.5 μm, olive brown when fresh in deposit, smooth, obscurely inequilateral in profile, inamyloid.

Observations   The name *subaureus* means somewhat golden yellow.

72   *Suillus subaureus*   About one-half natural size

Leccinum

The field character for this genus is the dark colored (often black), rough ornamentation of the stalk. This ornamentation is often white in young fruiting bodies, but soon darkens to brown and finally blackish. In a few species it is coal black in young fruiting bodies. The tubes are white in most species when young and are often merely dark brown when mature. A number of species are mycorrhiza-formers with birch. *Leccinum* is an Italian word (*leccino*) for fungus.

Key to Species

1. Stalk ornamentation black in button stages and on to maturity . . . . 74. *Leccinum atrostipitatum*
1. Stalk ornamentation white or pale brown at first, blackening on aging 2
   2. Cap orange red and margin appendiculate; cut flesh slowly becoming grayish lilac and finally nearly black . . . . 75. *L. insigne*
   2. Cap gray brown, margin not appendiculate; cut flesh unchanging or in time merely slightly brownish . . . . 73. *L. scabrum*

Leccinum scabrum   73

Identification marks   The edge of the cap scarcely projects beyond the tubes; the cap surface is viscid when moist, and is dull brown to dull yellowish brown. The cut context of the cap and upper part of the stalk do not change color significantly on exposure to air. The flesh of the stalk stains slowly to a dingy tan when cut. *L. scabrum* is to be regarded as a "collective" species.

Edibility   Edible, but not highly rated.

When and where   This and a number of more or less similar species are associated with birch. All of these fruit during the summer and fall. *L. scabrum* is common and widely distributed in North America wherever, apparently, birches (the genus *Betula*) occur.

73 *Leccinum scabrum*   About two-thirds natural size

Spores 15–19 x 5–7 μm, dark yellow brown in deposit, in profile ventricose-inequilateral, smooth, pale tawny in iodine (weakly dextrinoid?).

Observations *Scabrum* means rough; in this species it refers to the ornamentation of the stalk.

---

74 Leccinum atrostipitatum

Identification marks The cap cuticle at first extends beyond the tubes about 5 mm, and this band becomes broken into flaps as the cap expands. The ornamentation of the stalk is black at first (not pale and then darkening with age), and the cap is orange buff to orange brown or duller. The cut flesh changes from white to slightly reddish and then black.

Edibility Reports on this species are not at all favorable, but to our knowledge there have been no fatalities. Apparently the disturbances were of the gastrointestinal type. Not recommended.

When and where Scattered to gregarious, and associated with birch (particularly white birches). We have no records of it from under yellow birch or dwarf birches. It fruits during the summer and fall east of the Great Plains.

Spores 13–17 x 4–5 μm, dull yellow brown in deposit, somewhat inequilateral in profile, smooth, inamyloid.

Observations *Atrostipitatum* means black stalk. In this species the stalk is blacker when young than it is in age.

74 *Leccinum atrostipitatum*   About one-half natural size

---

75 Leccinum insigne

Identification marks The cap is red to orange; its margin is decorated at first with flaps of the cap cuticle which extend beyond the tubes. When the fruiting body is cut in half lengthwise, the white flesh—at least in or near the apex of the stalk—turns lilac grayish and finally nearly black. The stalk ornamentation is pallid at first but soon darkens to nearly black.

Edibility   Edible and good. It darkens when cooked, and thus does not make a dish appealing to one's aesthetic sense.

When and where   It fruits under aspen from spring on into the fall. It is to be expected in North America where large- and small-toothed aspens grow. It is frequently confused with *L. aurantiacum*.

Spores   13–16 x 4–5.5 μm, yellow brown in deposit, smooth, in profile somewhat inequilateral, mostly lemon yellow in Melzer's solution.

Observations   *Insigne* means distinctive or outstanding.

75   *Leccinum insigne*   About two-thirds natural size

Boletus

The spore deposit color is dull yellow brown to olive brown, and the tubes at maturity are typically dingy olive to olive ochraceous, though they may be very bright yellow at first. The stalk is often ornamented with a reticulum, but this may be such a fine netting that it is best seen with a hand lens. Usually it is best developed over the apex of the stalk. The tube mouths are red to dark brown in one group of species, and it is in this group that most poisonous species are known. The stalk may be roughened to somewhat squamulose, but this ornamentation does not darken as in the genus *Leccinum*. The spores are smooth as seen under the light microscope. *Boletus* in our Latin dictionary means the best kind of mushroom. In Greek it means a clod (of earth).

Key to Species

1. Pores red when young 2
1. Pores not red at first 5
  2.   Stalk coarsely reticulate; cap apple red and viscid at first . . . . .
  . . . . .76. *Boletus frostii*
  2.   Not as above 3

76   Boletus frostii

Identification marks   The coarsely reticulate stalk, apple red viscid cap, deep red tube mouths which bear droplets of a yellow fluid when young, and the change to blue of injured parts are distinctive. The stalk is often as red as the cap.

Edibility   It is reported as edible, but we strongly advise following the rule about not eating any bolete with red pores.

When and where   It prefers thin, sandy soil under scrub oak in the Great Lakes region. It is in this habitat that it fruits in abundance during the hot,

76   *Boletus frostii*   About one-half natural size

humid weather of midsummer. We have never found it associated with conifers. It fruits from July through September, depending on the weather, and is to be expected in the area east of the Great Plains.

Spores 11–15 x 4–5 μm, olive brown in deposit, narrowly inequilateral in profile, boat-shaped in face view, smooth, inamyloid, ochraceous in KOH.

Observations The species was named in honor of Charles Christopher Frost, an early American mycologist.

Boletus subvelutipes 77

Identification marks The stalk is not reticulate; instead, it is covered by minute branlike particles. Injured areas turn blue instantly. The cap is velvety and bright ochraceous at first; in age the whole fruiting body is dingy brown. The tube mouths are orange red, becoming paler in age. The base of the stalk may or may not be somewhat hairy.

Edibility Dangerous. Follow the rule and do not experiment with boletes with red tube mouths (see "Observations" below).

When and where This is one of the early-fruiting boletes. In the Great Lakes region it is often abundant by mid-June. It prefers open hardwood stands of trees twenty to forty years old. *Boletus luridus* often occurs with it. We suspect its range to be the area east of the Great Plains.

Spores 14–18 x 5–6.5 (8) μm, olive brown when moist in deposit, in profile strongly inequilateral, smooth, many dextrinoid.

Observations In some areas the cap typically is as indicated above, but specimens with reddish caps when young also occur. The species is rather variable in the color of the cap, the development of tomentum at the base of the stalk, and the degree of redness of the pores at various stages of development. *Subvelutipes* means with a somewhat velvety stalk.

Boletus pulcherrimus 78

Identification marks This beautiful bolete is at once recognizable by the brilliant scarlet tube mouths, the olive brown cap, the reticulate stalk with its varied red and yellow colors, and the broken flesh staining blue. The stalk is thick but not bulbous at first, as in *B. satanus*. *B. satanus*, in addition to the large bulb, has a pallid cap.

Edibility To be regarded as POISONOUS because of its close relationship to *B. satanus*, and in line with the rule against eating boletes with red pores.

When and where It is rare, but still a feature of the Pacific Coast rain forest. After warm heavy fall rains following a moist summer it does fruit in quantity—but these conditions are not often realized.

Spores 13–16 x 5.5–6.5 μm, inequilateral in profile, subelliptic in face view, smooth, ochraceous in KOH.

Observations In a previous edition of the *Guide*, this species is treated under the name *B. eastwoodiae*. Unfortunately, it recently was found that the type collection of *B. eastwoodiae* is a collection of *B. satanus*. This necessitated giving a new name to the species previously known under the name *B. eastwoodiae*. *Pulcherrimus* means beautiful.

77 *Boletus subvelutipes*   About one-half natural size

78 *Boletus pulcherrimus*   About one-half natural size

79   Boletus luridus

Identification marks The orange red tube mouths, reticulate and more or less cylindric stalk, the quick change to blue when injured, and the yellowish to clay colored, dry, unpolished cap are distinctive.

Edibility POISONOUS, or at least to be so regarded. Dr. Rolf Singer, who doubtless knows this species as well as any person, does not concur with authors who list it as edible. His opinion is based on personal experience.

When and where In the upper Great Lakes region it seems to occur with *B. subvelutipes* in the same woods at the same time of year. Apparently it is not as abundant in North America as earlier reports indicate. It has appeared very sporadically in Michigan.

Spores 12–17 x 5.5–7 μm, olive brown in deposit, smooth, somewhat inequilateral in profile, about tawny in KOH, somewhat dextrinoid.

Observations *Luridus* means a pale dingy yellow.

79 *Boletus luridus*   About one-half natural size

Boletus variipes   80

Identification marks The habitat on soil under hardwoods, reticulate stalk, lack of changes to blue or green where injured, white coating over the young tubes, dry cap when young and fresh soon becoming areolate-rimose, and dark to pale gray brown color are distinctive. The stalk is often inflated at the base and the interior punky.

Edibility Edible, but not choice (as previously reported). Some collectors

80 *Boletus variipes*   About one-half natural size

state that it is bitter when cooked. In contrast to *B. edulis*, the stalk is seldom usable.

When and where   Under scrub oak on poor soil after heavy summer rains east of the Great Plains. Like *B. edulis*, it is a collective species. A number of the closely related populations are common in the Southeast.

Spores   12–16 (18) x 3.5–5.5 µm, dull olive brown in deposit, smooth, narrowly inequilateral in profile, yellow in KOH, weakly dextrinoid.

Observations   The differences of opinion as to the edibility of this species may be correlated with variability in taxonomic characters. *Variipes* means with a variable stalk; in this instance the stalk varies from equal to strongly clavate.

---

81   Boletus edulis
(Steinpilz)

Identification marks   The cap is slightly viscid when fresh and moist, but soon dries. Typically there is no change to blue on injured parts, the stalk is covered with a very fine reticulum, and the pores at first are covered by a thin white layer of hyphae. There are various color varieties. In Colorado the mature cap typically is dull red; in Idaho bread-crust brown; and in Michigan var. *ochraceus* has a yellow cap, and var. *clavipes* is reddish cinnamon.

Edibility   Edible, and one of the very best.

When and where   In North America it is to be sought in conifer forests. In the Rocky Mountains it fruits in July and August, and in the Northwest in the fall. East of the Great Plains it fruits both in the summer and fall. Like so many other species, its fruiting depends on the amount of precipitation, and some years it apparently does not appear.

Spores   (13) 14–19 x 4–6.5 µm, olive brown to fuscous olive in deposit, in profile elongate-inequilateral, smooth, pale tawny in KOH, mostly inamyloid to weakly dextrinoid.

Observations   *Edulis* means edible.

---

82   Boletus mirabilis

Identification marks   This is one of the few boletes found on rotting logs and stumps. It is known by its rough dark brown to dark red brown cap, pale yellow to greenish tubes which stain mustard yellow, and reddish stalk which may or may not show reticulations. The cap seems almost granulose at times.

Edibility   Edible and choice, but be sure the specimens are young and fresh. This fungus is attacked by a white mold, and such material should not be saved for table use.

When and where   It occurs solitary to clustered on rotting conifer logs, especially hemlock, in the fall in the Pacific Northwest. It is one of the mycological features of the Olympic National Park. It is rare east of the Great Plains, but in the Great Lakes area and the Southeast, *Boletus projectellus*, a very closely related species, is often fairly abundant.

Spores   19–24 x 7–9 µm, olive to olive brown in deposit, smooth, somewhat inequilateral in profile, in Melzer's solution some faintly clouded grayish and some weakly dextrinoid.

Observations   *Mirabilis* means admirable or marvelous.

81a *Boletus edulis*   About one-half natural size

81b *Boletus edulis*   About one-half natural size

82 *Boletus mirabilis*   About one-third natural size

83   Boletus pallidus

Identification marks The cap when young is a beautiful off-white but becomes dingy and finally dull brown. The tubes are pale greenish yellow and stain dingy blue. The stalk lacks distinctive markings and is colored at first about like the cap.

Edibility Edible and considered good. Bitter specimens sometimes occur, but, according to some authors, the bitter taste disappears in cooking.

When and where It is a common species east of the Great Plains, and fruits in abundance in the hot, humid midsummer weather. It frequents moss beds along the edges of bogs but is probably associated with oak and beech.

Spores 9–15.5 x 3–4.5 μm, olive brown in deposit, smooth, inequilateral in profile, greenish hyaline in KOH, inamyloid to weakly dextrinoid.

Observations *Pallidus* means pallid (off-white).

83 *Boletus pallidus*   About one-half natural size

84   Boletus chrysenteron

Identification marks The cap is 3-10 cm broad, the color is at first dull olive to olive brown, usually with a red zone along the margin; red tints develop in the cracks as the cap becomes areolate. The tubes are dingy pale yellow and stain greenish to blue. The stalk is dry and not marked distinctly.

Edibility Edible, but there are many closely related, untested species. Do not eat any that are covered by a moldy growth; the latter is a parasite.

When and where It is not uncommon in second growth hardwood stands east of the Great Plains, and under aspen in the Rocky Mountains. It appears during summer and fall, but not in large numbers.

Spores 9–13 x 3.5–4.5 (5) μm, olive brown in deposit, smooth, narrowly inequilateral in profile, bright yellow in KOH, yellow in Melzer's solution.

Observations The specific epithet *chrysenteron* is derived from two Greek words meaning gold and intestine. The application of this to the above species is not readily apparent to us.

84 *Boletus chrysenteron*   About two-thirds natural size

Boletus zelleri   85

Identification marks   The cap is 4-12 cm broad, dark olive brown beneath a whitish bloom, and develops red tones in age. The surface is slightly slippery when the bloom is removed. Typically, the surface does not become areolate. The flesh is yellow and the tubes greenish yellow, but where injured they stain slightly to blue. The stalk is yellowish at first but becomes dull red variously in age.

Edibility   Edible and choice. In recent years it has become a favorite in the Pacific Northwest.

When and where   It is characteristic of the rain forests of the Pacific Northwest, where it is often found in stream valleys where alder is present. It fruits during the fall and on into the winter.

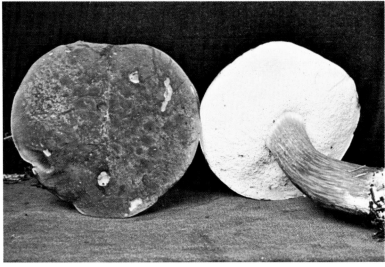

85 *Boletus zelleri*   About natural size

Spores 12–15 x 4–6 μm, olive brown in deposit, smooth, somewhat in-equilateral in profile, weakly dextrinoid.

Observations This species was named in honor of Professor S. M. Zeller of Oregon State University.

---

86   Boletellus russellii

Identification marks The coarsely shaggy-reticulate stalk and the rimose-areolate cap surface are striking characters. The stalk is typically long in relation to the width of the cap. The flesh is yellow and does not stain blue where injured.

Edibility Edible, but not highly rated. The flesh of the cap grows quite soft in age, and little is left after the tubes are removed.

When and where It is a species of our southern hardwood forests, favoring well drained soil and fruiting during hot, wet weather in the summer and fall. It extends as far north as southern Canada.

Spores 15–20 x 7–11 μm, olive brown in deposit, longitudinally grooved, in face view more or less elliptic, in profile somewhat inequilateral, somewhat dextrinoid, dark yellow brown in KOH.

Observations When perfectly fresh the base of the stalk is viscid. Mr. Frost named this species after Mr. John Lewis Russell, who first collected it.

86   *Boletellus russellii*   About one-half natural size

---

87   Strobilomyces floccopus
(Old Man of the Woods)

Identification marks Hardly any one is likely to misidentify this species after seeing it once. The coarse wartlike patches on the cap, the ashy white pores which stain red when bruised and then blacken, the shaggy, cottony veil, and reticulate blackish spores (if a microscope is available) are diagnostic.

Edibility Not poisonous, but apparently few people like it.

When and where Solitary to scattered in hardwood or mixed habitats, common but never in abundance, summer and fall east of the Great Plains.

Spores 9.5–15 x 8.5–12 μm, black in deposit, nearly globose, reticulate, the ridges up to 1.7 μm high, dextrinoid.

Observations *Strobilomyces* pertains to a pine cone, hence the species has been called the "pine cone fungus." *Floccopus* means woolly stalk, a feature due to the loose organization of the veil-remnants on the stalk.

87 *Strobilomyces floccopus*   About one-half natural size

Gilled Agaricales

All the families of the fleshy fungi having gills on the underside of the cap are grouped in part of this order. The fleshy pore fungi (Boletaceae) constitute the remainder. One of the principal features used in the recognition of the families of the gilled mushrooms is the color of the spore deposit. Be sure to have the spore deposit on white paper so that delicate color tones can be observed. The keys are based as much as possible on field characters, but accurate observations on the color of the spore deposit must be made before one may feel that his/her identification of a collection is final. Also, when checking spores for the amyloid reaction with Melzer's solution, scrape spores from the deposit and make the test on a glass slide with a white paper beneath it. Paper itself gives an amyloid reaction.

Key to Families and Genera

1. Spore deposit white, yellowish, orange, or pink 2
1. Spore deposit ochraceous orange to rusty brown, chocolate brown, black, or dull red 6
  2. Fruiting bodies mostly with thick fragile stalks lacking veil remnants; spores amyloid; gills attached to stalk and both rigid and brittle; typically terrestrial .... Russulaceae
  2. Not as above 3
3. Gills waxy and clean in appearance .... Hygrophoraceae (see also *Laccaria*)
3. Gills not as above 4
  4. Gills attached to stalk (if one is present); in old caps the gills may have broken away from the stalk .... Tricholomataceae
  4. Gills typically free from stalk; cap and stalk typically cleanly separable 5
5. Outer veil well-developed; membranous, a fragile membrane, powdery, or a slime veil .... Amanitaceae
5. Outer veil, if present, intergrown with inner veil (hence ring on the stalk ragged at times, sometimes thick and more or less double) .... Lepiotaceae
  6. Spore deposit dull reddish to reddish cinnamon or vinaceous 7
  6. Spore deposit brown, chocolate color, or black 8
7. Gills free from stalk; cap and stalk cleanly separable .... Pluteaceae
7. Gills attached to stalk (but often seceding in age in some); stalk and cap not cleanly separable .... Rhodophyllaceae
  8. Gills thickish, broad, and usually decurrent; spores more or less boletoid in shape .... Gilled Mushrooms Related to Boletaceae (see also *Paxillus*)
  8. Not as above 9
9. Spore deposit tawny to rusty brown to ochraceous or cinnamon brown to earth brown 10
9. Spore deposit chocolate brown to black or dark vinaceous brown 11
  10. Fruiting bodies very soft-fleshed if large; if small, stalk exceedingly fragile .... Bolbitiaceae
  10. Not as above .... Cortinariaceae and Related Genera

11. Stalk cleanly separable from cap; gills free or practically so; ring on stalk usually present and membranous .... Agaricaceae
11. Not as above 12
    12. Fruiting bodies with gills that liquify after spores have been discharged; or fruiting bodies very fragile (especially the stalks) but gills at maturity gray brown to chocolate brown to black ... . Coprinaceae
    12. Fruiting bodies not especially fragile, stalks rather pliant if slender; gills never liquifying .... Strophariaceae

Gilled Mushrooms Related to Boletaceae

Phylloporus, *Gomphidius*, and *Chroogomphus* are the genera treated here by the inclusion of one species in each. These genera are closely related to the boletes, especially in their spore morphology and gill structure. The hymenophore, however, is gill-like rather than porelike, so they are placed here as intermediates. It is such fungi as those placed in each of the above genera that have led specialists to include the family Boletaceae in with the Agaricales. *Phylloporus* as a genus connects up to *Boletus* in the vicinity of *B. subtomentosus* and similar species. *Chroogomphus* appears to be closely related to *Suillus*.

Key to Species

1. Cap dry, dull red to olivaceous .... 90. *Phylloporus rhodoxanthus*
1. Not as above 2
    2. Cap slimy, rose red to dull red; context white .... 88. *Gomphidius subroseus*
    2. Caps thinly viscid but soon dry, orange ochraceous at first; context ochraceous .... 89. *Chroogomphus vinicolor*

Gomphidius subroseus   88

Identification marks   The medium sized caps (3–6 cm broad) which are glabrous, slimy, and at first bright to dull pinkish red are characteristic. The context of the cap is white, and both the odor and taste are mild. The stalk is whitish down to the yellow base and is coated at first by a thin veil of slime.

Edibility   It is reported as edible and good.

When and where   It fruits from July to November in the northern United States and southern Canada. It has been reported under hemlock and the true firs but appears to favor Douglas fir.

Spores   (11) 15–20 x 4.5–7 μm, smoky brown in deposit, in profile somewhat inequilateral, smooth, inamyloid.

Observations   *Subroseus* in this instance means rather similar to *Gomphidius roseus*. Literally it means somewhat rose colored. *Gomphidius* refers to a large wedge-shaped nail.

88   *Gomphidius subroseus*   About natural size

89   Chroogomphus vinicolor

Identification marks   The caps vary considerably in size but mostly are 1–8 cm broad, and are thinly viscid at first. The colors are variable. The caps are orange ochraceous at first and finally become dark dingy yellow brown and frequently become flushed salmon pink to vinaceous red. The gills are distant to subdistant, broad, decurrent, and more or less dull ochraceous to orange ochraceous. The stalks are ochraceous to orange ochraceous and (3) 4–12 mm thick.

Edibility   Presumed to be edible, but we have no data on it.

When and where   Scattered under pine and less often under other conifers; it is known from Maine to Washington and, especially in California, has a prolonged fruiting season during the rainy season.

89   *Chroogomphus vinicolor*   About one-half natural size

Spores 17–23 x 4.5–7 μm, dark smoky brown in deposit, subfusiform in profile, smooth, inamyloid.

Observations *Vinicolor* means wine color; here it is used to cover a broad range from pale dingy pink to dingy rose red to purplish. *Chroogomphus* means a colored *Gomphus*.

Phylloporus rhodoxanthus   90

Identification marks The cap is dry, dull, and red to olive or reddish brown. The gills are thickish and yellow as well as often being intervenose, and are usually decurrent. The mycelium around the base of the stalk is white in some varieties and yellow in others.

Edibility Edible and reported good, but we have little information on which of the North American varieties were tested.

When and where The genus is found in the forested areas of the United States and Canada. Fruiting bodies are mostly solitary to scattered and appear during wet seasons in the late summer and fall. The species *P. rhodoxanthus* apparently forms mycorrhiza with both conifers and hardwoods.

Spores 9–12 x 4–5.5 μm, olive brown in deposit, smooth (under light microscope), somewhat inequilateral in profile, yellow in KOH, inamyloid.

Observations *Rhodo* indicates a rose color; *xantho* indicates yellow. The genus name is derived from words meaning gill and pore; hence, this is the gilled pore fungus.

90   *Phylloporus rhodoxanthus*   About natural size

Hygrophoraceae

In this family the gills have a clean, more or less waxy appearance, and in many species have a somewhat waxy feel. Under the microscope one sees other features which aid in identifying the family, namely the typically long, narrow basidia correlated with a divergent arrangement of the hyphae of the gill trama for the type genus, *Hygrophorus*. In *Camarophyllus* and *Hygrocybe* (along with minor genera segregated from them), the gills are thick, rigid, and the waxiness is more apparent than in *Hygrophorus*. *Camarophyllus* has the hyphae of the gill trama very intricately interwoven, whereas in *Hygrocybe* they are parallel or nearly so.

Key to Species

1. Cap with a sharply conic umbo; stalk 6–12 cm or more long, 3–6 (12) mm thick, not blackening where injured . . . . 91. *Hygrocybe acutoconica*
1. Not as above 2
    2. Cap dull orange red, orange to yellowish when faded; gills distant and decurrent; stalk white and dry . . . . 92. *Camarophyllus pratensis*
    2. Not as above 3
3. Gills orange cinnamon to vinaceous brown (at maturity) . . . . 93. *Hygrophorus kauffmanii*
3. Gills some other color than in above 4
    4. Gills soon spotted dingy vinaceous red, close; cap streaked with vinaceous red . . . . 94. *Hygrophorus russula*
    4. Gills and cap white or whitish; stalk dry and often pointed below . . . . 95. *Hygrophorus sordidus*

---

91   Hygrocybe acutoconica

Identification marks The very acutely conic cap, lack of black stains on bruised areas (especially the base of the stalk), and the dry stalk are diagnostic. The color of the cap may be red, orange, yellow, or intergradations

91 *Hygrocybe acutoconica*   About two-thirds natural size

of these. The differences are caused, we think, by different concentrations of the pigments in different caps.

Edibility   Not known. *H. conica*, a very closely related species which stains black where bruised, has been reported as poisonous; but recently it has been found to be edible at least for some people.

When and where   *H. acutoconica* fruits during the summer and early fall on humus in deciduous and mixed coniferous stands or in brushy places. It is not rare but is seldom found in large numbers. It is widely distributed in North America and also occurs in Europe.

Spores   9–15 x 5–9 μm, white in deposit, some with a medial constriction, ellipsoid to elongate, smooth, inamyloid.

Observations   *Hygrocybe* means moist head; the specific epithet means sharply conic.

Camarophyllus pratensis   92

Identification marks   The surface of the cap is dry, usually more or less unpolished, and dull orange red to reddish orange, slowly fading to buffy yellow. The gills are distant and extend down the stalk (are decurrent) and do not become spotted. No veil is present. The hyphae of the gill trama are intricately interwoven—a character not ascertainable in the field.

Edibility   Edible, but rather tasteless—as reported by some who have tried it.

When and where   In spite of the specific epithet *pratensis*, which means of the fields and meadows, this fungus is nearly always found in association with woody plants here in North America. In the Northwest it occurs in pastures and also in stands of conifers. In the Great Lakes area it is most often found under hardwoods. It is widely distributed throughout the Northern Hemisphere.

Spores   5.5–8 x 3.5–5 μm, white in deposit, ellipsoid to subglobose, smooth, not amyloid.

Observations   *Camarophyllus* is derived from words meaning vault and leaf.

92 *Camarophyllus pratensis*   About two-thirds natural size

Hygrophorus kauffmanii

Identification marks   The color of the mature gills is the single most distinctive character of the species: they are a dull deep reddish pecan brown. The late fall fruiting period, the canescent only slightly viscid cap, the vinaceous rufous to pecan brown color tones of the cap when the bloom is rubbed off, and the dry stalk are also important.

Edibility   We have no data on it.

When and where   Scattered to gregarious under hardwoods, especially oak, in moist depressions of the forest floor. In the southern Great Lakes region it can be found regularly once one has located an established mycelium. Most people miss seeing it because it fruits in autumn and merges with the color of the fallen leaves. Its general range is doubtless east of the Great Plains.

Spores   7–9 x 4–5.5 μm, white in deposit, ellipsoid, smooth, inamyloid.

Observations   This species illustrates the dangers of assuming that color of the spores can be judged reliably from the color of the mature gills. *Hygrophorus* means bearer of moisture. The specific epithet is in honor of Professor Calvin H. Kauffman of the University of Michigan, who discovered the fungus.

93   *Hygrophorus kauffmanii*   About one-half natural size

---

94   **Hygrophorus russula**

Identification marks   The distinctive characters for this species include the mild, pleasant taste, the wine red disc of the cap with the color radiating in streaks, the yellow stains developing on injured places, the dry stalk, the close gills which are initially pale pinkish white and broadly adnate, and the habitat under oak. There is no veil. The entire fruiting body is often almost completely covered with wine red discolorations in age and in this stage is too old to be used for human consumption.

94 *Hygrophorus russula*   About one-half natural size

Edibility   Edible and choice, but be sure you have young, actively developing fruiting bodies. In our estimation it is the best of the Hygrophoraceae for table use.

When and where   It fruits year after year in the same location. Its area is the hardwood forest belt east of the Great Plains. In Michigan it favors open, grassy oak stands, where it forms large fairy rings during late summer and early fall.

Spores   6–8 x 3–4.5 (5) μm, white in deposit, ellipsoid, smooth, inamyloid.

Observations   We have a number of species in North America which stain like the above. *H. purpurascens* has a distinct veil and is common in the Rocky Mountains under spruce. It is bitter, as is *H. amarus*—a very bitter Rocky Mountain species that often becomes yellow by maturity. *H. erubescens* has more or less decurrent (distant to subdistant) gills. It also occurs under conifers. *Russula* means reddish.

Hygrophorus sordidus   95

Identification marks   The large size (8–20 cm) of the cap, which is white or with a cream buff tinge over the disc, the dry stalk usually narrowed to a more or less pointed base, and the subdistant white gills with their waxy appearance distinguish this species in the field. There is no veil. It is most likely to be mistaken for a *Clitocybe* or a *Tricholoma*. In the latter the gills are notched at the stalk, and the stalk is not narrowed to a point below. The large white species of *Clitocybe* present more of a problem, but, again, most have a clavate to bulbous base. If a microscope is available, the divergent gill trama of the *Hygrophorus* will distinguish it at once.

Edibility   Edible and highly rated. It is popular in southeastern Michigan with those who have learned to recognize it.

When and where   It grows in open, ordinarily dry, grassy oak groves, especially on hillsides near the bottom of the slope, and appears during late summer and early fall east of the Great Plains.

Spores   6–8 x (3.5) 4–5.5 μm, white in deposit, ellipsoid, smooth, inamyloid.

95 *Hygrophorus sordidus*   About two-thirds natural size

Tricholomataceae

The numerous genera and species of the fungi classified here are characterized by white to pale lilac drab or pale buff to yellowish spore deposits, and by the gill trama being composed of hyphae typically parallel to interwoven in arrangement or, rarely, slightly divergent but never convergent. Also, the gills typically are not waxy in appearance or consistency. In other words, with the exclusion of the Hygrophoraceae, nearly all the white-spored mushrooms found in North America which have the gills attached to the stalk belong here. This is a large and diverse assemblage of mushrooms.

Key to Genera and Species

1. Partial veil well-developed and typically leaving a membranous ring when it breaks, or outer and partial veils combined (intergrown) 2
1. Partial veil lacking or fibrillose to cortinate 7
    2. Cap surface and sheath on stalk more or less orange-granulose; on hardwood logs, etc. .... 102. *Cystoderma granosum*
    2. Not as above 3
3. Gill edges serrate; stalk tough and fibrous; on wood of conifers ....
.... 96. *Lentinus lepideus*
3. Not as above 4
    4. Spores from deposit amyloid 5
    4. Spores from deposit inamyloid 6
5. Stalk typically 2–4 cm thick above the middle, more or less pointed below; veil forming a "double" annulus (lower and upper edges flare out) .... 98. *Catathelasma imperialis* & *C. ventricosa*
5. Stalk equal to bulbous; veil double as evidenced by a colored outer layer .... *Armillaria*

6. Fruiting in clusters, black rhizomorphs present around and adjacent to the base of the stalks . . . . 97. *Armillariella mellea*
6. Not as above . . . . see *Hygrophorus*, *Tricholoma*, & *Armillaria*
7. Gills with a waxy appearance, rigid and brittle, violaceous to vinaceous red to dull pink; stalk rather fibrous . . . . *Laccaria*
7. Not as above 8
8. Stalk absent; gills orange; spore deposit pink . . . .
. . . . 139. *Phyllotopsis nidulans*
8. Not as above 9
9. Stalk absent to eccentric 10
9. Stalk typically central 12
10. Gills at maturity with serrate edges; spores amyloid; consistency tough . . . . 138. *Lentinellus vulpinus*
10. Not as above 11
11. Gills crowded, orange to yellow; stalk well-developed . . . .
. . . . 109. *Omphalotus illudens*
11. Gills close to subdistant; white to pallid or grayish stalk present or absent, but if present it is eccentric and poorly developed . . . . . *Pleurotus*
12. Gills yellow to orange and dichotomously forked; cap soft to the touch . . . . . (see also *Omphalotus illudens*) . . . .
. . . . 110. *Hygrophoropsis aurantiaca*
12. Not as above 13
13. Stalk velvety and becoming dark brown over lower third; cap slimy if moist; clustered on dead wood of hardwoods . . . .
. . . . 111. *Flammulina velutipes*
13. Not as above 14
14. Spores from deposits amyloid; stalk typically 1 cm or more thick
. . . . *Leucopaxillus*
14. Not as above 15
15. Gills decurrent (often broadly adnate at first); spores not amyloid . . .
. . . . (see also *Lyophyllum*) . . . . . *Clitocybe*
15. Not as above 16
16. Stalk fleshy and about 1 cm or more thick; gills typically notched at attachment to the stalk . . . (see also *Lyophyllum*) . . . . . *Tricholoma*
16. Stalk cartilaginous to tough and pliant 17
17. Fruiting bodies thin and pliant, drying out and reviving readily as weather changes occur . . . . 118. *Marasmius oreades*
17. Fruiting bodies not reviving repeatedly . . . .
. . . . *Collybia*, *Clitocybula*, & *Mycena*

Lentinus lepideus   96
(Scaly Lentinus)

Identification marks The scaly cap, white flesh, the ring on the stalk, the scales beneath the ring, the yellow stains which develop in age or where handled, and an odor somewhat reminiscent of licorice, along with the occurrence on conifer wood, are characteristic. The scales on the cap are brownish. Variation in this species is great. Old specimens often have a disagreeable taste, and their gills are often bright yellow. The ring on the stalk and the scales on the cap are obliterated on specimens that have stood for a long time. The fruiting bodies decay slowly.

Edibility   Edible—some people like it. Be sure you have young fruiting bodies; old ones have a disagreeable taste.

When and where   It is almost always on wood of conifers and very widely distributed. It fruits during the spring, summer, and fall during cool, moist weather. When railroad ties were cut from conifer logs, one could find this species rather regularly fruiting from the ties.

Spores   9–12 x 4–5 μm, white or nearly so in deposit, smooth, subcylindric, inamyloid.

Observations   *Lentinus* means tough or pliant; *lepideus* means scaly.

96   *Lentinus lepideus*   About one-third natural size

---

97   Armillariella mellea
(Honey Mushroom)

Identification marks   The concept of this species here in North America is a collective one. The essential field characters are the somewhat floccose ring on the stalk, the clustered habit of the fruiting bodies, the occurrence on wood of both conifers and hardwoods, the gills attached to the stalk, and either a white or yellowish spore print.

In one of the variations, each stalk narrows downward and the stalks are more or less fused at the base, thus forming a coherent cluster. The cap in this variant has strong yellow tones, at least on the margin, and the spore deposit is yellowish. We have seen whitish and almost fuscous brown variants of this variation. It usually fruits late in August in the Great Lakes region; the clusters may appear terrestrial, but are actually attached to buried wood.

In another variation, which usually fruits late in the fall, the stalk is slightly enlarged at the base, the clusters are often on wood which is above ground, the caps often lack any yellow tints (they are usually dingy to dark brown), and the spore print is white. The caps are quite squamulose at first.

Edibility   Edible and popular, but do not eat it raw. Unless carefully prepared the slime may annoy some people—pickled specimens are often very slimy.

When and where   The species is to be expected in the Northern Hemisphere in forested areas during the late summer and fall, or in winter in the South.

97 *Armillariella mellea*   About one-half natural size

Spores 7–9 x 5–6 μm, white to yellow in deposit, smooth, ellipsoid, inamyloid.

Observations With the variability of this fungus here in North America in mind, we are not surprised to find confusing reports on its effects when eaten. Unfortunately, it would not make a good species for the commercial trade—assuming it could be fruited on a controlled regime. Most of the attention given to this species in North America has been on how to eliminate it. The generic name is a diminutive of *Armillaria*. The specific epithet means honey colored.

Catathelasma imperialis & C. ventricosa   98

Identification marks These monsters of the mushroom world at times have caps over 40 cm broad. In *C. imperialis* the cap is a dingy yellow brown (more or less date brown) and slightly viscid. In *C. ventricosa* the cap is white becoming dingy to grayish. The gills are distinctly decurrent, close, and in age are finally broad. The ring (for both) has been termed "double" in the technical literature, but the collector should not expect to see two rings equally distinct. The buttons are about the size of baseballs and very hard.

Edibility Both are edible, but not highly rated.

When and where These species are more abundant in the central Rocky Mountains than in any other area in which we have collected, but they are widely distributed in the Northern Hemisphere. Conifer forests, especially spruce-fir stands, are preferred. Fruiting, as one would expect, follows periods of heavy rain.

Spores 11–14 x 4–5.5 μm, somewhat inequilateral in profile, smooth, amyloid, hyaline in KOH (for *C. imperialis*); 8–11 (14) x 4–4.5 μm (for *C. ventricosa*).

Observations The generic name is derived from "to run down" (referring to the decurrent gills). The specific epithet *imperialis* means, essentially, the head of the group (the king of the mushrooms). *Ventricosa* means inflated (usually in the middle).

98 *Catathelasma ventricosa*　　　　　　About one-half natural size

Armillaria

The veil is typically double in the sense that it is two-layered, the outer layer usually being distinctly colored. It leaves a membranous ring on the stalk. The spore deposit is white, and the spores may be amyloid or not. The species apparently form mycorrhiza with conifers or hardwoods. Two very famous edible species belong here: the white matsutake of the Pacific Northwest and the true matsutake of Japan. The latter is very close to *Armillaria caligata. Armillaria* means a ring, a reference to the annulus left by the broken veils.

Key to Species

1. Cap with vinaceous brown, broad, appressed scales, finally becoming merely fibrillose-streaked with brown fibrils . . . . 99. *Armillaria caligata*
1. Not as above 2
　　2. Cap white at first, slowly staining cinnamon tan . . 100. *A. ponderosa*
　　2. Cap with yellow, orange, and olive tones in various proportions
　　　 . . . . 101. *A. zelleri*

99 Armillaria caligata
(Booted Armillaria)

Identification marks The broad, vinaceous brown to dark cinnamon brown covering of appressed fibrils both over the cap and over the membranous ring about halfway up the stalk, the white spore deposit, and the gills being attached to the stalk make a distinctive combination of characters.

The cuticle of the cap breaks up into appressed scales or patches or simply separates into brown fibrils more or less radially arranged. In a young fruiting body the cuticle of the cap is continuous with the colored fibrils on the under (outer) side of the ring and the "boot" of the stalk. One variety has an odor like that of *A. ponderosa*, another has an odor somewhat like that of bitter almonds, and a third no odor at all. The Japanese matsutake is one of the varieties of this collective species.

Edibility   Edible. It is highly rated by some Europeans and is especially popular among Orientals here in North America.

When and where   Fruiting occurs in the late summer and fall, generally in deciduous woods east of the Great Plains to the Atlantic Coast, but to a lesser extent in the conifer forests of our western states. It occurs scattered to gregarious.

Spores   6–7.5 x 4–5 μm, white in deposit, ellipsoid, inamyloid, smooth.

Observations   *Caligata* refers to a soldier's boot; here it must refer to the sheath that "boots" the base of the stalk.

99   *Armillaria caligata*   About one-half natural size

Armillaria ponderosa   100
(White Matsutake)

Identification marks   This large white mushroom gradually develops cinnamon stains as it ages, and in age is quite discolored. The cap may be up to 35 cm broad and covered with cinnamon colored patches of tissue. The gills are white and slowly stain vinaceous cinnamon. The faint spicy-aromatic odor is also distinctive.

Edibility   Edible and collected commercially for use in oriental-style cooking, especially in the Pacific Northwest.

When and where   It is associated with 2-needle pines more often than with other kinds of trees. It fruits during late summer and fall after heavy rains in the Great Lakes region, where it often grows with both Norway and jack pine. It is found mostly with lodgepole pine in the Northwest. It is also known from the Adirondack Mountains of New York; in fact, it was originally described from this region.

Spores 5.5–7 x 4.5–5.5 μm, smooth, inamyloid, broadly ellipsoid.

Observations The specific epithet means large and heavy, and is a very appropriate name for this species.

100 *Armillaria ponderosa*   About one-half natural size

101   Armillaria zelleri

Identification marks This is a large species with caps 5–15 cm or more broad. The cap surface is viscid at first but is soon dry and breaks up into small scales. The colors are orange, olive, and orange brown to yellowish in varying proportions. The gills are off-white but finally stain rusty brown. The strong odor and taste resemble that of fresh meal (farinaceous). The colored layer of the cap is continued on the stalk from the annulus down.

Edibility Edible (at least for some people), but not recommended. There are usually better species available when this one fruits.

101 *Armillaria zelleri*   Nearly natural size

When and where Typically it is abundant in the pine forests of the Pacific Northwest and is frequent in the Great Lakes region in jack pine stands.

Spores 4–5.5 x 3.5 μm, white in deposit, ellipsoid, smooth, inamyloid.

Observations By the time the cuticle of the cap has broken up to form squamules or scales, the viscidity is no longer detectable. This species is named in honor of Professor S. M. Zeller of Oregon State University.

Cystoderma granosum 102

Identification marks The caps are large for the genus (4–9 cm); the fruiting bodies are found on wood of deciduous trees; the surface of the cap is dry, granulose, and bright orange; and the veil leaves a granulose sheath on the stalk terminating in a persistent ring.

Edibility We have no data on it.

When and where It is found clustered to gregarious on wood of deciduous trees in the summer and fall east of the Great Plains, sometimes in abundance.

Spores 4–5 x 3 μm, white in deposit, ellipsoid, amyloid, smooth.

Observations In the older literature this species is treated under the name *Lepiota granosa* or *Armillaria granosa*. *Cystoderma* refers to the inflated to globose cells that form the cuticle of the cap; the specific epithet refers to the somewhat powdery (granulose) appearance of the cap.

102 *Cystoderma granosum*   Nearly natural size

Clitocybe

The classical concept of this genus calls for species with white to pale yellow or buff spore deposits, more or less fleshy stalks centrally attached to the cap, and broadly adnate to decurrent gills. Most species lack a veil, and the spores of most are inamyloid. Those species which "glow in the dark" are now placed in *Omphalotus*. *Clitocybe* means a sloping head or cap.

Key to Species

---

103 Clitocybe nuda
(Blewits)

Identification marks The spore deposit is a pale pinkish tan, not rusty brown. The cap is smooth, moist, violaceous to blue at first, gradually becoming dingy brownish. The gills are violaceous at first (somewhat like the cap). The base of the stalk is more or less flared to form a bulb, but no veil is present (the blue Cortinarii have a cobwebby veil).

Edibility Edible and highly regarded, but old specimens may have a bad flavor. Do not eat it raw.

When and where It fruits from late summer on into the fall and winter across the continent in hardwood and conifer forests, in grassy places, and particularly around compost piles or rubbish heaps of woody debris. It is cosmopolitan and abundant.

103 *Clitocybe nuda*   Nearly natural size

Spores 6–8 x 4–5 μm, pale pinkish tan in deposit, narrowly ellipsoid, inamyloid.

Observations This species has been known as *Tricholoma nudum*, *Lepista nuda*, *Rhodopaxillus nuda* and *Gyrophila nuda* in the past. *Nuda* means naked.

Clitocybe clavipes 104

Identification marks The cap is 2–7 (9) cm broad, flat or with a slight central umbo; the surface is glabrous and dull olive brown, grayish brown, or dingy yellow brown. The gills are long-decurrent, pallid to cream buff, and not spotted. The stalk is 4–10 (12) mm thick at apex and 10–35 mm at the base (it is clavate). The surface is fibrillose-streaked, but there is no veil.

Edibility Not recommended. As this revision of the *Guide* was being written, an authentic report appeared that this species caused the same type of intoxication as that caused by *Coprinus atramentarius* (see p. 18).

When and where This species is one of the very abundant species in our pine plantations (under 5- and 2- to 3-needle pines) in the Great Lakes region east and southward. We have not seen it abundant in the West. It is widely distributed in North America, but is rare under hardwoods.

Spores 6–7 (8) x 4–5 μm, white in deposit, ellipsoid, smooth, inamyloid.

Observations *Clavipes* refers to the enlargement near the base of the stalk and means a club-shaped foot.

104 *Clitocybe clavipes*   About two-thirds natural size

Clitocybe dealbata 105

Identification marks The cap is small (1–4 cm broad), and the disc is often somewhat depressed at maturity. The surface is dry and shining to dull white, and in age may be more or less concentrically rivulose. The gills are

105 *Clitocybe dealbata*   About natural size

very narrow and crowded, as well as more or less decurrent. The stalk is short (2–3 cm long) and dingy white to (finally) slightly discolored.

Edibility POISONOUS. The symptoms are characteristic of muscarine poisoning. The cases of poisoning by this species often are caused by the accidental inclusion of its fruiting bodies with those of the fairy ring, *Marasmius oreades*, since the two often fruit together at the same time and place.

When and where Fruiting occurs on lawns in with groups of the fairy ring (see above) as well as on wasteland, woods borders, etc., in the summer and fall. It is cosmopolitan.

Spores 4–5.5 x 2.5–3 μm, white in deposit, mostly ellipsoid, inamyloid.

Observations It is best for the casual collector not to experiment with any of the small to medium sized white species in this genus. *Dealbata* means whitewashed, referring to the appearance of the fresh caps.

106   Clitocybe robusta

Identification marks This is a large white *Clitocybe* with a pale yellow spore deposit. The caps measure 5–15 cm broad, and the gills are adnate to short-decurrent. When specimens are taken into a warm room the odor which develops reminds one more of skunk than anything else.

Edibility Edible, but not palatable, according to some reports. The most closely related species, *C. nebularis*, is not recommended for the same reason—poor flavor.

When and where It grows scattered to gregarious under hardwoods and in mixed forests after heavy rains in the fall. It is widely distributed, though *C. nebularis* is the more common species in the Pacific Northwest. *C. robusta* is common east of the Great Plains.

Spores (5) 6–8.5 x 3–4 μm, pale yellow in deposit, ellipsoid, smooth, inamyloid.

Observations The name *Clitocybe alba* was used in the previous edition of the *Guide*, but *C. robusta* has priority. The specific epithet *robusta* means robust or stocky.

106 *Clitocybe robusta*

About two-thirds natural size

Clitocybe irina **107**

Identification marks   The large (up to 15 cm) caps which are silky, white, and discolor in age (much as in *C. subconnexa*) are important. The margin may be somewhat cottony and is often grooved at first. Usually the flesh has a distinctive fragrant odor, but, especially in material from Michigan, the odor may be pungent to absent. The gills become grayish vinaceous by maturity. The young fruiting bodies are whitish all over and are gregarious rather than clustered. The stalks are thicker than those of *C. subconnexa*.

Edibility   Edible and enjoyed by many people, but cases of "upsets" are known. Here, as for *C. subconnexa*, use only young white fruiting bodies.

When and where   Common and widely distributed in the Northern Hemisphere. It fruits after heavy rains from late August on into the fall. We have found it abundant under locust (*Robenia*), and it has also been found under

107 *Clitocybe irina*

About one-half natural size

conifers. Mostly, however, it occurs in oak and beech woods or along their borders.

Spores 7–9 (10) x 4–5 μm, dingy pale pinkish buff in deposit, ellipsoid, slightly verrucose, inamyloid.

Observations Other names for this species are *Tricholoma irinum* and *Lepista irina*. *Irina* means of or belonging to the iris—no doubt a reference to the typical fragrance.

---

108   Clitocybe subconnexa

Identification marks It fruits in dense clusters and when young is satiny white. However, by the time it is mature, it has discolored to buff to some extent, and in age (in wet weather) is dingy pale vinaceous brown. The taste becomes unpleasant in old specimens. The gills are crowded, narrow, and soon become pale pinkish buff to dingy vinaceous buff. They are somewhat separable from the cap tissue. There is no veil. The stalk is fleshy and unpolished.

Edibility Edible, but use it only when the caps are fresh and white. One of our acquaintances, who likes it and collects it regularly, warns us *not to keep leftovers* since by the next day the flavor has become disagreeable.

When and where It is to be expected during late summer and fall east of the Great Plains. It is common and fruits in abundance, often in large clusters.

Spores 4.5–6 x 3–3.5 μm, vinaceous buff in deposit, ellipsoid, verrucose, inamyloid.

Observations The clustered habit helps distinguish this species from the other large white species of *Clitocybe* that may fruit at the same time. The specific epithet refers to the slight connection between the clustered fruiting bodies.

---

109   Omphalotus illudens
(Jack-O-Lantern Fungus)

Identification marks The clustered habit of growth with the stalks narrowed toward the base and often fused, the orange yellow cap gills and (usually) stalks, the crowded narrow descending (decurrent) gills, and the lack of a veil are distinctive. When perfectly fresh, collected, and taken into a dark room, the gills typically are luminescent; hence the common name. The spore deposit is usually yellowish.

Edibility POISONOUS. Nausea and vomiting are violent for a few hours, but the patient recovers—however, the experience is very disagreeable.

When and where It fruits during the late summer and early fall, usually as the weather dries up following heavy rains. It grows on wood and usually fruits from the underground parts of a stump or old tree. Oak is the preferred substratum. The species is rather frequent east of the Great Plains.

Spores 3.5–5 x 3.5–4.5 μm, pale yellow to nearly white in deposit, sub-globose to globose, smooth, hyaline, inamyloid.

Observations *O. olearius* has spores 4.5–7 x 4.5–6.5 μm. Some workers consider *O. illudens* a synonym of *O. olearius*. In the previous edition of the *Guide* the name *Clitocybe illudens* was used. *Illudens* means emitting light. *Omphalotus* refers to the depressed disc of the cap.

108   *Clitocybe subconnexa*   About two-thirds natural size

109   *Omphalotus illudens*   About one-half natural size

Hygrophoropsis aurantiaca   110

Identification marks   The very crowded to close gills which are forked and
are yellow to brilliant orange, the lack of a veil, and the often eccentric stalk
are distinctive. The color of the cap is variable, being blackish to sepia brown,
dark brown toned orange, dull orange yellow, or actually whitish. The texture of the flesh of the pileus is soft and dry.

Edibility   Not recommended. Leading authorities now state that the species
is edible. However, these authorities have not tried all the different variations
of the species we find in North America, and knowing what we do about the

distribution of poisons in a single species from different localities, we urge caution in trying it. Some recent authors still list it as being upsetting to some people and not to others.

When and where It occurs on humus, on burned areas, on fairly rotten conifer logs and stumps, and (rarely) on hardwood. It is a "dry weather" species, i.e., abundant during rather dry seasons when other fungi are scarce. It occurs across the continent in late summer and fall.

Spores 5–6 x 4μm, nearly white in deposit, ellipsoid, smooth, dextrinoid.

Observations In the previous edition of this *Guide* the name *Clitocybe aurantiaca* was used. The specific epithet means orange, the generic name *Hygrophorus*-like.

110 *Hygrophoropsis aurantiaca*   Near natural size

111   Flammulina velutipes
(Winter Mushroom)

Identification marks The viscid, smooth, yellowish orange to orange brown cap, the velvety stalk which is yellowish when young but nearly black in age, and occurrence on elm and aspen make a distinctive combination of characters. The gills are pallid to yellowish, and the fruiting bodies revive somewhat when moistened. One may find large clusters of small caps, small clusters of large caps, or intermediates.

Edibility Edible. It is an important species for the casual collector because it appears when few other fungi are available. The slime layer of the cap should be wiped off before cooking. Discard the stalks.

When and where East of the Great Plains it is found mostly on elm; in the Rocky Mountains it grows mostly on aspen. It fruits in early spring, late fall, and in winter if a prolonged "warm" spell is encountered. In the mountains it fruits in the summer. It is often found on living trees, where it is apparently a wound parasite.

Spores 7–9 x 3–4 μm, white in deposit, oblong, smooth, inamyloid.

Observations *Flammulina* means pertaining to *Flammula*; *velutipes* means velvet stalk (foot).

111 *Flammulina velutipes*   Nearly natural size

Collybia

This genus has long been a problem to specialists and is difficult to identify in the field because of the diverse mushrooms included in it originally. There was no unifying set of field or microscopic characters that made it readily recognizable. Recently, however, considerable progress has been made on this group, but the details are beyond the scope of a field guide. We offer here a key to the selected "collybioid" species illustrated. *Collybia* means a small coin, probably a reference to the small caps of many species.

Key to Species

1. Fruiting in large clusters on conifer logs 2
1. Not as above 3
   2. Caps blackish when young, gray on disc at maturity, stalks pallid . . . . 112. *Clitocybula familia*
   2. Caps dark to pale vinaceous brown when moist; stalks reddish brown but paler than cap . . . . 113. *Collybia acervata*
3. Odor strong (heavily fragrant); cap vinaceous red to vinaceous brown; gills yellowish and finally stained vinaceous brown . . . .
  . . . . 114. *Collybia oregonensis*
3. Not as above 4
   4. Gills and/or cap stained reddish brown; taste bitter; stalk 8–20 mm thick, with a distinctly cartilaginous cortex; on rotten wood . . . . 115. *Collybia maculata*
   4. Not as above 5
5. Spore deposit pale buff; cap dark reddish brown; gill edges often serrate; growing scattered under conifers . . . . . . 116. *Collybia butyracea*
5. Spore deposit white 6

6. Growing on or near decaying hardwood slash or debris (often clustered on sawdust piles); gills close and thin . . . .
. . . . 117. *Collybia dryophila*
6. Growing in fairy rings on grassy areas, rarely in conifer plantations; gills broad and subdistant . . . . 118. *Marasmius oreades*

---

112 Clitocybula familia

Identification marks The large loose clusters on old conifer logs, the gray to blackish caps seldom depressed on the disc, the whitish gills, and the grayish to pallid stalks distinguish it. The spores are white in deposit and amyloid. No veil is present.

Edibility Edible and good. As Kauffman pointed out, it is seldom infested with insect larvae.

When and where During late summer and early fall it can be found on decaying conifer logs, often during rather dry seasons in the northern and western states and in adjacent areas in Canada.

Spores 3.5–4.5 μm, white in deposit, globose, hyaline, amyloid.

Observations This species was treated as a *Collybia* previously. *Collybia abundans* was described as a closely related species with a depressed cap but also occurring on wood. It is also edible. The specific epithet *familia* refers to the large loose cluster, and the epithet *abundans* refers to the habit of fruiting in abundance. The generic name means a small *Clitocybe*.

112 *Clitocybula familia*   Nearly natural size

---

113 Collybia acervata

Identification marks The fruiting bodies are found in large compact clusters (bundles) on very old rotten conifer logs and around stumps. The caps are 2–4 (5) cm broad, glabrous and at first a dark reddish brown which fades to vinaceous buff and eventually to pallid (whitish). The gills are pallid to pale vinaceous. The stalks are about the color of the young moist caps, and are bound together by a pallid mycelium. No veil is present.

Edibility   POISONOUS, at least to some people. We have a report from the Pacific Northwest of students made ill by it. Because of the bitter taste it is not a desirable species.

When and where   It is very widely distributed in conifer forests generally. In the higher Rocky Mountains of Colorado it fruits in the summer, but on the Pacific Coast it is a fall and winter species. East of the Great Plains it fruits mostly in September and October.

Spores   5–6 x 3 μm, white in deposit, narrowly ellipsoid, smooth, inamyloid.

Observations   The specific epithet means in clusters.

113   *Collybia acervata*   About two-thirds natural size

Collybia oregonensis   **114**

Identification marks   The 5–10 cm broad cap, the dark to medium vinaceous brown to vinaceous red color, the bitterish taste, the odor of benzaldehyde (a heavy fragrance), and the yellowish gills becoming pallid and

114   *Collybia oregonensis*   About two-thirds natural size

finally stained vinaceous brown constitute a distinctive group of characters. It grows on rotten conifer stumps and debris.

Edibility   To our knowledge it has not been tested, and we advise against experimenting with it.

When and where   It is native to the Pacific Northwest, where it is found in the fall, solitary to scattered on conifer logs, stumps, and debris.

Spores   6–8 x 3.5–4 μm, ochraceous to orange buff in deposit, ellipsoid, smooth, inamyloid.

Observations   This species is closely related to *C. maculata*, but differs in the color of the cap and the odor. The specific epithet refers to the state of Oregon, where the species has been found on numerous occasions.

---

115   Collybia maculata

Identification marks   The cap is large (5–10 cm), whitish, and appearing as if frosted but soon naked and becoming pale cinnamon over the disc, at times with watery spots near the margin; the margin long remains inrolled. Reddish to rusty stains typically develop by late maturity on the cap, gills, and stalk. The stalk is white at first, subradicating, and 5–12 cm x 8–20 mm. No veil is present. The taste is bitter.

Edibility   Edible according to some authorities, but the bitter taste makes it undesirable for the table. Also, it is a collective species, and we have no detailed data on the different varieties.

When and where   It occurs throughout the fruiting season—spring, summer and fall—on wood, mostly of conifers, and on debris. The most luxuriant fruitings seen to date were on piles of cone debris around spruce trees. It is to be expected in the area west of the Great Plains, and to the east of them in at least the northern area. It also occurs in the South, but we have no estimate on its frequency.

Spores   4.5–6 x 3.5–4.5 μm, whitish to pinkish buff in deposit, ellipsoid to subglobose, smooth, hyaline, inamyloid.

Observations   We have never seen yellow stains on the typical variant. *Collybia scorzonera* is yellow overall, and is regarded as a variety of *C. ma-*

115   *Collybia maculata*   About natural size

culata by some. We have found caps of var. *maculata* 20 cm broad with stalks 2 cm thick on cone debris in Colorado. *Maculata* means spotted.

Collybia butyracea   116

Identification marks   This is a medium sized species with the caps 3–5 cm broad, and a pale buff spore print. The cap surface is slippery but not sticky, and the color is typically dull, dark to pale red brown. A brownish gray variety (var. *asema*) also occurs, often with the type variety. The gills are close, and their edges are usually eroded by maturity. The stalk is naked and paler than the cap. No veil is present.

Edibility   Edible, according to reports, but apparently not popular.

When and where   It is found solitary to scattered under conifers, especially in white pine plantations. It is widely distributed and is most abundant during late summer and fall after heavy rains. Var. *asema* is most abundant in the Pacific Northwest, but has been observed in the Upper Peninsula of Michigan.

Spores   7–9 x 4–4.5 μm, cream buff in deposit, oblong to drop-shaped, smooth, hyaline, inamyloid.

Observations   *Butyracea* refers to the slippery feel of fresh caps.

116   *Collybia butyracea*   Slightly under natural size

Collybia dryophila   117

Identification marks   This species differs from *C. butyracea* in having a white instead of yellowish spore deposit, and more often occurs in bunches on decaying hardwood material. It often develops secondary growths on the cap and/or stalk which are merely masses of tissue of the species. At one time these masses were thought to be a parasite on the *Collybia*.

Edibility Edible. Kauffman reported it as delicious fried with egg and bread crumbs. Miller reported it as poisonous, and we have one report which substantiates this. Apparently the situation is comparable to that known for a number of species: some people can eat it, and some cannot.

When and where It occurs gregarious to clustered on rich humus, around chip-dirt, and especially around old sawdust piles and slash of hardwoods. It is cosmopolitan and fruits both in the spring and fall.

Spores 5–6 x 3 μm, white in deposit, oblong to ellipsoid, smooth, inamyloid.

Observations *Dryophila* means oak-loving, but the species is not limited to this substrate.

117 *Collybia dryophila*   About natural size

118   Marasmius oreades
(Fairy Ring Mushroom)

Identification marks This is not an easy species to characterize because it lacks outstanding positive features. The color of the cap varies from nearly brick red at times to dull brown or paler to nearly white. The cap is glabrous and smooth or uneven; the gills are broad, somewhat distant, and pallid to white. No veil is evident on even the youngest fruiting bodies. The stalk is pallid and woolly over the lower fourth to nearly smooth near the apex. Beware of any fungus of this stature with pink gills at maturity, and, in particular, beware of a small white mushroom with close narrow gills which often grows with the *Marasmius*. It is *Clitocybe dealbata*, and is poisonous (see p. 131).

Edibility Edible and popular. One can usually find it in his or her own lawn, but do not pick it on lawns where chemicals have been used to kill weeds or eradicate fungi (such as this one).

When and where Open grassy places such as lawns and golf courses are its favorite habitat. We have also found it in pine plantations, and to a lesser extent under plantings of spruce. The fruiting bodies usually come up in a circle or arc, which indicates the extent of the mycelium producing them.

The species is a pest to those caring for lawns, but it may be expected wherever lawns are maintained.

Spores 7–9 x 4–5 μm, white in deposit, inequilateral in profile, inamyloid.

Observations The epithet *oreades* refers to a mountain nymph; the genus name means to become dry.

118 *Marasmius oreades*   About two-thirds natural size

Laccaria

This is one of the more readily recognized genera of mushrooms on a field basis. Members of this genus have thickish, violet purplish to vinaceous red or flesh pink gills that are attached variously to a somewhat tough, fibrous stalk. The spore deposit is white or pale lilac. The species vary greatly in size; one has caps up to 20 cm broad, and in another they are only 3–6 mm broad. *Laccaria* is derived from the word *lac*, the secretion of an insect which is (or was) the basis of lacquer.

Key to Species

1. On sand dunes or barren sand generally; gills deep violaceous; stalk about 1 cm thick near apex, base enlarged from included sand
. . . . .119. *Laccaria trullisata*
1. Not as above 2
    2. Stalks 1–2 cm thick; caps purple umber when moist, nearly white faded; growing under hardwoods in well drained situations
. . . . .120. *L. ochropurpurea*
    2. Stalks less than 1 cm thick; caps and gills some shade of vinaceous (pinkish) red . . . . .121. *L. laccata*

119　Laccaria trullisata

Identification marks　The somewhat distant, broad, purplish to violaceous gills, white spore deposit, and habitat on sand distinguish this species. No part of the fruiting body is ever slimy.

Edibility　The question is academic: it is impossible to get rid of all the sand.

When and where　Characteristically solitary to scattered on sand dunes and other areas of barren sand. It is not infrequent on the dunes of the Great Lakes shore lines. It fruits in the summer and early fall after heavy rains, and a hump in the sand is often the only clue available to the collector hunting for it.

Spores　16–22 x 6–9 μm, oblong to cylindric, inamyloid, smooth or nearly so.

Observations　*Trullisata* refers to the shape of the stalk, which was thought to resemble a bricklayer's trowel because of the enlargement of the part buried in the sand. The fungus, of course, does not live on pure sand; it may be forming mycorrhiza with any one of a number of dune plants.

119　*Laccaria trullisata*　　　　　　　　　　About natural size

120　Laccaria ochropurpurea

Identification marks　This is a striking species with caps up to 20 cm broad. They are purplish brown to purplish umber when moist and fresh but grayish to white when faded. The gills are persistently purple long after the cap fades. The stalk is thick, coarse, fibrous, and usually scaly near the apex. The colors of the stalk are about like those of the cap and fade like the latter. There is no veil.

Edibility　Edible, according to reports, but of inferior flavor. Cook it slowly if you try it.

When and where　This mushroom grows in the area east of the Great Plains in hardwood forests, often in thin woods on hard-packed soil. It fruits from July to October mostly during seasons or in localities where other mushrooms are not abundant. We have not found it west of the Great Plains.

Spores 6–8 μm, white to faintly lilac in deposit, globose, echinulate, inamyloid.

Observations The specific epithet means ochraceous and purplish, but in the populations we have sampled there was very little by way of ochraceous tints.

120   *Laccaria ochropurpurea*   About one-half natural size

Laccaria laccata   121

Identification marks This common nondescript mushroom has few definite characters for its field identification, and there are relatively few critical technical descriptions available in the North American literature—in spite of its being one of our most cosmopolitan and easily recognized mushrooms.

121   *Laccaria laccata*   Near natural size

The pale pinkish to pinkish red (flesh color) subdistant gills with their clean waxy appearance, the more or less reddish cap, and the dingy reddish stalk are distinctive. The cap is smooth when moist but furfuraceous when faded. There is no veil.

Edibility Edible, but not recommended. It is difficult to find enough for a meal. The stalks are fibrous and should be discarded, and, apparently, the flavor of what is left is not good.

When and where This species is cosmopolitan: summer and fall it is found at high and low elevations, in bogs and dry woods, open areas, etc., from Alaska to Mexico and from Nova Scotia to California.

Spores 7.5–10 x 7–8.5 μm, white in deposit, globose to broadly ellipsoid, echinulate, inamyloid.

Observations *Laccata* means appearing varnished, in this case referring to the waxy-appearing gills.

Leucopaxillus

The species of *Leucopaxillus* have spores with amyloid ornamentation, a feature which distinguishes this genus from *Tricholoma* and *Clitocybe*. In the field, species of *Leucopaxillus* have copious white mycelium around the base of the stalk and in the surrounding duff. The fruiting bodies have a rather dry context as compared to those of species of *Tricholoma* and *Clitocybe*. They do not rate highly as edible fungi because most of them are too bitter—even when cooked. *Leuco-* means pale or pallid; hence the name means a pale *Paxillus*.

Key to Species

1. Cap buff to pale clay color; gills yellowish, but dark brownish red when dried .... 122. *Leucopaxillus tricolor*
1. Caps white at first; gills white to pallid, not discoloring when dried (as above) 2
   2. On humus under hardwoods in late spring or early summer; disc of cap vinaceous buff at maturity .... 123. *L. laterarius*
   2. On humus and often on very rotten wood under conifers, late summer and fall; disc of cap more or less cream buff at maturity .... 124. *L. paradoxus*

122   Leucopaxillus tricolor

Identification marks The fruiting bodies of this species are gigantic. The caps are often up to 30 cm broad. They are broadly convex to flat or finally broadly depressed. The surfaces are matted-fibrillose and dry; the margins are often grooved-striate, as in *Paxillus involutus*. The caps are buff to light dingy yellow brown or (in age) darker. The gills on dried specimens are dark

122   *Leucopaxillus tricolor*   About one-third natural size

dull vinaceous red, but when fresh they are a pale dull yellow. The stalks are thick and clavate.

Edibility   Kauffman (*The Agaricaceae of Michigan*, 1918) lists it as edible under the name *Clitocybe maxima*, but it is not clear whether this report applies to the European material of *C. maxima* or the fungus Kauffman actually described under that name. Not recommended.

When and where   Solitary to scattered in moist rich hardwood forests east of the Great Plains, late summer and fall. We find it mostly following heavy rains during late summer and early fall.

Spores   6–8 x 4–5.5 μm, white in deposit, broadly ellipsoid, and covered with minute amyloid warts.

Observations   *Tricolor* means of three colors.

Leucopaxillus laterarius   **123**

Identification marks   This is a medium to large mushroom with a dull, dry cap with the margin often ribbed or grooved and the disc faintly tinged vinaceous buff. The taste raw is very bitter. The fruiting bodies are rather dry in consistency throughout, and a copious white mycelium permeates the surrounding duff.

Edibility   Inedible because of the taste. We have no data as to whether or not it is truly poisonous.

When and where   In the Great Lakes region it is one of the first large terrestrial species to fruit, usually in late June or early July. It is found from the Great Lakes area eastward. We have never seen it in large numbers, but it is collected nearly every season.

Spores   3.5–5.5 x 3.5–4 μm, white in deposit, globose to broadly ellipsoid, amyloid, ornamented with minute warts.

Observations   This species is seen by many hikers and wild-flower enthusiasts, but is seldom illustrated. *Laterarius* means pertaining to brick, but the color of the cap is not that usually associated with brick.

123 *Leucopaxillus laterarius*   About two-thirds natural size

124   Leucopaxillus paradoxus

Identification marks   The spores are amyloid; the raw flesh has a disagreeable taste; the cap is whitish with a pinkish buff disc by maturity, and its surface is dry and unpolished; the gills are close and white; and a copious white mycelium will be noted around the base of the stalk and in the surrounding humus.

Edibility   Inedible because of the taste and, in addition, not recommended because of the danger of confusing it with white species of *Clitocybe*.

When and where   Under conifers (often with spruce) across the continent, August to December, common during some seasons.

Spores   5–7.5 x 3.3–4.5 μm, white in deposit, mostly ellipsoid, amyloid, ornamented.

Observations   In the previous edition of this *Guide* it was described as *L. albissimus* var. *paradoxus*. *Paradoxus* means strange or unexpected.

124 *Leucopaxillus paradoxus*   About one-half natural size

Mycena

These attractive, thin-stalked mushrooms have a fragile to cartilaginous stalk, attached gills, white spore deposits, and generally conic caps. The cap margin is straight at first or only slightly bent in toward the stalk. The cap has very little context, so the species do not rate as edible fungi. Some of the species fruit in a densely gregarious pattern on needle carpets under conifers. Apparently these species are among the first to attack the fallen conifer needles and initiate the cycle of reducing the needles to humus. Some species fruit in the spring, but most fruit after the first heavy fall rains. The generic name is derived from an ancient word for fungus.

Key to Species

1. Stalk viscid when fresh 2
1. Stalk dry when fresh 3
    2. Stalk yellow; cap olive to brownish olive; on duff under conifers, late fall . . . . 125. *Mycena viscosa*
    2. Stalk orange, cap and gills orange to yellow; on wood of hardwoods, especially on beech, spring and fall . . . . 126. *M. leaiana*
3. On wood of conifers; fruiting in the spring as the snow melts; stalk with copious white tomentum on lower portion . . . . . . 127. *M. overholtsii*
3. On hardwood debris; fruiting in late summer and fall; stalk generally naked to the strigose base . . . . 128. *M. galericulata*

Mycena viscosa   125

Identification marks   The olive brown canescent cap, yellow slimy stalk (it slips through the fingers readily), crenate cap margin, and a rather disagreeable taste raw are distinctive, along with the habitat under conifers and the late fall appearance.

125 *Mycena viscosa*   About two-thirds natural size

Edibility   Not recommended.

When and where   The appearance of this species usually indicates that the season for mushrooms is about over for the year. In the Great Lakes area it is abundant in conifer plantations, especially those of pine, but it is widely distributed in northern regions and mountain conifer forests. If a species appearing rather similar to it is found under hardwoods late in the season, it is probably *Mycena griseoviridis*. The latter has less yellow in the stalk.

Spores   9–11 x 6.5–8 μm (from 2-spored basidia), white in deposit, dropshaped to subovoid, smooth, amyloid; spores from 4-spored basidia are 8–10 x 5–6.5 μm.

Observations   *Viscosa* means very viscid or slimy.

---

126   Mycena leaiana

Identification marks   This beautiful mushroom has an orange yellow cap which is shiny and more or less viscid when fresh, yellow gills with orange margins, and a yellow to orange stalk with an orange-frosty covering at first. When the fruiting body is broken, a slight amount of an orange juice can be squeezed out. It lives on hardwood substrates, especially that of beech (*Fagus*).

Edibility   We have no data on its edibility and therefore do not recommend it.

When and where   This species fruits both in the spring and fall on hardwood, especially beech, in the area east of the Great Plains. It is curious that it has not been found, to our knowledge, on alder or other hardwoods in the Pacific Northwest.

Spores   7–9 (10) x 5–6 μm, white in deposit, ellipsoid, smooth, amyloid.

Observations   This is an easy species to grow and fruit in culture. The senior author has produced fruiting bodies in culture; some were white, others yellow, and most were the typical orange color. The species is named in honor of Mr. Lea, an Ohio mushroom collector.

---

127   Mycena overholtsii

Identification marks   It is found on old conifer logs and stumps in the mountains in the spring as the snow melts—part of the log is often still covered with snow. The caps are 1.5–5 cm broad, fuscous to grayish brown and often hoary at first. The stalks are pallid and in clusters, each with white mycelium and copious tomentum around the base and extending up the stalk for some distance.

Edibility   As stated previously, we consider it dangerous to experiment with species of *Mycena*. We have no data on this one.

When and where   It is a feature of the "snowbank mushroom flora" of the spruce-fir zone in the Rocky Mountains. The fruiting period is quite prolonged, especially following a heavy snow pack.

Spores   6–7 x 3.5–4 μm, white in deposit, narrowly ovate to oblong or pipshaped, smooth, amyloid.

Observations   This species is named in honor of Lee Oras Overholts, who first collected it while studying the Polyporaceae.

126　*Mycena leaiana*　　　　　　　　　　　About two-thirds natural size

127　*Mycena overholtsii*　　　　　　　　　About one-fourth natural size

Mycena galericulata　　　　　　　　　　128

Identification marks　The cap is large for the genus (2–7 cm broad), the umbo is obtuse, and the color gray to dull brown (in age). The cartilaginous, naked stalk, along with the habitat on rotten wood, also aid in characterizing it. In age the gills often are flushed pale rose, but not so the cap surface, which may be actually blackish in buttons.

Edibility　Edible, according to a number of earlier American authors, but it is not clear as to which species, *M. galericulata* or *M. inclinata*, they tested. We do not recommend it—at least for the present.

When and where It is found on decaying wood of hardwoods east of the Great Plains in the fall, and is fairly common late in the season. In the western area it is found mostly on hardwood and is very robust. *M. rugulosiceps* of Kauffman is now considered a synonym of *M. galericulata*. It represents a geographical variant of the latter.

Spores 8–11 x 5.5–7 μm, white in deposit, ellipsoid, smooth, amyloid.

Observations A *galericulum* is a small peaked cap.

128 *Mycena galericulata*   About two-thirds natural size

Tricholoma

This genus is rather easy to recognize in the field. The important field characters are the notched gills that are initially, at least, attached to the stalk; the fleshy stalk; the white spore deposit; and the terrestrial habit. It is a large genus containing good edible species and some that are poisonous. *Lyophyllum* is a closely related genus distinguished on chemical characters. The one species of *Lyophyllum* that we include is keyed out with the species of *Tricholoma*. *Tricholoma* is derived from words meaning hair and fringe.

Key to Species

1. Caps viscid at first (check young, fresh caps) 2
1. Caps dry to moist but not viscid 6
  2. Gills soon stained reddish brown 3
  2. Gills not staining as above 5
3. Stalk with a superior orange zone but lacking any veil fibrils .... 136. *Tricholoma aurantium*
3. Stalk not as above 4
  4. Growing under cottonwood in arcs or densely gregarious .... 129. *T. populinum*
  4. Growing under conifers, scattered or gregarious .... 130. *T. pessundatum*
5. Disc of cap streaked with gray or darker fibrils; gills white at first .... 131. *T. sejunctum*
5. Disc of cap merely brownish; gills distinctly yellow at first .... 132. *T. flavovirens*
  6. Caps white at first, pale crust brown in age .... 133. *T. venenata*
  6. Not as above 7
7. Cap glabrous and moist; growing in dense clusters .... 137. *Lyophyllum multiceps*
7. Not as above 8
  8. Caps whitish on margin, creamy gray to gray over the disc; appressed squamules usually present on disc; stalk 1–2 cm thick .... 134. *T. pardinum*
  8. Caps differently colored from above choice; cap reddish brown and fibrillose .... 135. *T. vaccinum*

Tricholoma populinum 129
(The Sandy)

Identification marks It fruits in great clusters or densely gregarious under cottonwood trees, especially on sandy soil. The cap is viscid and dull reddish cinnamon over the disc. The margin is paler, and the odor and taste are farinaceous. The gills stain a dingy reddish brown in age, but the spore deposit is white.

Edibility Edible and popular in the Pacific Northwest. It was described from Europe.

When and where It is found late in the fall in rings or arcs clustered or gregarious near cottonwood trees, especially on sandy soil, which gave rise to the common name. See also comments under *T. pessundatum*.

Spores 5–5.5 x 3.5–4 μm, white in deposit, ellipsoid, smooth, inamyloid.

Observations Again, we should like to emphasize that when collecting for table use, collect only under cottonwood. There are "look-alikes" that grow under conifers and other hardwoods, and neither their taxonomy nor their edibility has been critically studied here in North America. *Populinum* refers to *Populus*, the genus to which cottonwood belongs.

129 *Tricholoma populinum*   About two-thirds natural size

130 *Tricholoma pessundatum*   About one-half natural size

131 *Tricholoma sejunctum*   About two-thirds natural size

Tricholoma pessundatum 130

Identification marks   The distinctly viscid, reddish to reddish brown cap; the white gills which become reddish spotted in age; and the practically white stalk, along with the habitat under pine, are distinctive. Also, the taste is strongly bitter-farinaceous. The fruiting bodies at times remain practically buried in the pine straw of the forest floor.

Edibility   "Mildly" poisonous; not recommended.

When and where   It is most abundant in the Great Lakes region under red and jack pine late in the season after heavy rains. It also occurs in the Pacific Northwest, at times in considerable quantity.

Spores   4.5–5.5 x 3–3.5 μm, white in deposit, smooth, ellipsoid, inamyloid.

Observations   This species is included as a representative of a group of Tricholomas, including *T. albobrunneum* and *T. populinum*, which contains an edible and a poisonous species. This pattern is frequently encountered in the fleshy fungi; that is why empirical tests do not work. *Pessundatum* apparently means ruined.

Tricholoma sejunctum 131

Identification marks   The cap is viscid when young, the disc streaked or coated with dark appressed fibrils, and the broad marginal area is yellowish. Occasionally the cap is yellowish overall. Typically the cap is umbonate, and the margin spreading. The gills are white at first, but near the cap edge are often yellow in age. The taste of the raw flesh is somewhat disagreeable to farinaceous.

Edibility   Kauffman listed it as edible, but in Europe in recent times cases of poisoning have been traced to it, and the image of the species is now somewhat tarnished. In view of this we do not recommend it.

When and where   It is common in its various forms and is found in both hardwood and conifer forests during the summer and fall. It is difficult for the beginner to identify correctly, since a number of "look-alike" species occur. This species (including its variants) is widely distributed in North America.

Spores   6.5–8 x 4.5–5.5 μm, white in deposit, ellipsoid, smooth, inamyloid.

Observations   The word *sejunctum* means separable.

Tricholoma flavovirens 132
(Man-on-a-Horse)

Identification marks   Pay attention to the slightly viscid cap, which is pale brownish over the disc with the remainder yellow, and the yellow gills and stalk. The stalk can vary to nearly white. No veil is present. Collections with white gills belong in a different species, *T. leucophyllum*.

Edibility   Edible and considered choice but be critical in making your identifications. Our greatest objection to this species is that it is found in abundance under pine on sandy soil, and it is almost impossible to remove all the sand.

When and where In the Great Lakes area we have found it mostly with 2-needle pines and with aspen. It fruits mostly in the fall and is a common and widely distributed species in the conifer forests of North America.

Spores 6–7.5 x 4–5 μm, white in deposit, ellipsoid, smooth, inamyloid.

Observations In sandy soil, specimens have much sand adhering to the cap because of the viscidity of the latter. To avoid this it is better to collect in pine woods with a thick carpet of lichens and fallen pine needles. We suspect that most casual collectors have not distinguished between this species and *T. leucophyllum*, so if the latter is poisonous, we should have had evidence by this time. *Leucophyllum* means pale leaves (gills), and *flavovirens* means greenish yellow.

132 *Tricholoma flavovirens*   About two-thirds natural size

133 Tricholoma venenata

Identification marks In the specimens we have identified as belonging to this species, the fruiting body is white at first, but, on injury or on aging, the cap becomes buff to pale crust brown, at least over the disc. The cap

133 *Tricholoma venenata*   About one-half natural size

surface is dry and matted-fibrillose, the gills and stalk become crust brown where injured, and the odor and taste are mild.

Edibility   POISONOUS; it has caused severe gastrointestinal upsets.

When and where   It is to be expected in the lower Great Lakes area on low, rich hardwood stands in late summer and fall. It is not considered common, or at least not commonly recognized because of the color changes that normally take place.

Spores   5.5–7 x 4–5 μm, white in deposit, broadly ellipsoid, smooth, inamyloid.

Observations   *Venenata* means poisonous.

Tricholoma pardinum 134

Identification marks   The fine fibrillose scales of the cap (which are creamy gray to dark gray against the paler flesh), the whitish, smooth stalk, and the lack of a veil (check buttons) are features to note. Here, again, however, one cannot make accurate distinctions between all the related species in the group on field characters alone. These fungi are difficult for specialists and amateurs alike.

Edibility   POISONOUS. Any gray- to white-gilled mushroom with gray, bluish gray or grayish brown, dry, fibrillose caps should be avoided by beginners. Some of these are very common in conifer plantations, and some of these are edible. *T. pardinum* may cause severe gastrointestinal upsets.

When and where   This fungus occurs in the fall under conifers in the northern United States and in Canada as well as in the mountains of the West. During warm, wet seasons it is often quite abundant. In Colorado it fruits during late July into August.

Spores   8–9 x 5–6 μm, white in deposit, ellipsoid, smooth, inamyloid.

Observations   *Pardinum* means pertaining to panthers.

134   *Tricholoma pardinum*   About one-half natural size

135   Tricholoma vaccinum

Identification marks   The cap is densely covered with reddish cinnamon fibrils, groups of which become aggregated to form appressed squamules. The gills are pallid but soon stain vinaceous brown as does the stalk. At times the fibrils on the cap become darker in aging, and in some caps they appear almost granulose. These variations are currently under study.

Edibility   According to some reports it is edible but not good, and it also has been listed as suspected. We do not recommend it.

When and where   Scattered to gregarious under conifers. It is common in the western mountains during late summer and fall, and often abundant, even occurring in large clusters. It is also common in conifer forests east of the Great Plains.

Spores   6–7.5 x 4.5–5 μm, white in deposit, broadly ellipsoid, smooth, inamyloid.

Observations   *Vaccinum* means pertaining to cows; in this case, it probably refers to the color.

135   *Tricholoma vaccinum*   About two-thirds natural size

136   Tricholoma aurantium

Identification marks   The viscid cap which soon becomes dry, its orange tan color, the white context with its strong farinaceous odor and taste, and the colored zone near the apex of the stalk are distinctive. There is no veil connecting the cap margin to the stalk, but the colored zone near the apex of the stalk makes one suspicious that a rudimentary veil exists. The gills become stained rusty brown by maturity.

Edibility   Not recommended because of a bitter taste along with the farinaceous component. We have no data on it.

When and where   Gregarious in mixed conifer and hardwood forests; often abundant during wet periods in late summer and early fall in the Rocky Mountains, the Great Lakes area, and eastward.

Spores 4–5 x 3–4 μm, white in deposit, smooth, ellipsoid, inamyloid.

Observations There is considerable color variation from olive to orange to orange brown in the caps. *Aurantium* means orange.

136 *Tricholoma aurantium*   About one-half natural size

Lyophyllum multiceps *(L. decastes* group)   **137**

Identification marks The species typically fruits in large clusters. The caps measure 4–12 cm broad and vary from pallid to tan or grayish tan. The gills are adnate becoming somewhat decurrent, and are whitish at maturity. There is no veil, and injured areas do not stain black in this species. If the

137 *Lyophyllum multiceps*   About one-half natural size

gills are pinkish or reddish cinnamon at maturity, the specimen is likely to be an *Entoloma* and should be discarded if you are collecting for the table.

Edibility Edible and choice—but be sure you check the color of the spore deposit or the color of mature gills.

When and where It fruits in large clusters—especially around old sawdust piles, on waste soil, or along hedges or even under ornamental plantings —late summer and fall after heavy rains, but occasionally in the spring also. At times it fruits along woods roads in great profusion. It is widely distributed in North America.

Spores 5–8 μm, white in deposit, globose, smooth, inamyloid.

Observations As American authors have pointed out, there is grave danger in using this species for food if one does not collect carefully and check the color of the spore print. *Multiceps* means many-headed; *decastes* signifies groups of ten, an allusion to the clustered manner of growth. *Lyophyllum* is derived from "I loosen" and "leaf." In many areas this is referred to as the fried chicken mushroom.

138   Lentinellus vulpinus

Identification marks The caps basically are fan-shaped, but often occur in shelving masses two to four caps high. As a cap ages the surface near the place of attachment becomes coarsely hairy with dark vinaceous brown hairs, and this condition may finally spread to near the cap margin. The taste, as we find it, is not only disagreeable but strongly acrid. The spore deposit is amyloid.

Edibility Inedible. We have no data on whether or not it contains any actual poisonous compounds.

When and where It is commonly found on larger pieces of debris—logs and stumps of hardwoods—in the summer and fall, especially east of the Great Plains; it is often abundant.

Spores 3–4 x 2–3.5 μm, white in deposit, subglobose, very minutely ornamented, strongly amyloid.

Observations Collectors may mistake this species for an oyster mushroom, but it is tougher than the true oyster mushroom, and the gills at maturity

138 *Lentinellus vulpinus*   About one-half natural size

have jagged edges. The taste, of course, is very different. *Vulpinus* means pertaining to a fox, possibly an allusion to the color of the surface hairs. *Lentinellus* means a small *Lentinus*.

Phyllotopsis nidulans   139

Identification marks   This is a pleurotoid (*Pleurotus*-like) species with a pink spore deposit, medium sized caps with dry fibrillose surfaces which are usually bright orange yellow (but slowly fade), and bright orange to pinkish orange gills which in age are merely yellowish. The odor resembles that of old, somewhat spoiled cabbage—with a definite sulphur component.

Edibility   Apparently not actually poisonous, but clearly undesirable as far as the casual mushroom hunter is concerned. Not recommended.

When and where   We find it both on conifer and on hardwood, but its favorite, if it may be said to have one, is the wood of the small-toothed aspen (popple wood). It is to be expected in the forested areas of Canada and the United States in late summer and fall.

Spores   6–8 x 3.5–4 μm, bright pink in deposit, sausage-shaped in profile, cylindric in face view, smooth, inamyloid.

Observations   *Nidulans* means partly encased or lying in a cavity. *Phyllotopsis* means resembling *Phyllotus*.

139   *Phyllotopsis nidulans*   About three-fourths natural size

Pleurotus

The "pleurotoid" habit is an important feature of this genus. This term refers to the fact a stalk may be absent, or if one is present, it is eccentric to lateral. Consequently, the fruiting body is often fan-shaped or ear-shaped. The spore print may be lilac gray, pale buff, or white. These species typically fruit on decaying wood of coniferous or deciduous trees. The two widely used edible species are included here. *Pleurotus* is derived from words meaning side and ear, perhaps a reference to the way the fruiting bodies are attached to the wood.

Key to Species

140   Pleurotus ostreatus
(Oyster Mushroom)

Identification marks   The gills are white to pallid and often fuse where they extend down the stalk. The whole fruiting body is soft and fleshy. Many related wood-inhabiting mushrooms are tough, and some of these have jagged or serrate gill edges. In the oyster the cap is smooth and naked and varies in its numerous variants from white to brown or almost black. The spore print of the true oyster is lilac gray after excess moisture has evaporated from it. Dark colored specimens are usually found in the fall and the whitish ones in June and July, but there are numerous exceptions.

Edibility   Edible and popular. The base of the cap, including the stalk (if present), is tough and should be discarded. Beetles hiding between the gills are rapidly removed by briefly immersing the specimens in water, or better, by simply holding the specimens with gills facing downward and tapping the top of the cap sharply with a blunt object.

When and where   It is widely distributed, abundant, and fruits during late spring, summer, and fall, or even in the winter in the South. It is to be expected wherever hardwoods occur in the United States and Canada.

140   *Pleurotus ostreatus*   About one-half natural size

Spores 7–10 x 3.5–4 μm, pale lilac gray in air-dried deposit, oblong in face view, smooth, hyaline in KOH, inamyloid.

Observations According to the dictionary *ostreatus* means rough or scabby, or pertaining to an oyster. The latter seems the more appropriate, since the cap of the species is smooth.

Pleurotus porrigens   141
(Angel's Wings)

Identification marks The habitat on old conifer logs, the shining white to milk white caps 2–8 cm wide, the gills soon becoming yellowish, the lack of a true stalk, and the white spore deposit are diagnostic.

Edibility Edible, and popular in the Pacific Northwest. It is abundant there and in the Great Lakes area also. Many people prefer it to the true oyster mushroom.

When and where See above.

Spores 6–7 x 5–6.5 μm, white in deposit, subglobose to globose, smooth, inamyloid.

Observations We continue to use the generic name *Pleurotus* for this species until better-tested generic concepts are available. Singer first used the name *Pleurocybella porrigens*, but has now changed to *Nothopanus*. There are problems here that go beyond the scope of a field guide. *Porrigens* apparently means stretching out.

141   *Pleurotus porrigens*   About two-thirds natural size

Amanitaceae

The casual collector should not eat any *Amanita*. In fact, no one should eat any *Amanita* until he/she has studied the genus carefully using all the technical characters by which mycologists distinguish the various species. It is fortunate that the species of this genus have such a distinctive aspect in the field that any collector can soon learn to recognize the genus at sight. We include a significant number of the common species, and a few not so common, to help the user grasp what we call the "field aspect" of the genus.

Amanitas have three essential characters that can be studied without a microscope: 1) an outer veil, 2) free gills, and 3) a white or nearly white spore deposit. In addition, many species also have a ring or annulus on the stalk.

The outer veil completely covers the button stage and breaks as the cap expands and the stalk elongates. Depending on the consistency of this veil, it may break in one of several different ways. For example, it may form a cup or volva at the base of the stalk, as in *A. virosa* and *A. phalloides*. In *A. calyptroderma* it breaks leaving a large piece on the cap, with the remainder around the base of the stalk as a volva. In *A. pantherina* and related species it breaks up into numerous pieces scattered over the cap, and a collar like zone is left at the apex of the bulb. This zone marks the line along which the outer veil broke. In some other species the outer veil is very fragile and is not attached to the stalk at all. No volva is formed, but the remains of the veil (pieces of soft, fragile tissue) may adhere to the stalk or the soil around its base. The pieces of veil left on the cap in such species may be the only proof that an outer veil was present at first, but even this evidence is easily washed away. For this group, at least, one can readily see why the collector should obtain both old and young specimens for identification purposes.

In most species of *Amanita* the gills are not attached to the stalk, or they just barely reach it. Furthermore, the stalk can often be pulled or twisted so that it separates rather easily from the cap. The gills vary in color from species to species, but in most are white to only slightly colored, and the degree of pigmentation is not of great taxonomic value. The spore deposit is white or nearly so.

Many species have a ring or annulus on the stalk. It arises from a thin layer of tissue that extends from the cap margin to the stalk and acts as a cover for the young gills until about the time the spores are mature. When this veil finally breaks, it typically does so along the cap margin, leaving a thin skirt around the upper part of the stalk. This skirt is the ring or annulus. A number of Amanitas do not have such a partial veil and were placed in a separate genus, *Amanitopsis*, in the older literature. In some species with a partial veil, the tissue is thin and powdery and no annulus is formed.

The following key is to the genus *Amanita*; one species of *Limacella* is keyed out with the Lepiotaceae.

Key to Species

Amanita spreta   142

Identification marks   The cap is usually glabrous, sulcate-striate on the margin in age, and typically lead color to grayish brown. The gills are usually attached to the stalk by a line. The stalk is cylindric, 8–15 cm long, deeply inserted in the sandy soil, and has a small saccate volva at the base which

142 *Amanita spreta*   About two-thirds natural size

is easily lost in the collecting process. The ring is tinged gray to concolor with the cap on its outer (under) side.

Edibility   Not recommended! We have no documented cases of poisoning, but we do have one authentic report that it is edible, from a person who ate it. Doubts have been raised recently as to its rating as poisonous, because the related species are mostly edible.

When and where   Scattered under scrub oak in particular, in the Great Lakes region and both east and southward; fruiting during hot humid weather in the summer and early fall.

Spores   10–12 x 6–7.5 μm, white in deposit, obovoid, smooth, inamyloid.

Observations   *Spreta* means despised, i.e., the despised *Amanita*.

---

143   Amanita citrina

Identification marks   The cap is pale greenish yellow to greenish. The veil remnants are thin and often have a grayish tinge; they are often absent in mature caps. The stalk has a distinct basal bulb, often cleft longitudinally as in *A. brunnescens*. The ring is typically well formed and at times is vinaceous gray on the edge and lower side.

Edibility   Edible, but the flavor is not pleasant. It has a rather astringent taste, according to those who have eaten it. In keeping with our policy on species of *Amanita*, we do not recommend it.

When and where   In the hardwood and mixed conifer-hardwood stands east of the Great Plains, in the summer and fall. It appears in varying amounts, but is available almost every season and is a very persistent mushroom once it starts to produce fruiting bodies.

Spores   7–9 μm, white in deposit, globose, smooth, amyloid, apiculus inconspicuous.

Observations   *Citrina* means citron colored or greenish yellow.

143   *Amanita citrina*   About three-fourths natural size

Identification marks   The cap is a dark gray brown and, rarely, has thin patches of gray veil material, sometimes as floccose warts. The margin is not striate. The gills are pallid to ash color, and the edges are crenulate. The bulb is usually prominent as in *A. brunnescens* and *A. citrina*. The ring is gray on the lower surface, and the outer-veil remnants are grayish.

Edibility   Questionable; therefore, one should refrain from eating it.

When and where   Scattered on rich humus in conifer forests in the fall, both west and east of the Great Plains. We frequently find it on almost completely decayed hemlock logs.

Spores   7–10 μm, white in deposit, smooth, globose, amyloid.

Observations   *A. brunnescens* has a blacker cap when young and soon shows pallid areas on or near the margin. *Porphyria* means purplish: this species has a slight purplish tint to the gray when in full vigor.

144   *Amanita porphyria*   About natural size

Identification marks The outstanding combination of features for this species is the occurrence under hardwoods, the blackish to gray brown to nearly white cap, and the large bulb with longitudinal clefts (as if someone had removed a wedge-shaped piece of tissue). The remains of the universal veil resemble irregular small patches of veil tissue rather than well-defined warts on the cap. These are often absent by maturity or in old age. The ring and the stalk are white. A white variety of the species has been described, but it does not appear to be constant.

Edibility At one time this species was mistaken for a variation of *A. phalloides* and listed as poisonous, but "the tide has turned," and indications at present are that it is edible. However, more testing is needed before it can be recommended to the public as an edible species. This testing should be done by qualified chemists.

When and where East of the Great Plains it is found with hardwoods, especially in sandy aspen and oak woods. It is very abundant during wet seasons, and in Michigan it is one of the indicators that the summer flora has begun to appear, in contrast to the spring flora of *Mycena* and *Collybia*.

145 *Amanita brunnescens*   Natural size

Spores   8–10 μm, white in deposit, globose, smooth, amyloid.

Observations   *A. citrina*, *A. brunnescens*, and *A. porphyria* are very close-ly related, and all three, at times, have a cleft bulb. *Brunnescens* means be-coming brown, and refers to brownish stains often present on the stalk.

Amanita rubescens   146
(The Blusher)

Identification marks   The warts on the cap left by the broken universal veil, the brownish to gray or dingy clay brown cap often stained dingy vinaceous brown or red in age, the gills often flushed pink, and the stalk with its vina-ceous red stains at least in the lower portion in age are distinctive. There is no distinct cuplike volva—the veil breaks into small patches, and these usu-ally adhere to the surrounding dirt when the specimens are gathered. The spores are amyloid.

Edibility   Edible and choice, but "out of bounds" for anyone who has not studied *Amanita* for at least several seasons.

When and where   It is rare west of the Great Plains and common east of them. It fruits through the summer into the early fall in a solitary, scattered,

146   *Amanita rubescens*   About natural size

or gregarious pattern. There are a number of variations of this species based in part on color: one is nearly white and is frequent along the south shore of Lake Superior; one having strong olive tones occurs in southeastern Michigan. In the south, however, an even more complex variation is encountered.

Spores   8–10 x 5–6 μm, white in deposit, smooth, ellipsoid, amyloid.

Observations   *A. flavorubescens* is a yellow species which stains red in the base of the stalk. *A brunnescens* tends to stain brown, not reddish. *Rubescens* means becoming reddish.

---

147   Amanita flavoconia

Identification marks   The cap and the remains of the outer veil are chrome yellow, the stalk is also chrome yellow, and there are chrome yellow pieces of the outer veil around the base of the stalk. The ring is also yellow. It may seem at times to resemble a small specimen of *A. muscaria*, but the spores are amyloid.

Edibility   It has been reported to contain the cyclopeptide toxins; this would put it in the very dangerous group. We lack chemical studies on the closely related species.

When and where   This species is common in the region of the Great Lakes and both eastward and southward, but does not occur in large numbers at one time. It often fruits during relatively dry summers when other fungi are not numerous. We have not found it in the West, but would expect it in southern Oregon.

Spores   7–9 x 5–6.5 μm, white in deposit, broadly ellipsoid, amyloid, smooth.

Observations   *A. flavorubescens*, which could easily be confused with the above species, finally stains red on the stalk as in *A. rubescens*. *Flavoconia* refers to the bright yellow color of the warts left on the cap by the broken veil.

---

148   Amanita muscaria
(Fly Mushroom)

Identification marks   The outer veil is intergrown with the base of the stalk and does not form a free cup as in *A. virosa* or *A. bisporigera*. The expanding cap causes the part of the outer veil covering the cap to break up in small patches or warts (often looking like particles of cottage cheese). There are usually one to three bracelets of outer veil tissue on the stalk just above the bulb. The spores are not amyloid. Color variants are common: dark red, orange red, orange, yellow, pale yellow, and white. Fruiting bodies with red caps are more numerous in the western United States and in the Gulf Coast area, but are also known from the Great Lakes region. The orange to yellow variations are common in the Great Lakes area, but are known both in the West and the Gulf Coast area. The most extensive fruiting of the white variation that we have seen was along the south shore of Lake Superior in the fall of 1978.

Edibility   POISONOUS to most people. The species is the cause of considerable controversy because of certain cults, the members of which eat the fruiting bodies to experience the "visions" and other mental derangements its poisons (muscimol and ibotenic acid) produce. Contrary to previous popular beliefs, the principal poison is not muscarine, as the specific epithet might suggest.

147 *Amanita flavoconia*   About natural size

148a *Amanita muscaria*   About half natural size

148b *Amanita muscaria*   About half natural size

When and where   It is common in conifer forests throughout North America, and, at least in the Great Lakes area, it is also found under aspen. It has a late spring and a fall fruiting period. In the Rocky Mountains it is a summer-fruiting species.

Spores   9–12 x 7–9 μm, white in deposit, broadly ellipsoid, inamyloid.

Observations   A saucer of milk with a cap of *A. muscaria* soaked in it can be used to stun or kill flies, hence the specific epithet and the common name. As with a number of poisonous species (see *Gyromitra esculenta*), some people can eat this species and suffer no ill effects; others parboil the specimens and discard the liquid, and suffer no ill effects from eating the material so prepared. So, again, one advising the public cannot promise an individual who wants to eat the fungus that he/she will or will not suffer ill effects from eating it, but statistics are definitely in favor of being poisoned. *A. muscaria* is one of the more controversial mushrooms treated in this *Guide*.

149   Amanita pantherina
(Panther Fungus)

Identification marks   The cap is gray brown to dingy yellow to dark yellow brown or nearly cinnamon brown. In a mature cap the margin is tuberculate-striate. The outer veil breaks up much as in *A. muscaria*, and the warts are firm and well-formed. The outer veil is intergrown with the stalk and terminates above the bulb as a tight-fitting collar. There is a group of variations with this last feature, and it is to be regarded as a danger signal—all are poisonous.

Edibility   This is one of the most common POISONOUS species in the Rocky Mountains and the Pacific Northwest, and the one most frequently involved in poisonings. The variant in the Northwest is said to be chemically different from the type (European) material. It causes poisonings with symptoms quite similar to those caused by *A. muscaria*.

When and where   It fruits early in the season in the northern Rocky Mountains, during the summer in Colorado, and during the spring and fall in the Pacific Northwest. Years ago it was particularly abundant on the Tacoma prairies in the Puget Sound area of Washington.

Spores   8–12 x 6–7 μm, dull white in deposit, ellipsoid, smooth, inamyloid.

Observations   *Pantherina* means pertaining to a panther.

149   *Amanita pantherina*   About one-half natural size

Identification marks   The cap is more or less covered with brownish conic warts, its margin is short-striate, and the ground color is whitish to yellowish. The stalk may be up to 18 cm long and 1 – 2 cm thick near the apex. A prominent bulb with grayish brown scales on it, representing the remains of the outer veil, is usually well developed. The ring is nearly apical, pendant, thin, and often shredded. It often develops dingy yellow to clay color stains. The stalk is often rooting beneath the bulb, which tapers to a point if no pseudorhiza is present.

Edibility   We have no data on it, and suggest not experimenting with it or any other species of *Amanita* until one has gained substantial experience in the identification of the species using the technical literature.

When and where   It is usually found scattered under oak where there is a ground cover of *Vaccinium* (blueberry) bushes. It is not abundant, but is one of our most conspicuous species. It fruits mostly during late summer and fall after heavy rains. Its range appears to be east of the Great Plains, and it is most abundant in the Southeast and Gulf Coast regions.

Spores   8–11 x 6–7.5 μm, white in deposit, ellipsoid, smooth, amyloid.

Observations   This species was named in honor of Professor G. F. Atkinson of Cornell University.

150   *Amanita atkinsoniana*   About one-half natural size

Identification marks   The fruiting body is whitish overall, or the disc of the cap may become yellowish; the volval remains on the cap are soft, and the warts often collapse, or pieces of the volva become blocked out into warts, but these never become separated. The flesh also is soft as well as fragile. The stalk often is deeply rooted in the sandy soil. The annulus is soft and fragile, and often is soon obliterated. The volva is also soft and floccose, and any remnants around the base are soon evanescent.

Edibility   We have no data on it, and do not recommend it.

When and where   In the Great Lakes area it occurs in stands of scrub oak on very poor sandy soil in a scattered to gregarious pattern during wet, hot summer weather. It is fairly abundant at times. Its range in North America still remains to be determined.

Spores   10–14 (16) x (4.5) 5–6.5 (7.5) μm, white in deposit, elongate-oblong to cylindric, smooth, amyloid.

Observations   The soft tissue of all parts makes it difficult to collect and transport the fruiting bodies properly—in a sense this is a significant taxonomic character. *Baccata* means set with pearls.

---

152   Amanita fulva

Identification marks   The cap is glabrous and fulvous (reddish tan); the margin for some distance toward the center is sulcate-striate; there is no annulus; and the volva is membranous, white to pale tan, and soft and easily broken. The stalk is pallid to pale tan and covered with whitish pruina (it often appears frosted).

Edibility   Edible, according to reports, but not recommended to beginners.

When and where   This species, common east of the Great Plains, is sometimes very abundant in bogs or at their edges. During wet seasons it occurs on well-drained soil. It fruits from midsummer into the fall and may be solitary, scattered, or gregarious. It also occurs in our Southwest under conditions of exceptionally heavy precipitation.

Spores   8–12 μm, white in deposit, globose or nearly so, smooth, inamyloid.

Observations   *Fulva* means tawny.

---

153   Amanita bisporigera & A. virosa
(Destroying Angel)

Identification marks   The fruiting bodies of these species are a small to large pure white mushroom with a glabrous cap, a cuplike volva at the base of the stalk with the sides collapsing on the stalk but actually remaining unattached to it, a superior to apical annulus, and gills almost or just touching the apex of the stalk. Typically, there are no remains of a veil on the surface of the cap. The two species are recognized mainly on microscopic characters. As the name indicates, *A. bisporigera* has 2-spored basidia; *A. virosa* has mostly 4-spored basidia. In *A. bisporigera*, the spores measure 7–9 μm and are globose. In 2-spored *A. virosa*, they are 8.5–11 μm. We regard the two species as distinct from each other because in *A. virosa* the spores from such 2-spored basidia as are present are larger than the spores from the basidia of *A. bisporigera*. Also, the fruiting bodies of the latter are consistently smaller and more slender than those of *A. virosa*, but here intergradation frequently occurs.

Edibility   DEADLY POISONOUS, of the *A. phalloides* type. The symptoms are delayed in appearance; no sure cure for this type is known.

151 *Amanita baccata*   About two-thirds natural size

152 *Amanita fulva*   About one-third natural size

153 *Amanita virosa*   About one-fourth natural size

When and where Both are primarily northern in distribution but rare in the Pacific Northwest; they are common east of the Great Plains especially in the Great Lakes region and down into the Southeast. *A. bisporigera* fruits mainly during late summer and early fall, and *A. virosa* in the fall—often quite late.

Spores (see above), amyloid in both species and smooth.

Observations *Virosa* means with a bad odor; *bisporigera* refers to the presence of 2-spored basidia.

---

154 Amanita phalloides

Identification marks The cap varies form olive gray on the disc to paler olive or olive yellow over the margin. Pale olive yellow caps rather closely resemble caps of *Amanita citrina*. The volva is a membranous cup containing the bulb of the stalk. The spores are amyloid. The cap is glabrous, and an ample ring is present near the apex of the stalk.

Edibility DEADLY POISONOUS. It contains toxic cyclopeptides which destroy the liver, and the symptoms are often quite delayed. There is no sure cure for poisoning by this species.

When and where Under conifers and hardwoods. It is relatively rare in North America, and has frequently been misidentified over here. It is now known from a number of areas including both coasts as well as Pennsylvania and Ohio. The picture of its distribution in North America is changing with every passing mushroom season.

Spores 7–10 x 6–8.5 μm, white in deposit, subglobose to practically globose, smooth, amyloid.

Observations The fact that at this time the species is expanding its territory in North America makes it necessary for every collector to expect it even in his or her "old" collecting grounds. Every collector should learn the diagnostic features of this species for, as a mycophagist, it is his worst enemy. *Phalloides* means phalluslike.

---

155 Limacella lenticularis var. fischeri

Identification marks The cap is 4–10 cm broad, glabrous, slightly viscid, and a very pale dull tan to whitish. The gills are white, free from the stalk, and crowded. The stalk is about 1 cm thick, solid, whitish, and near the apex bears a large membranous white ring. The taste is slightly mealy.

Edibility Probably edible. *L. lenticularis* var. *lenticularis* in Europe is recommended by some investigators.

When and where After periods of heavy rain in September this mushroom is common in the Great Lakes area in and along the borders of swamps forested with elm, ash, and soft maple. It has a rather short fruiting period.

Spores 3–4.5 x 2–3 μm, white in deposit, smooth, ellipsoid, inamyloid.

Observations *Lenticularis* refers to the shape of a lentil. *Limacella* means slimy.

154 *Amanita phalloides*   About one-half natural size

155 *Limacella lenticularis* var. *fischeri*   About two-thirds natural size

Lepiotaceae

The members of this family have free gills, a cap that is more or less cleanly separable from the stalk, and a partial veil that forms an annulus (which may be evanescent). The spore deposit is white except in *Chlorophyllum*, where it is green to olive. Unlike previous editions of the *Guide*, we are now recognizing only two genera, *Chlorophyllum* and *Lepiota*, in this family. *L. naucina*, *L. procera*, and *L.*

rhacodes are sometimes placed in *Leucoagaricus*, while *L. birnbaumii* and *L. cepaestipes* have been placed in *Leucocoprinus*. However, when *Lepiota* is subdivided, technical characters outside the scope of a field guide become involved. We think it more important for the beginner to get a "feel" for the group as a whole than to become mired in these technicalities. *Limacella lenticularis* var. *fischeri* is keyed out with the Lepiotaceae because it looks more like a *Lepiota* than an *Amanita*. (Technically, it belongs in the Amanitaceae.) *Lepiota* means scaly ear.

Key to Species

156   Chlorophyllum molybdites

Identification marks   The cap varies from fibrillose to fibrillose-scaly, the brown scales being on a whitish ground color. The scales are formed by the breaking up of the cuticle. The caps may reach a diameter of 30 cm. The spore deposit is dull green on white paper. The gills are white then yellowish, and only after the spores mature are they olivaceous. The ring is thick but ragged at the edge, and a volva is lacking.

Edibility POISONOUS, but some people can eat it with no ensuing discomfort. It should never be sold on markets, as happened once in Michigan. Recently a collection of *Lepiota naucina* was found with olive gills, but it gave a white spore deposit. Poisoning by *C. molybdites* usually takes the form of nausea, vomiting, cramps, and diarrhea.

When and where Typically it is a southern species, but extends northward to the Great Lakes area. It often forms large "fairy rings," and before artificial turf was introduced for football fields, it was a common sight on the playing fields of the South and Southeast.

Spores 9–12 x 6.5–8 μm, green in deposit, ellipsoid, smooth, with an apical pore, dextrinoid.

Observations Although some people eat this species deliberately, it is more often mistaken for *Lepiota procera* or *L. rhacodes*. As discussed above, a spore deposit will distinguish them readily. *Chlorophyllum* means a pale green leaf (gills in the case of a mushroom); *molybdites* pertains to lead —just what application this has to the North American collections seems obscure.

156   *Chlorophyllum molybdites*   About one-fourth natural size

Lepiota naucina   157

Identification marks The grayish to entirely white fruiting bodies of this species can be rather easily confused with the white species of *Amanita*, including *A. virosa*. There is no good reason for doing this, but it is done. Be sure to check the base of the stalk to see that a volva or cup *is not* present. In age the caps are grayish, and in some races they are pale gray when young. The gills slowly become pinkish gray to (finally) a dingy vinaceous red. The edge of the ring is not ragged as in *Chlorophyllum molybdites*.

Edibility Edible and of excellent flavor, but *not* recommended. Two considerations are involved in the above statement: first, some who have eaten the species for years have finally been poisoned by it; second, people continue to make erroneous identifications and collect and eat white species of *Amanita* instead.

When and where   It is found scattered to gregarious on lawns, pastures, golf courses, and grassy waste land. It fruits during the summer and early fall and is cosmopolitan.

Spores   7–10 x 5–6 μm, white in deposit, ellipsoid, smooth, dextrinoid, apical pore present.

Observations   We have found a white-spored *L. naucina* in which the gills became olive green by maturity. We did not test these specimens for edibility. *Naucinus*, as reported by McIlvaine, seems to have no appropriate translation. Rea gives its meaning as nutty.

157   *Lepiota naucina*   About one-half natural size

---

158   Lepiota rhacodes

Identification marks   The large cap with its coarse, often recurved, brown scales; the thick stalk which is white and rapidly stains brown from handling; the large movable ring; and the white spore deposit distinguish it. The stalk is not tapered to a point at the base as in most specimens of *L. americana*.

158   *Lepiota rhacodes*   About one-fourth natural size

Edibility   Edible and choice, but not recommended because of the danger of mistaking it for *Chlorophyllum molybdites*—particularly if sterile specimens of the latter are encountered.

When and where   It is widely distributed in North America, but it cannot be said to be either common or abundant. When it does fruit, however, large numbers of fruiting bodies often are produced. It is frequently collected in the Pacific Northwest, and in recent years numerous collections from the region of the Great Lakes have been made. It appears during the late summer and fall.

Spores   8–10.5 x 5–7 μm, white in deposit, ellipsoid to somewhat ovoid, dextrinoid, with a distinct apical pore.

Observations   *Rhacodes* means ragged—a very appropriate epithet for this species.

Lepiota procera   159
(Parasol Mushroom)

Identification marks   In the button stages the stalk is roughened by minute grayish brown particles much the same as those covering the cap. As the cap expands, the cuticle is broken into large scales which finally weather away somewhat. The cap may reach 20 cm broad, the ring has a jagged outer edge and is usually movable up and down the stalk, and the spore deposit is white. The stalk is characteristically long and slender.

Edibility   Edible and choice. It is sought out by connoisseurs. It keeps well and usually does not become wormy quickly.

When and where   It grows in woods and waste places under brush, etc., from late summer through early fall. Its area is that east of the Great Plains, but it is spotty within this range. It is often abundant in New England, but in Michigan we have seen it in abundance only in pine plantations.

Spores   Large (14–18 x 9–12 μm), white in deposit, ellipsoid, smooth, with an apical germ pore, dextrinoid.

Observations   *Procera* means tall, in this instance tall in relation to the diameter of the stalk.

159   *Lepiota procera*   About one-fourth natural size

160 Lepiota americana

Identification marks The cap measures 3–15 cm broad, becoming scaly in age; the ground color is pallid but stains red and finally brown; and when dried the whole cap is dull red. The stalk is typically enlarged near the base and then tapered to a point (or a short pseudorhiza) below the enlargement. The stalk stains yellowish, then red, and finally brown. The ring is well-formed.

Edibility Edible and a favorite with most who have tried it. However, poisonous species occur in *Lepiota*, and so one must be very critical in making identifications. We recommend this species only to experienced collectors. The rather similar European *Lepiota badhami* is reported poisonous.

When and where Usually clustered on decayed hardwood stumps, sawdust, and on humus, in summer and early fall. We collect it nearly every season in southern Michigan, but it is not common. Its area appears to be primarily east of the Rocky Mountains, but it is also known from the Pacific Coast.

Spores 9–11 (12) x (5) 7–8.5 μm, white in deposit, broadly ellipsoid to subglobose, dextrinoid, wall thick, and pore apical.

Observations *Americana* means of or pertaining to America.

160 *Lepiota americana*   About one-half natural size

161 Lepiota rubrotincta

Identification marks The cap is pinkish red to dark red, about 3–6 cm broad, and the surface becomes rimose near the margin as the cap expands. The gills are white, as is the stalk, but the annulus usually has a reddish edge. The fruiting bodies typically are small to medium sized. In the Pacific Northwest the fruiting bodies are often larger and the color of the cap duller, but intergradations are often encountered. This western material has been known under the name *L. rubrotinctoides*.

Edibility   Edible, or at least so reported. We have no data on it.

When and where   Solitary to scattered on humus and soil under either conifers or hardwoods, August and September, and rather common at times from the Great Lakes eastward and southward. The dull colored variant is common in the Northwest in September and early October.

Spores   7–10 x 4.5–5 μm, white in deposit, ovoid-pointed, apiculus prominent, smooth, inamyloid.

Observations   *Rubrotincta* means tinted red; *rubrotinctoides* means resembling rubrotincta.

161   *Lepiota rubrotincta*   Nearly natural size

Lepiota clypeolaria   162

Identification marks   The most conspicuous feature is the ragged appearance of the stalk up to the line where the veil broke. The texture of this material is very soft, and it is readily removed or damaged in the collecting process or by weathering. The cap is dry and floccose to lacerated-scaly except for the disc. There is no truly membranous ring on the stalk.

Edibility   Not recommended. There are numerous varieties of this species, and these have not been tested individually either by chemical analysis or by simply eating them. The current literature on the species is divided as to its edibility.

When and where   It fruits from late summer on into the fall or early winter under either hardwoods or conifers. It is widely distributed and to be expected in one or more of its varieties in wooded areas of both Canada and the United States.

Spores   10–17 x 4–6.6 μm, white in deposit, subfusoid in profile view, smooth, somewhat dextrinoid.

Observations   *Clypeus* refers to a type of shield used by the Romans.

162 *Lepiota clypeolaria*   Nearly natural size

163   Lepiota cepaestipes

Identification marks The entirely white fruiting body when nearly mature, the thin flesh, the typically clustered habit, the finely squamulose to mealy cap surface which in age becomes sulcate-striate near the margin, and the stalk often staining yellow where handled are the principle characters of this species. The stalk is often clavate to a pinched off (somewhat pointed) base. The very young buttons are typically pale gray over at least the disc.

Edibility Edible, according to most reports. We have not tried it. There are conflicting reports, and again, within this group both poisonous and edible species are known.

163 *Lepiota cepaestipes*   Nearly natural size

When and where   It fruits during the summer and early fall in large clusters on compost piles, around sawdust piles, and on rich soil generally. It is widely distributed in the Northern Hemisphere. The best fruiting we have seen was in an area used by the city to dump leaves swept from the city streets in the fall. Here, on a leaf pile the size of a small house, this species practically covered the pile.

Spores   7–10 x 6–8 μm, white in deposit, broadly ellipsoid, apical pore present, weakly dextrinoid.

Observations   The cap colors vary from nearly white to yellow to pale tan to tawny in this group of species: *L. birnbaumii*, for instance, is regularly bright yellow. *Cepaestipes* means onion-foot—referring to the base of the stalk.

Lepiota birnbaumii   164

Identification marks   The fruiting bodies are bright yellow overall, and become conspicuously sulcate-striate when expanded, but otherwise closely resemble those of *L. cepaestipes*. The bright yellow color, however, is a very constant character. In our material, the striations on the margin of the cap do not show distinctly until the caps are old.

Edibility   We have conflicting data on it, and consequently do not recommend it.

When and where   This is the "greenhouse" species in the northern United States and southern Canada, where it often fruits in orchid pots and even on bins of "sterilized" soil. The specimens illustrated are from such soil. In the Gulf Coast area this species and species closely resembling it occur "wild" on debris in the woods, on compost, in pastures, etc. A seasonal pattern of fruiting is difficult to establish for the group.

Spores   8–11 x 5–7 μm, whitish in deposit, ovoid to ellipsoid, dextrinoid, thick-walled, apical pore evident.

Observations   This species has been erroneously called *Lepiota lutea* in the past. It was named in honor of Mr. Birnbaum, who gave specimens to Corda, who described the species.

164   *Lepiota birnbaumii*   Nearly natural size

Pluteaceae

In this family the spore deposit is some shade of pink to reddish cinnamon, the gills are free from the stalk, and the latter is usually cleanly separable from the tissue of the cap. The hyphae of the gill trama are "convergent," but this cannot be determined in the field. The spores are smooth and neither angular nor nodulose, a feature which distinguishes the family from the Rhodophyllaceae.

Pluteus is the largest genus in the family. Its species are found mostly on decaying wood and are often abundant early in the summer season. The most important commercially grown species is *Volvariella volvacea*, the padi straw mushroom of the Orient. Most of the species in the family are scavengers, but *Volvariella surrecta* is parasitic on fruiting bodies of *Clitocybe nebularis*. *Pluteus* means a shed or penthouse; possibly the shape of the cap was thought to resemble a shed's roof.

Key to Species

1. Volva prominent; cap fibrillose; growing on rotting wood of hardwoods . . . . 165. *Volvariella bombycina*
1. Volva absent 2
   2. Cap brilliant scarlet . . . . 166. *Pluteus aurantiorugosus*
   2. Cap blackish at first; growing on wood; stalk 1 – 2 cm thick . . . .
   . . . . 167. *P. magnus* & *P. cervinus*

---

165   Volvariella bombycina

Identification marks   The yellowish to nearly white, dry, fibrillose cap; the lack of a ring on the stalk; the very membranous-pliant brown volva that forms a persistent "cup" around the base of the stalk; the pink gills at maturity; and the habitat on wood of hardwoods together are distinctive.

165 *Volvariella bombycina*   About two-thirds natural size

Edibility   Edible, but rare; we have not seen more than a dozen collections over the years.

When and where   It fruits in the summer and fall, often from knotholes on living trees. We assume it causes a rot of the heartwood of the tree. It apparently favors maple, and is widely distributed.

Spores   6.5–9 x 5–6.5 μm, pink in deposit, mostly ovoid, smooth, inamyloid.

Observations   *Volvariella gliocephala*, another large species, is indicated as poisonous. Here again we have closely related species, one edible and one poisonous. *Bombycina* means silky. *Volvariella* is a diminutive of *Volvaria*.

Pluteus aurantiorugosus   166

Identification marks   The gills are free and yellowish before becoming pink from the spores, the cap is a brilliant scarlet, the stalk is slender, and the species is found on rotten wood of hardwoods, especially that of beech and maple.

Edibility   Of no significance; we have no records of it being tried.

When and where   We find it only rarely, and then usually on standing trees with a very advanced rot of the heartwood—one reaches into the hollow of the tree to gather the fruiting bodies. It is a late summer and fall species with a range, apparently, east of the Great Plains.

Spores   6–7 x 4.5–5 μm, dull pink in deposit, ovate in profile, mostly elliptic in face view, smooth, pale yellow in KOH, inamyloid.

Observations   This is perhaps the most brilliantly colored species in the genus and, as such, is a mycological curiosity. The specific epithet refers to the brilliant red to orange of the cap and the way it is wrinkled on some specimens.

Pluteus magnus & P. cervinus   167

Identification marks   The blackish cap with the surface often wrinkled when young, the whitish free gills which become dull pink in age, the stalk and cap readily separable, and the absence of a veil distinguish it from other species in the field. We treat it here as a single species because, in the past, both have been included under the name *P. cervinus* in the sense of a collective species. The final resolution of this problem rests on the interpretation one places on a large number of additional variations now known for the Great Lakes region.

Edibility   Both *P. magnus* and *P. cervinus* are edible and rather popular (under the name *P. cervinus*). We have no reports of trouble from eating them.

When and where   *P. magnus* consistently is found on sawdust piles, mostly of hardwood origin. Here it often fruits in large clusters and with stalks up to 2 cm thick. The young caps are black and coarsely wrinkled. *P. cervinus* usually occurs solitary or gregarious on rotting wood, mostly of hardwoods. It is smaller, browner, and has a more slender stalk. Fruiting occurs during spring, summer, and fall anywhere in North America north of Mexico where dead wood is available.

Spores 5–6.5 x 4.5–5 μm, dull reddish in air-dried deposit, mostly ellipsoid to ovoid, smooth, slightly pinkish in KOH, inamyloid.

Observations *Magnus* means large; *cervinus* means pertaining to a deer.

166 *Pluteus aurantiorugosus*   About natural size

167 *Pluteus cervinus*   About natural size

Agaricaceae

The field characters of *Agaricus*, the only genus of the family treated here, are: presence of a ring or annulus on the stalk; lack of a cup-like volva at the base of the stalk; gills free from the stalk and the latter readily separating from the cap; and gills pink to wine red when young in most species, becoming some shade of dark chocolate color by maturity (as the spores mature). The spores, individually under the microscope and in spore deposits, are a chocolate brown to blackish. The color of the spores can be determined in the field from spores deposited on the apex of the stalk or on the ring.

Every collector should learn to recognize this genus at sight, as it contains many popular species. From the technical standpoint, the species are very difficult to identify. As yet we have no adequate treatment of the North American species in spite of the fact that our commercially grown species belongs in this genus. Not all the species are edible, however, so the collector should not become careless and eat just any *Agaricus* he may happen to find. According to one authority the name *Agaricus* is derived from the Greek *Agaricon*, the name for fungi; according to another, it was derived from the name of a town, *Agara*.

Key to Species

1. Fruiting body staining yellow where injured 2
1. Fruiting body not staining yellow where injured 3
    2. Annulus with yellow to brown droplets on underside; cap ashy gray over disc . . . . 173. *Agaricus placomyces*
    2. Annulus lacking yellow to brown droplets on underside; disc of cap white to pale buff . . . . 172. *A. sylvicola* & *A. arvensis*
3. Cap tawny from the fibrils of the cuticle; annulus double . . . .
  . . . . 171. *A. subrufescens*
3. Not as above 4
    4. Cap fibrillose with appressed patches of dark vinaceous brown fibrils; staining red slowly where injured . . . . 170. *A. pattersonae*
    4. Not as above 5
5. Cap white and smooth; ring double (flared at both the upper and lower edges) . . . . 169. *A. bitorquis*
5. Cap white or with some brownish fibrils; annulus a single membrane (no patches on the underside) . . . . 168. *A. campestris*

Agaricus campestris   168
(Meadow Mushroom or Champignon)

Identification marks   The cap is dry and fibrillose, typically white but at times with brownish fibrils; the gills are bright pink before becoming chocolate color from the spores; and the ring on the stalk is a thin layer of tissue representing the remains of the veil. No volva is present at the base of the stalk. The ring, because of its delicate texture, is often obliterated.

Edibility   Edible and choice. It can be prepared as one prepares the commercially grown mushroom. There are numerous cookbooks giving recipes for using it.

When and where   It fruits in pastures, meadows, and grassy places—generally from sea level to high in the mountains above timberline—and is most abundant from late summer on into the fall, depending on the geographic location and the elevation. It is widely distributed in North America, and like most common species is quite variable.

Spores 6–7.4 x 4.5–5 μm, chocolate brown under the microscope, ellipsoid, smooth.

Observations The cultivated mushroom has 2-spored basidia; *A. campestris* has mostly 4-spored basidia. *Campestris* means of the meadows.

168 *Agaricus campestris*   Nearly natural size

169   Agaricus bitorquis

Identification marks This mushroom is white overall save for the pink gills which become chocolate in age. The ring on the stalk is in the shape of a wide band curved outward at the lower edge and flaring out at the upper edge. This feature distinguishes it from *Agaricus campestris*. In addition, *A. bitorquis* fruits most abundantly in the spring and comes up on hard-packed soil such as old driveways, school yards, parking areas, etc.

169 *Agaricus bitorquis*   About two-thirds natural size

Edibility   Edible and choice. The flavor is excellent and the flesh is firm. It keeps well, and cooks up nicely. Attempts have been made to grow it commercially.

When and where   Mostly in pastures. Generally fairly common east of the Great Plains; along the Pacific Coast it has been found in large cities, particularly in areas used by carnivals and circuses.

Spores   4.5–6 x 4–5 μm, dark chocolate brown in deposit and under the microscope, broadly ellipsoid to subglobose, smooth.

Observations   In North America the names *A. edulis* and *A. rodmani* have been used for this species, but apparently the name *bitorquis* was published a few weeks ahead of *A. rodmani* and so has priority. *Edulis* means edible; *rodmani* means Mr. Rodman's *Agaricus*; and *bitorquis* means two collars—referring to the double ring.

Agaricus pattersonae   170

Identification marks   The cap is covered by long, dark, almost chestnut brown to dark vinaceous brown fibrils which become grouped into fascicles (bundles) as the cap expands. The ring is "double"—somewhat like that of *A. bitorquis*. The flesh is hard and firm and the stalk short and thick. Bruised areas slowly stain red.

Edibility   Edible and choice. The flesh is firm and well flavored.

When and where   It was described from California but also has been found in the Great Lakes region. It fruits in the summer and fall in habitats normally unattractive to mushrooms—hard-packed soil along city streets and in parking lots, much as for *A. bitorquis*. The type was collected under *Eucalyptus*.

Spores   6.5–8 x 4.5–5.5 μm, smooth, broadly ellipsoid, dark chocolate colored in KOH.

Observations   *Pattersonae* refers to Ms. Patterson, the collector, who found it in the San Francisco Bay region.

Agaricus subrufescens   171

Identification marks   The cuticle of the cap is ochraceous tawny to tawny and it breaks up into appressed, fibrillose scales. The sheath of veil tissue on the stalk breaks up into floccose patches, as does the outer (under) layer of the membranous ring.

Edibility   Edible and popular.

When and where   Solitary to gregarious in rich humus or around piles of organic debris in the fall, especially around compost heaps; in fact, it may be worth some study by gardeners for use in compost heaps. It is to be expected east of the Rocky Mountains. West of the Great Plains *Agaricus augustus* and *A. perrarus* occur more frequently, and have rather similar cap colors and scale patterns. *A. augustus* is highly prized as an edible species. *A. perrarus* occurs under Sitka spruce on the Pacific Coast, and is often confused with *A. augustus*.

Spores   6–7.5 x 4–5 μm, chocolate brown in deposit, ellipsoid, chocolate brown in KOH, smooth, no pore visible under ordinary magnifications.

Observations   *Subrufescens* means becoming somewhat tawny.

170 *Agaricus pattersonae*   About one-half natural size

171 *Agaricus subrufescens*   About one-half natural size

172   Agaricus sylvicola & A. arvensis

Identification marks   These are collective species. To a considerable extent, species differences in this group involve differences in spore size. The field characters of the group are a tendency to stain yellow when bruised, white fruiting bodies (with the exception of the gills), and the patches of tissue on the underside of the usually ample ring. The stalk is often flattened at the base, and the base may be bulbous or flanged (abruptly bulbous).

Edibility   There are some "mildly" poisonous species in this group, so we do not recommend it to those without considerable experience in the genus. Most of the species are edible and choice.

When and where   They are found scattered to gregarious in conifer and hardwood forests in the summer and fall, are widely distributed in North America, and can be found during almost every season.

Spores   5–6.5 x 4–4.5 μm, chocolate brown in KOH (about the same in deposit), more or less ovoid to ellipsoid in *A. sylvicola*.

Observations   *Agaricus arvensis* has spores 7–9 x 5–6 μm. It is usually found in pastures. A variety growing in the woods caused a case of mild poisoning. The fruiting bodies are much more robust than those of *A. sylvicola*. *Sylvicola* means woods-loving.

172   *Agaricus sylvicola*   About two-thirds natural size

Agaricus placomyces   173
(Flat-Capped Agaricus)

Identification marks   The droplets on the underside of the ring, which are yellowish becoming brown and when dried leave brown spots, and the thin coating of grayish fibrils over the cap which finally form minute appressed squamules are the important characters. Yellow stains develop on injured areas, and these eventually become brown.

Edibility   Because of confusion over the identity of this species, it has received a "bad" reputation. Apparently it is edible; at least the reports of poisoning to come to our attention have been attributable to *Agaricus meleagris*, a "European species" very common in North America.

When and where   It occurs scattered to gregarious on rich humus in low hardwood forests, especially around old sawdust piles and rubbish heaps, from the Great Plains eastward, during summer and fall. We have seen no authentic specimens from west of the Great Plains.

Spores   4–5.5 x 3.5–4 μm, chocolate brown in deposit, ellipsoid, smooth, dark brown in KOH.

Observations   Peck, who described the species, emphasized the brown droplets on the underside of the ring and the fine squamules on the cap. *A. meleagris* lacks the brown droplets and has more numerous and more conspicuous dark brown to blackish scales on the cap. *Placomyces* means a flat cake: the disc of the cap in this species is flattened.

173   *Agaricus placomyces*   Nearly natural size

Rhodophyllaceae

As for the Pluteaceae, the spore deposit is pink to reddish cinnamon, but the spores (under the microscope) are seen to be variously angular to nodulose. The gills are attached to the stalk, but in mature or old specimens may have broken away and, hence, appear to be free. In the field, the collector can rely on the color of the spore deposit, since it is often observed either on the apex of the stalk, on a cap, on duff around the fruiting body, or on the attached gills in young specimens. The largest genus is *Entoloma* (*Rhodophyllus* in the sense of Quélet). It contains over 200 species in North America, as currently estimated. Most species are found on humus or rotten logs practically reduced to humus. We suspect that most of them are mycorrhiza formers. *Entoloma abortivum* is the only recommended one in that genus. Some species are truly poisonous. The two species of *Clitopilus* keyed out here are the best edible ones in that genus. The spore characters, if a microscope is available, will allow the two genera to be readily distinguished. *Rhodophyllus* means red leaf (red gills); *Entoloma* means within a fringe; *Clitopilus* means a cap with a declivity (depressed on the disc).

Key to Species

1. Fruiting body *Clitocybe*-like (disc flat to depressed); gills whitish then pink, close, decurrent; growing solitary to scattered on humus; odor and taste strongly farinaceous . . . .
. . . . 174. *Clitopilus prunulus* & *C. orcella*
1. Not as above 2
    2. Growing near or around old hardwood stumps and logs; cap

drab gray, dry; whitish "abortive fleshy masses" occurring along with the mushroom-type of fruiting body or independent of them
.... 175. *Entoloma abortivum*
2. Not as above 3
3. Stalk 10–15 mm thick, cap pallid to grayish tan and up to 20 cm broad .... 178. *E. sinuatum*
3. Stalk 2–4 mm thick; cap typically sharply conic 4
    4. Fruiting body more or less salmon color .... 176. *E. salmoneum*
    4. Not colored as in above choice 5
5. Fruiting body bright yellow .... 176. *E. murraii*
5. Fruiting body with a dark brown cap .... 177. *E. aprile*

Clitopilus prunulus & C. orcella 174

Identification marks The close decurrent gills with a vinaceous tone at maturity, the gray to whitish cap, the strong farinaceous odor of the crushed flesh, and the reddish spore deposit are distinctive. There is no veil, and under the microscope the spores are seen to be finely grooved more or less longitudinally. The stalk is often eccentric.

Edibility Edible and choice. The danger in using these species for the table rests on the possibility of mistaking them for an *Entoloma*. All of the latter have angular spores.

When and where They are found solitary to scattered on humus in woods, and often on sandy soil, late in the summer and fall. Ordinarily they do not fruit in large numbers, but in the Pacific Northwest it is often easy to collect enough for a meal. Their distribution east of the Great Plains is spotty.

Spores 9–13 x 5–7 μm, reddish in deposit, subfusoid, with distinct longitudinal grooves as seen with an oil-immersion lens.

Observations In the area east of the Great Plains a whitish, slightly viscid variation occurs more frequently than the gray one with a dry cap. It is often referred to as *Clitopilus orcella*. The gray, dry-capped variation is *C. prunulus*. A common name applied to both is *mousseron*. Intermediates between the two "species" are common during some seasons, so we treat them here as variants within a collective species. *Prunulus* means a little plum.

174 *Clitopilus prunulus*   Nearly natural size

175　Entoloma abortivum

Identification marks　The cap is 3–12 cm broad, the surface is dry, fibril-lose, and pale to dark gray or grayish brown. On some caps one observes watery spots near the margins. The gills are decurrent and pale gray but finally dingy reddish from the spores. The stalk is solid and colored on the surface more or less like the cap. The taste is distinctly farinaceous.

In an area where the typical mushroom-type of fruiting bodies occur, masses of fungous tissue 1–8 cm thick also can occur. Some of these may be attached to "normal" fruiting bodies. For years these masses of tissue were designated as "carpophoroids," but they are now regarded as fruiting bodies of the *Entoloma* which have been parasitized by *Armillariella mellea*, the common honey mushroom (see pl. 97).

Edibility　Both the normal and parasitized fruiting bodies are edible, but the latter apparently are soon spoiled by bacterial or yeast action. Use only those that are firm and not watery within.

When and where　In low hardwood stands on or around very decayed logs and stumps; abundant during September and October in the Great Lakes region, eastward, and southward.

Spores　8–11 x 5–6 μm, reddish in deposit, angular-elongate (nearly ellip-tic in outline).

Observations　The very appropriate name *Rhodophyllus* is "illegal," so to comply with the International Rules we use *Entoloma* here. The specific epithet refers to the "aborted" masses of tissue.

175　*Entoloma abortivum*　　　　　　　　　　　　　Nearly natural size

176　Entoloma salmoneum & E. murraii

Identification marks　The salmon color of young to mature caps, their sharply conic shape, and the "straight" margin of each cap are features of *E. salmoneum*. *E. murraii* is like it, but bright yellow instead of salmon color. The spore deposits are typical of the genus (dull reddish).

176a *Entoloma salmoneum*   About natural size

176b *Entoloma murraii*   About natural size

Edibility   *E. salmoneum* is to be regarded as POISONOUS, and, in view of the similarity of *E. murraii*, the latter should also be avoided.

When and where   Scattered to gregarious on moss under conifers and second growth hardwoods, from the Great Lakes area eastward and southward. It is often found in large numbers after heavy rains in late August in the Great Lakes area and the Northeast. *E. murraii* is, apparently, a rare species.

Spores   9–12 μm on a side, reddish salmon in deposit (in both species), square in optical section.

Observations   *Salmoneum* refers to the color of the flesh of salmon; *murraii* refers to the collector: Murray's *Entoloma*.

---

177   Entoloma aprile

Identification marks   The cap is sharply to obtusely conic, 1.5–4 cm broad, glabrous, hygrophanous, and a very dark bister or date brown. The margin is quite opaque when moist. Odor and taste are not distinctive. The gills are grayish brown before becoming colored from the spores. The stalk is 1.5–3 mm thick, naked, and paler than the cap.

Edibility   Not recommended. Some authors indicate it is edible, but we have no data on North American collections and, over here, the related species are poisonous.

When and where   Under bracken fern, weeds, and brush along country roads and in cutover pine lands in the Great Lakes area; early in the spring —at the time the morels and lorchels are fruiting. It is rather common in its habitat if warm spring rains come near the end of April.

Spores   9–12 x 7–10 μm, angular-tuberculate, not amyloid.

Observations   The specific epithet indicates the early fruiting period of this species.

---

178   Entoloma sinuatum (= E. lividum)

Identification marks   The large cap (up to 20 cm), ivory white in color at first but becoming yellowish to dull tan or finally at times grayish brown; the gills at first having a slight yellowish tint; and the stalk 10–20 mm or more thick are distinctive. Young specimens are likely to be (and apparently have been) mistaken for a *Tricholoma*.

Edibility   POISONOUS. Deaths have been associated with poisoning by this species, but in the reported cases the patient was already weakened from other causes. The symptoms develop soon after eating and include severe disturbances of the digestive system.

When and where   In North America the members of this genus generally can be found in forested areas, either conifer or hardwood, during the spring (rarely), summer, and fall. In the Great Lakes region, *E. sinuatum* often fruits late in August or early September under hardwoods and can often be collected in quantity. It is an attractive species and a temptation to the "pot-hunter." It is to be expected generally east of the Great Plains.

Spores   8–10 x 7–8.5 μm, dull reddish in deposit, angular (subspherical in outline).

Observations   *Sinuatum* means wavy; *lividum* means livid (lead color). Current opinion seems to be that the names *E. sinuatum* and *E. lividum* apply to a single species. As far as the casual collector is concerned, the question is academic; he/she should avoid both.

177 *Entoloma aprile*   About natural size

178 *Entoloma sinuatum*   About one-half natural size

Cortinariaceae and Related Genera

Both young and mature specimens must be used for recognition of genera in this group, since the gills can be almost any color when young, depending on the species. Only selected species can be included here, and greatest reliance must be placed on the photographs in making identifications. In *Cortinarius*, *Hebeloma*, and most species of *Galerina*, the spores are ornamented.

Key to Genera and Species

Cortinarius

This is the largest genus in the Agaricales, and contains about 800
species in the United States and Canada. The presence of a cortina
(a cobwebby partial veil), and a rusty brown spore deposit are the
two major field characters for the genus. Nearly all the species are
terrestrial and presumed to be mycorrhiza formers. Not much is
known of their edibility, though two apparently seriously poisonous
species, *C. gentilis* and *C. orellanus*, are known. Until we know the
species better, it is going to be next to impossible to document which
ones are poisonous and which are not. Collectors will soon notice
that in this genus there is one large aggregation of species associated with hardwoods, and a second associated with conifers. *Cortinarius* is named for the cortina (see above). In Latin it means a
curtain.

Key to Species

3. Cap surface smooth but very slimy; stalk with a broad marginate
    bulb at the time the cortina breaks . . . . 179. *C. atkinsonianus*
    4. Fruiting body dark violet; cap scaly; stalk 1–2 cm thick . . . .
        . . . . 181. *C. violaceus*
    4. Not as above 5
5. Either gills or cap red 6
5. Fruiting body lacking red colors; cap hygrophanous; moist cap about
    amber brown . . . . 184. *C. gentilis*
    6. Gills red, cap and stalk ochraceous . . . . 182. *C. semisanguineus*
    6. Gills and cap red, stalk ochraceous, red tones rather persistent
        . . . . 183. *C. phoeniceus* var. *occidentalis*

Cortinarius atkinsonianus   179

Identification marks   The cap is yellow and soon becomes tinted olivaceous and finally reddish tawny; it is slimy-viscid to the touch. The flesh
is lavender in color, and the gills are violaceous except for the edges, which
are at first olive yellow at times. The violet of the gills fades rapidly. The
stalk is violet and at the base has, at first, a broad marginate bulb. The outer
veil is olive yellow.

Edibility   Edible, according to Kauffman, who described the species and
tested it. Be sure of your identification, however, before you try it.

When and where   Gregarious or in fairy rings on rich soil under hardwoods.
If heavy rains occur in late August, this species usually fruits in abundance.
Its area appears to be the hardwood forests east of the Great Plains.

Spores   13–15 x 7–9 μm, rusty cinnamon in deposit, elliptic in face view,
distinctly roughened.

Observations   The species is named in honor of Professor G. F. Atkinson
of Cornell University, who studied mushrooms there from 1892 to 1918. We
have eaten this species on a few occasions and rate it highly—the flesh is
firm and keeps its lavender color when cooked. Because of the complexity
of the genus *Cortinarius* in regard to identification of species, we recommend
the above species only to competent mycologists.

179   *Cortinarius atkinsonianus*   About one-third natural size

180   Cortinarius corrugatus

Identification marks   The cap is viscid, its surface very wrinkled, and its color pale to dark tawny or ochraceous tawny. The gills are dark violaceous at first but soon become brown. The stalk is 1–2 cm thick and varies considerably in length. It is about the color of the cap. The basal bulb is viscid at first but soon becomes dry; it vanishes as the stalk elongates.

Edibility   It has been listed as edible. We do not recommend it. It is variable in its important characters, and misidentifications are almost sure to occur.

When and where   It is often common during the summer and early fall in beech-maple forests east of the Great Plains. It can be found almost every season, often in large numbers.

Spores   12–15 x 7–9 μm, mostly elliptic in face view, coarsely roughened, dark rusty brown in KOH.

Observations   *Corrugatus* means having wrinkles, in this instance referring to the surface of the cap.

180   *Cortinarius corrugatus*   About one-half natural size

181   Cortinarius violaceus

Identification marks   This species is often misidentified, but there is no reason for this if one remembers that hundreds of Cortinarii have blue or violet colors somewhere on the fruiting body. The dark violaceous color overall, the squamulose cap, and the production of a vinaceous red pigment from tissue placed in a weak solution of KOH (caustic potash) constitute the set of diagnostic characters.

Edibility   Edible, but not one of the best, at least as far as North American variants go. Some of these have a bitter taste when cooked, according to reports that have reached us.

When and where   In Europe it is said to grow under hardwood, but in North America it is found mostly under conifers. In the Pacific Northwest it favors old-growth stands, and is a feature of the Olympic National Park. In the Great Lakes region it has recently turned up in cutover areas that have come back to a mixture of fir, pine, aspen, and alder. It also occurs under pine in the Southeast.

Spores   12–17 x 8–10 μm, mostly ellipsoid, rusty brown in KOH, ornamented with warts and wrinkles over most of surface.

Observations   *Violaceus* refers to the violet color.

181   *Cortinarius violaceus*   About one-half natural size

Cortinarius semisanguineus   182

Identification marks   This is a small to medium sized species with an ochraceous brown, dry, fibrillose cap; a yellowish stalk; and rusty red gills even in mature specimens. KOH dropped on a fresh cap quickly stains the spot inky violet. The stalk is often reddish at the base.

Edibility   Not recommended. We have no data on it.

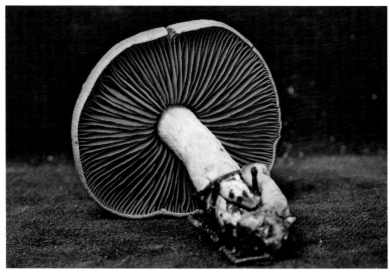

182   *Cortinarius semisanguineus*   About natural size

When and where   It is common under conifers in the late summer and fall in the Great Lakes region eastward and in the Northwest, but seldom in large numbers. We have a few records of it from oak woods with an undergrowth of blueberry bushes (*Vaccinium* species). Other northern fungi were found in the same area. No conifers were present.

Spores   (5) 6–8 x 3–4.5 μm, ellipsoid, faintly ornamented, rusty brown in KOH.

Observations   This and the following two species illustrate patterns of pigment distribution in the genus. *Semisanguineus* means partly blood red.

---

183   Cortinarius phoeniceus var. occidentalis

Identification marks   One of the species of the subgenus *Dermocybe* of *Cortinarius*, this one is characterized by the deep red cap and gills and the yellowish stalk. In *C. semisanguineus* only the gills are red (pl. 182). In *C. sanguineus* the cap, gills, and stalk are all red. The type and localization of pigment in the species of this group of Cortinarii are important taxonomic features.

Edibility   Not recommended. At least one species, *C. orellanus*, of this subgenus is reported as deadly poisonous.

When and where   It is found scattered to gregarious under conifers in the forests west of the Great Plains, but particularly in the Pacific Northwest, where we have seen it in quantity on numerous occasions.

Spores   7–8 x 4–5 μm, mostly ellipsoid, nearly smooth, rusty brown in KOH.

Observations   The trama of cap and gills flush rose color in KOH. *Phoeniceus* refers to the purple red color made famous by the Phoenicians. *Occidentalis* means western.

---

184   Cortinarius gentilis

Identification marks   The cap is small, glabrous, and a bright, somewhat polished yellow brown when moist. The stalk is about cinnamon colored, and usually a yellow, fibrillose, often inconspicuous band of veil remnants is present in young material. It is the type of fruiting body that occasioned the coining of the term "little brown mushroom"—usually abbreviated "LBM"—a term applying to several hundred species with fruiting bodies of this general type, many of them poisonous.

Edibility   POISONOUS, at least we assume so because of reports from northern Europe. It is supposed to have a slow-acting poison that can be fatal. It is said the appearance of symptoms can be delayed up to 14 days.

When and where   Gregarious, often in large numbers on moss and the needle carpet under conifers. It is widely distributed in northern regions, and common in the Northwest during the fall season.

Spores   7.5–9 x 6–7 μm, broadly ellipsoid, minutely ornamented, rusty brown in KOH.

Observations   *Gentilis* means of the same race. *C. orellanus*, another species that causes a similar type of poisoning, has been reported from the Pacific Northwest. However, we have been unable to confirm its presence in North America.

183 *Cortinarius phoenecius* var. *occidentalis*   About natural size

184 *Cortinarius gentilis*   About natural size

Cortinarius armillatus   185

Identification marks   The medium to large dull reddish tawny caps which scarcely change color as moisture escapes, the red "bracelets" on the stalks, and the pale cinnamon gills of young caps are distinctive, as is also the appearance of the fruiting bodies in the vicinity of birch trees. The large spores furnish a laboratory check to eliminate a few other species with red veil remnants.

Edibility   Edible and choice. We have information that it is one of the very popular species in Canada.

When and where   We assume the mycelium forms mycorrhiza with birch, since the fruiting bodies are always near a birch tree. It is rare in the Pacific Northwest, where birch is of very spotty occurrence. It fruits in the fall, and its area is roughly the Great Lakes region eastward. It often occurs in quantity.

Spores 10–13 x 5.5–7.5 μm, rusty brown in deposit and in KOH, mostly ellipsoid, ornamented slightly.

Observations *Armillatus* refers to the bands of veil remnants on the stalk.

185   *Cortinarius armillatus*   About one-half natural size

Gymnopilus

The outstanding feature of this genus in the Cortinariaceae is the orange to orange rusty color of the spore deposit. The species mostly grow on wood (at least in North America), and feature orange to yellow or orange brown colors for the fruiting body. Some of the species contain hallucinogenic compounds, but the bitter taste of most species discourages collecting them for table use. The name means naked cap, but many of our species have scaly caps.

Key to Species

1.   Stalk with an annulus or annular zone; taste mild; on hardwood stumps and wood generally . . . . 186. *Gymnopilus validipes*
1.   Taste distinctly bitter 2
    2.   On conifer wood; stalk often greatly enlarged . . . 187. *G. ventricosus*
    2.   On wood of hardwoods . . . . 188. *G. spectabilis*

186   Gymnopilus validipes

Identification marks   The bright rusty color of the spore deposit is a generic feature. The cap is dry and fibrillose, the fruiting body is unicolorous, and the veil is a cortina and does not leave much of an annular zone or ring. The mild taste distinguishes it from *G. spectabilis*, which also grows on the wood of hardwood species.

Edibility POISONOUS: this was only recently discovered here in south-eastern Michigan. The victims ended up in the hospital. The active compounds were found to be psilocybin and psilocin.

When and where It inhabits wood of deciduous trees, and fruits during late summer and fall, either gregarious or in clusters. Because it has been confused with *G. spectabilis*, we cannot give meaningful data on its distribution. It was described from the state of New York.

Spores 7.5–10 x 4.5–5.5 μm, orange in deposit, mostly elliptic in face view, slightly ornamented (verrucose), dextrinoid.

Observations The poisoning by this species was accidental—the specimens were confused with those of *Armillariella mellea*. The victims recovered but did not enjoy their experience. *Validipes* means having a robust stalk (foot).

186 *Gymnopilus validipes*   About natural size

Gymnopilus ventricosus   **187**

Identification marks This is the giant *Gymnopilus* of the Pacific Northwest; it is frequently identified as *G. spectabilis*. It has the bitter taste of the latter, but lacks the compounds psilocybin and psilocin, which produce hallucinations. This, apparently, has been a disappointment to some collectors in that region. Its field characters are the large size, thick stalk, habitat on conifer wood, and the veil leaving a fibrillose ring high up on the stalk.

Edibility Not recommended. The taste, for one thing, is bitter, and most collectors will find it difficult to make a clear decision as to the species in this, the *G. spectabilis*, group.

When and where It is a late season species, but it may occur in the spring as well as in the fall. It favors old conifer stumps and dead trees but will be found on conifer wood generally. Its area to date appears to be the Pacific Northwest on down the coast into California.

Spores 8–10.5 x 4.5–5 (6) μm, zinc orange in deposit, ovate to elliptic in face view, slightly inequilateral in profile, wrinkled-warty.

Observations *Ventricosus* means enlarged and here refers to the very thick stalk (see photo).

187　*Gymnopilus ventricosus*　　　　　About two-thirds natural size

188　Gymnopilus spectabilis

Identification marks　The spore deposit is orange fulvous, a poorly formed ring is usually present near the apex of the stalk, the cap is fibrillose to more or less appressed-squamulose, the taste raw is decidedly bitter, and the whole fruiting body is a brownish orange.

Edibility　Not recommended: the bitter taste is persistent. Also, like *G. validipes*, *G. spectabilis* contains psilocybin and psilocin—in fact, because of the presence of these compounds, it is called "the big laughing mushroom" in Japan.

When and where　If one goes by reports in the literature, this species (as *Pholiota spectabilis*) occurs on conifers and hardwoods alike. The collection illustrated was from a conifer substrate. The fruiting period is late summer to late fall.

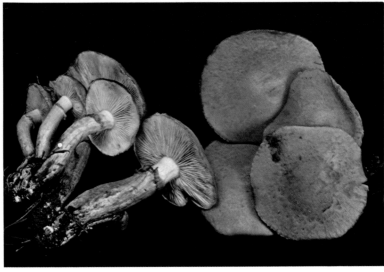

188　*Gymnopilus spectabilis*　　　　　About one-third natural size

Spores (7) 8–10 x 4.5–5.5 (6) μm, orange fulvous in deposit, mostly ellipsoid, slightly ornamented, dextrinoid.

Observations In Europe this species is reported on hardwood. On this basis our *G. luteus*, which has a bitter taste, may be the same as the European *G. spectabilis*. *Spectabilis* means notable or remarkable.

Crepidotus fusisporus var. rameus   189

Identification marks The cap measures (3) 10–30 mm broad, is roughly fan-shaped, the upper surface is dry and cottony, and the odor and taste are mild. The gills are white becoming pinkish buff in age, and the stalk is absent to rudimentary.

Edibility Not tested.

When and where On fallen branches of hardwoods, especially in slashings where the tops of the trees have been left to decay. Its area is that east of the Great Plains, and its fruiting time is June to August.

Spores 7–9 (10) x (3) 4–5 μm, pinkish buff in deposit, fusoid, nearly smooth, often in clumps as seen under microscope.

189 *Crepidotus fusisporus* var. *rameus*   About natural size

Observations The illustration is of a luxuriant fruiting. One might characterize the species of *Crepidotus* as resembling small oyster mushrooms. *Fusisporus* means with spores pointed at each end and inflated in the midportion; *rameus* means pertaining to branches. *Crepidotus* is derived from words meaning "a man's boot" and "ear."

190 Galerina autumnalis

Identification marks The distinguishing features of this most ordinary-appearing fungus are the dingy yellow brown thinly viscid cap, the pale tawny gills, the narrow bandlike ring near the apex of the stalk, and the darkening of the stalk from the base upward. Occurrence in clusters on wood is typical, but the fungus frequently occurs scattered to gregarious also. It grows on either conifer or hardwood substrates.

Edibility POISONOUS. It contains the cyclopeptide toxins which involve the liver and may cause death. Under no circumstances should one experiment with this species, or any fungus closely resembling it, in regard to edibility. It is the commonest potentially deadly species in the Pacific Northwest.

When and where It is widely distributed in forested areas of North America, and there are several variations of it, all, apparently, equally poisonous. Beware of "little brown mushrooms."

Spores 8.5–10.5 x 5–6.5 μm, rusty brown in deposit, ovate to elliptic, and with most of the surface minutely warty-wrinkled.

Observations This mushroom for some reason is confused with the honey mushroom; at least one case of this is on record. There is no danger of making this mistake if one checks the color of the spore deposit. A galerum is a helmetlike cap. *Autumnalis* means of the autumn, when, apparently, it was first collected. It also fruits abundantly in the spring.

191 Rozites caperata

Identification marks The spore deposit is rusty brown as in *Cortinarius*. The membranous ring left by the partial veil is prominent and persistent, and the stalk is thick and firm. The cap is usually orange brown to pale tawny and often in dry weather appears pallid from a thin silky coating over the disc. The cap is never viscid. This mushroom is difficult for the average hunter to identify because so many species have some of the diagnostic features stated here. Once acquainted with it, however, one will recognize it at a glance.

Edibility Edible and choice. It is a popular species in northern areas.

When and where It is common in the fall in conifer country in North America, especially west of the Great Plains. It is also common in the Great Lakes region, especially in jack pine stands, but it also occurs in mixed hardwoods (oak, hickory, beech, and maple). It is widely distributed in the Northern Hemisphere.

Spores 12–14 x 7–9 μm, rusty brown in deposit and in KOH, in profile somewhat inequilateral, minutely warty.

Observations The membranous partial veil distinguishes it from the Cortinarii. *Caperata* means wrinkled, a condition often evident in mature specimens of this species. *Rozites* (the genus) is named after a European mycologist, Ernst Roze.

190 *Galerina autumnalis*   Nearly natural size

191 *Rozites caperata*   About one-half natural size

Paxillus

The fleshy, often eccentric stalk, the yellow brown spore deposit, the
more or less pubescent cap margin when young, and the gills that
are readily separable from the cap tissue serve to identify the genus.
Paxillus means a small stake or peg.

Key to Species

1. Gills readily staining brown when injured . . . . 192. *Paxillus involutus*
1. Gills not staining as above . . . . 193. *P. atrotomentosus*

192 Paxillus involutus

Identification marks The gills are close, narrow, decurrent, and yellow when young but staining brown readily; they separate easily from the cap. Cross veins are often conspicuous between the gills. The cap is a medium dark dingy yellow brown, and the margin is often curled in and marked with short riblike lines or furrows. The edge of the cap may be slightly pubescent but is never bearded as in some species of *Lactarius*.

Edibility Dangerous. In Poland a study was made over a period of 10 years. In the 109 cases studied, 93 were hospitalized and there were 3 fatalities. Apparently, the mushrooms were not cooked sufficiently. NEVER EAT THIS SPECIES RAW. In the past it has rated as an edible species—and it is true that in North America it has been used for the table fairly frequently —but, on the basis of present information, we do *not* recommend it.

When and where This common northern species fruits in late summer and fall in conifer country, and is often abundant during dry seasons.

Spores 7–9 x 4.5–5 μm, dull brown in deposit, smooth, ellipsoid.

Observations In one drying-up bog in Michigan this species fruited in abundance for a ten-year period. *Involutus* refers to the curled-in cap margin of immature fruiting bodies.

192 *Paxillus involutus*   About one-half natural size

193 Paxillus atrotomentosus

Identification marks The stalk is thick, usually eccentric, and (over the basal area) covered with a velvety coating of dark brown tomentum. The cap is dry and unpolished and yellow brown or darker. The gills are readily separable from the cap. We have not seen it with truly blackish brown tomentum at the base of the stalk, as is often mentioned in the literature. This could be a feature which develops as the fruiting bodies age.

193 *Paxillus atrotomentosus*   About one-half natural size

Edibility Dangerous. There are conflicting reports on its edibility. Not recommended.

When and where Mostly it occurs around decaying conifer stumps or old trees. It is definitely associated with conifers, but is not a typical mycorrhiza former. It fruits during late summer and fall and is seldom found in large numbers. It is to be expected in regions where conifers grow naturally.

Spores 5–6 x 3.5–4 μm, yellowish in deposit, oval, smooth.

Observations *Atrotomentosus* means blackish tomentum—referring to the tomentum at the base of the stalk.

Phaeocollybia

Within the family Cortinariaceae, this genus is distinguished by its lack of veils and the presence of a long "taproot" (a pseudorhiza). The genus is a feature of the mushroom flora of the Pacific Northwest, but some species do occur sparingly east of the Great Plains. The name means dark *Collybia*.

Key to Species

Phaeocollybia kauffmanii   194

Identification marks This large fungus has a glabrous, viscid cap, at first reddish cinnamon but darkening to liver brown in age. The margin remains inrolled a long time. The stalk may be up to 2 cm thick near the apex, and it tapers down into a long pseudorhiza. The lower half is often purplish brown and the upper part pinkish brown. The cortex is very cartilaginous and the surface glabrous. There is no veil.

Edibility   Not known; at least we have no data on it.

When and where   It is a conspicuous mushroom in the Sitka spruce zone on our Pacific Coast. It fruits in the fall and can be found almost every season.

Spores   8–10 x 4.5–6 (7) μm, pale cinnamon brown in deposit, in profile somewhat inequilateral, slightly roughened.

Observations   It was named in honor of Professor C. H. Kauffman, of the University of Michigan, who first collected it.

194   *Phaeocollybia kauffmanii*   About one-half natural size

195   Phaeocollybia scatesiae

Identification marks   The fruiting pattern of several hundred specimens in a large, loose cluster is almost unique among our North American species. The long stalks (up to 18 cm x 7 mm or less thick) are also unusual. The yellowish gills when young, the lack of distinctive odor on fresh material, and the gray brown color of faded caps together are distinctive.

Edibility   Not known.

When and where   As stated above, it occurs in tremendous clusters late in the fall in the coastal conifer forests of the Pacific Northwest. The range for it has not yet been established.

Spores   8–9.5 x 5–6 μm, rusty brown in KOH, warty-rugulose, inequilateral in profile, ovate in face view, often beaked at apex.

Observations   *P. scatesiae* is named in honor of Mrs. Robert Scates of Post Falls, Idaho, who first discovered it. It differs from *P. californica* in a number of features. The latter has a pungent odor, grows in arcs or rings, has an apricot buff colored cap when faded (lacking gray tints), and its gills when young are brownish, not yellow.

195　*Phaeocollybia scatesiae*　　　　　　　　　　Nearly natural size

Hebeloma

Within the Cortinariaceae, *Hebeloma* can be distinguished in the field by the viscid to slimy (at first) cap; the frequently raphanoid (radishlike) taste and/or odor; the fibrillose veil (if one is present); and the spore deposit, which is clay colored (dull yellowish tan) or reddish rather than rusty brown. The genus is not recommended highly for table use, since poisonous species are known, and some of them are common. Species of *Hebeloma* are mycorrhiza formers and occur in both conifer and hardwood forests across the continent. *Hebeloma* is derived from words meaning youth and a fringe.

Key to Species

1. Veil copious and leaving conspicuous patches on the cap or stalk or on both .... 196. *Hebeloma strophosum*
1. Veil absent; stalk scaly from breaking up of the cuticle ....
.... 197. *H. sinapizans*

Identification marks This is a small to medium sized *Hebeloma* with a very copious veil and a stalk that darkens at the base and slowly but progressively upward. The cap is a dull, almost vinaceous brown where not obscured by veil remnants. The odor and taste are slightly pungent to radish-like, but they may be mild in some fruiting bodies.

Edibility Apparently not known (at least for American collections); therefore, not recommended. Some very similar species are thought to have caused cases of mild poisoning.

When and where It occurs in northern conifer forests and is sporadic—not appearing during many seasons, and then fruiting in great abundance for a year or two. We have found it in the Pacific Northwest, and in conifer (spruce) plantations in the Great Lakes area. It appears to have a spring and a fall fruiting period.

Spores 7.5–9 x 4.5–6 μm, dull clay color in deposit, nearly smooth, yellowish in KOH.

Observations The veil may leave a belt of soft veil material on the stalk, or nearly all of it may be left on the margin of the cap. *Strophosum* means a belt and refers to the zone of veil material often left on the stalk.

196 *Hebeloma strophosum*   About natural size

197   Hebeloma sinapizans

Identification marks *H. sinapizans* is a large *Hebeloma* lacking a veil but with a scaly stalk, pale to dark brown cap, and an odor and taste resembling that of radishes. The stalk does not discolor markedly at the base, and the young gills are pallid.

Edibility Not recommended. Reports on this species, as to edibility, are not good. In North America we have at least three very closely related species with the above characters.

When and where   In its various forms it fruits in the late summer and fall, often after heavy rains, in rather open woods of deciduous trees. We have found it very abundant under oak trees in cemeteries. It occurs generally in the forested areas of the United States and Canada.

Spores   11–13 x 7–8 μm, dull reddish brown in deposit, broadly ellipsoid, obscurely ornamented, dull brownish in KOH.

Observations   The genus is under critical study here in North America at the present time. The best the casual collector can do is to learn to recognize the genus and refrain from eating any species—even on a test basis. *H. crustuliniforme*, for instance, when young may be mistaken for a *Lyophyllum*, and is at least mildly poisonous. *Sinapizans* means mustard (presumably applying to the color of the cap, but certainly not the color of mustard as used in the United States).

197   *Hebeloma sinapizans*   About two-thirds natural size

Inocybe

Although one can soon learn to recognize this genus in the field, this is done by general aspect rather than by a set of definite characters. In general, small brown mushrooms with fibrillose, rimose, or scaly caps belong here. The genus is very large and common, and many of the species are poisonous, being rich in muscarine. It presents a problem to the pot-hunter. Finally, the species are among the most difficult to identify in the Agaricales. The name appropriately means fibrous head or cap.

Key to Species

1. Fruiting body yellow brown but hoary from a copious white veil . . . .
   . . . . 198. *Inocybe leucoblema*
1. Fruiting body white and surface of cap fibrillose, by maturity staining
   or flushed reddish . . . . 199. *I. pudica*

198   Inocybe leucoblema

Identification marks   The stalk is about 5–10 mm thick, the cap is 3–7 cm broad, and the margin of the cap near the edge is decorated with the remains of a fibrillose white veil. The remains of the veil at first sheath the stalk, but this layer is broken up by the elongation of the stalk as the fruiting body matures. The gills at first are olive ochraceous, and the ground color of the cap is a dingy pale date brown. The whole fruiting body has a very ragged appearance.

Edibility   Not recommended. We have no data on it, but the genus is a dangerous one, and experimentation is definitely discouraged.

When and where   It occurs gregarious to scattered in wet areas in the conifer forests of the western mountains. It is abundant in central Colorado, and less frequent east of the Great Plains.

Spores   9–12 x 5–6.5 μm, dull yellow brown in deposit, smooth.

Observations   The specific epithet refers to the white veil. The genus *Inocybe* is one of the large genera of the Agaricales. The species number in the hundreds, and the common clinical term for them is "LBMs" (see p. 204). Most of the species are not identifiable within the scope of a field guide.

198   *Inocybe leucoblema*   About two-thirds natural size

199   Inocybe pudica

Identification marks   The fruiting body is small to medium sized (the cap 2.5–6 cm broad, appressed fibrillose but not scaly), and at first is white overall. It very soon becomes flushed reddish ferruginous to salmon tinted over the disc of the cap or on the gills or more or less overall. The veil leaves only scattered fibrils on the stalk when it breaks.

Edibility   POISONOUS. It falls in the group of mushrooms having muscarine as the chief poison. Do not experiment with species of this genus!

When and where   This species is found in great abundance in the second growth stands of Douglas fir in the Pacific Northwest, but is wide-spread under conifers generally. East of the Great Plains it is to be expected in the Northeast and the Great Lakes area, in the summer and fall.

Spores   7.5–10 x 5–6 μm, smooth, dull yellow brown in KOH, elliptic in face view, subreniform in profile, no apical pore evident.

Observations   *Inocybe geophylla* is a closely related species that does not stain or flush reddish. It is also poisonous. *Pudica* means bashful or modest.

199   *Inocybe pudica*   About natural size

Strophariaceae

This family contains mushrooms with a violet tone to the spore deposit, and this color grades off to the dull yellow browns. Spores with a violet tint to the deposit show this same color in water mounts of fresh material, but if mounted in KOH they are yellow brown. In the field the members of this family are distinguished from the Coprinaceae, which also have dark spores, by their more pliant consistency and generally brighter yellow to red colors. The truly diagnostic differences are in the anatomy of the fruiting body. In the present revision we are including *Pholiota* in the family because of basic similarities in spore features as well as in the anatomy of the fruiting body.

In this family the spores all have an apical "pore," but in some it is too small to see with the light microscope. Since we assume all the species do have spores with an apical pore, this feature is omitted in the description of individual species. Because of the restriction a field key places on the user, we key out the species of the family in a single key. The important genera are *Pholiota*, in which the spore print is dull rusty brown; *Stropharia*, in which the print is usually purple brown, and the stalk has a membranous annulus; and *Psilocybe*, in which the veil is not membranous. *Naematoloma* was separated from *Psilocybe* because the hymenium contained a type of cystidium called a chrysocystidium. This is a microscopic character. All these genera intergrade; this is a major aspect of the family and is under investigation at present.

Stropharia pertains to a belt; *Pholiota* to a scaly ear; *Psilocybe* to a naked head; and *Naematoloma* to a fringe of fibrils.

Key to Species

1. Veil well-developed and remains usually obvious as remnants on cap or stalk 2
1. Veil absent to rudimentary and remains (if present) obscure 10
   2. Cap surface and sheath on stalk granulose and dry, cap orange to orange brown .... 200. *Pholiota aurea*
   2. Not as above 3
3. Spore deposit dark purple fuscous 4
3. Spore deposit more or less cinnamon brown 6
   4. Cap yellow; annulus seldom formed (veil remnants appendiculate on cap margin); on debris in the rain forests of the Pacific Northwest .... 206. *Stropharia ambigua*
   4. Not as above 5
5. Stalk densely white floccose below annulus from remnants of the veil; on wood of conifers .... 207. *S. hornemannii*
5. Stalk nearly naked; annulus thick, membranous and often divided radially into segments .... 208. *S. rugoso-annulata*
   6. Veil remnants variously disposed and both copious and cottony; on wood of cottonwood and other species of *Populus*; late fall .... 201. *Pholiota destruens*
   6. Not as above 7
7. Stalk conspicuously scaly; fruiting body picric acid yellow; cap viscid when fresh .... 202. *Pholiota flammans*
7. Not as above 8
   8. Cap slimy-viscid, scales of cap often gelatinizing .... 203. *Pholiota squarrosa-adiposa*
   8. Cap not slimy (slightly viscid in age in *Pholiota squarrosoides*) 9
9. Cap with lacerate-recurved scales; gills olive tinged at maturity .... 204. *Pholiota squarrosa*
9. Cap with conic scales at first; gills never olivaceous .... 205. *Pholiota squarrosoides*
   10. On wood of hardwoods; cap some shade of brick red at first; stalk 5–12 mm thick .... 212. *Naematoloma sublateritium*
   10. Not with all the above characters 11
11. On hardwood debris; stalk staining greenish to bluish where bruised (especially the base) .... 209. *Psilocybe caerulipes*
11. Not as above (on debris of conifers and not staining) 12
   12. Gills toned green at maturity, yellow at first ...... 210. *N. fasciculare*
   12. Gills pallid becoming purplish gray .... 211. *N. capnoides*

Pholiota aurea
(The Golden Pholiota)

Identification marks This is one of the most distinctive and beautiful of all the gilled fungi. The surface of the cap is yellow orange to orange or orange tan, is granular to rather powdery, and the margin of the cap is often decorated with veil remnants. A sheath extends from the flaring ring down to the base of the stalk, and its surface is colored like that of the cap and also is powdery to granular. The gills are yellowish at first and become pale tawny from the spores.

Edibility Edible for most people, but some cannot tolerate it. The disturbances are of the gastrointestinal type.

When and where Its area in North America appears to be from Alaska south along the coast. Generally it is rare, but it fruits in great abundance at times. It favors rich humus in conifer and hardwood stands. Three generic names have been and are still used for this species: *Phaeolepiota*, *Togaria*, and *Pholiota*.

Spores 10.5–13 (14) x 5–6 μm, pale tawny in deposit, yellowish to clay color in KOH, mostly elliptic in face view, in profile somewhat inequilateral, minutely ornamented, lacking a germ pore, inamyloid.

Observations *Aurea* means golden.

200 *Pholiota aurea*   About one-fourth natural size

Pholiota destruens

Identification marks This is a large, conspicuous species with whitish soft scales on the cap and copious, almost cottony veil remnants left hanging from the margin of the cap. The gills are pallid but soon become earth brown from the spores. The stalk is thick and hard, but the surface at first is copiously decorated from the veil remnants.

Edibility   Not poisonous, but we have yet to find anyone who has tried it who recommends it.

When and where   Our experience has been that it fruits in abundance on poplar stumps and logs, Lombardy poplar, and cottonwood in particular. The mushrooms grow out of the cut ends of the log or the surface of the stump. The best fruitings we have seen in either the Great Lakes region or the western mountains came after prolonged rainy weather late in the fall.

Spores   7–9.5 x 4–5.5 μm, cinnamon brown in deposit and KOH, smooth, in face view elliptic to ovate, in profile somewhat inequilateral.

Observations   *Destruens* means destructive, in this case no doubt referring to the rapid decay of the substrate.

201   *Pholiota destruens*   About one-half natural size

---

202   Pholiota flammans

Identification marks   The cap is 3–8 cm broad, very bright yellow (a picric acid yellow), and the surface is covered with fine recurved scales. In wet weather the surface is somewhat viscid. The stalk is also yellow and covered by recurved scales up to the fibrillose zone left when the veil breaks. Typically, it occurs on conifer wood.

Edibility   Not recommended. A poisonous species, *P. hiemalis*, also occurs on wood of conifers, and the two are easily confused.

When and where   Solitary to clustered on rotting conifer logs and stumps during late summer on into the fall. It is to be expected in areas where conifers grow in the United States and Canada. It is not infrequent in the Great Lakes area and eastward, and also in the Pacific Northwest.

Spores   4–5 x 2.5–3 μm, rusty brown in deposit, smooth, ochraceous in KOH, ellipsoid, inamyloid.

Observations   Previously we used the name *P. kauffmanii* for this species, but since European specimens were found to have an ixocutis like that of *P. kauffmanii*, we now use the earlier European name. *Flammans* means flaming.

202 *Pholiota flammans*   About one-half natural size

Pholiota squarrosa-adiposa   203

Identification marks The yellow slimy cap with conspicuous tawny scales, the pale yellow gills at first, and the scales on the stalk which are colored like those on the cap are diagnostic. The stalk gradually becomes amber brown over the lower portion.

Edibility Edible, but keep in mind that the rather similar *P. hiemalis* is poisonous.

When and where It is widely distributed mostly on decaying hardwood trunks, stumps, and slash. In the Pacific Northwest it is common on alder and maple, and less frequently on conifers. It fruits in the late summer and

203 *Pholiota squarrosa-adiposa*   About two-thirds natural size

fall, often in great abundance. *P. hiemalis* is found late in the fall on conifer wood. In the Great Lakes area, *P. aurivella* is likely to be confused with *P. squarrosa-adiposa*—both occur there. In *P. aurivella* the spores measure 7–10 x 4.5–6 μm.

Spores   6–7.5 x 4.3–5 μm, cinnamon brown in deposit, smooth, mostly ellipsoid.

Observations   This is the species usually reported in the literature under the name *Pholiota adiposa* in this country during the first half of this century. *Squarrosa-adiposa* as a name was designed to indicate that the species had some features of *P. squarrosa* and some of *P. adiposa*.

---

204   Pholiota squarrosa
(Scaly Pholiota)

Identification marks   The cap is dry and conspicuously scaly with recurved scales. The color varies from pale yellow to greenish yellow, except for the darker recurved scales. A greenish tone develops on the gills as the specimen ages. The stalk is at first covered with pale tawny scales much like those on the cap. The taste raw is mild at first but in old specimens it is quite rancid. One variation of the species has a garlic odor.

Edibility   Rated edible in many books, but poisonings have occurred, which were not typical of the coprine reaction, when an alcoholic beverage was consumed with or soon after eating the mushrooms. This, in addition to the change in flavor as the specimens mature, causes us to place the species in the "Not recommended" group.

When and where   It occurs in large clusters around the bases of conifer and hardwood trees in the late summer and fall. In the southern Rocky Mountains it occurs with equal frequency on aspen and spruce. It is widely distributed in North America. The form with the garlic odor is frequent in the Great Lakes area.

Spores   (5) 6–7.5 x 3.8–4.5 μm, dull rusty brown in deposit, smooth, elliptic in face view, in profile somewhat inequilateral or bean-shaped.

Observations   *Squarrosa* means with upright scales.

204   *Pholiota squarrosa*   About one-half natural size

Identification marks   The scales of the cap are spikelike in young specimens. Beneath this scaly layer (essentially of veil material) is one of gelatinized hyphae, and, as the cap ages, the gelatinous layer becomes more evident. The scales break down and become weathered away. The general
color is pale buff except for the tawny scales, and, unlike *P. squarrosa*, there
is no green tinge to the gills at any time. The ring on the stalk is usually
somewhat cottony and not a well-defined membrane.

Edibility   Edible and popular; many consider it the best edible species in the
genus.

When and where   It is common in late summer and fall on wood of hardwoods, and is equally abundant in the hardwood forests of the Northeast,
the Great Lakes, and the Pacific Northwest. In the Northwest it is found especially on alder, maple, and cottonwood.

Spores   4–5.5 (6) x (2.5) 3–3.5 μm, more or less cinnamon brown in deposit, smooth, in face view broadly elliptic, pale cinnamon in KOH.

Observations   *Squarrosoides* means like squarrosa.

205   *Pholiota squarrosoides* (old)   About two-thirds natural size

Identification marks   The medium to large size, the bright brownish to
yellow slimy cap with the margin hung with copious fragments of the broken
veil, the long, thick stalk (up to 30 cm long) decorated with white floccose
patches of tissue below the zone left by the broken veil, and the dark purplish
brown spore deposit are distinctive. The gills are white at first and become
dark purple brown from the spores. Sterile specimens are known, and in
these the gills are bright yellow.

206 *Stropharia ambigua*   About one-third natural size

Edibility   Not poisonous. One authority with considerable experience with this species stated that its flavor is poor (like old leaves).

When and where   It is common in the rain forest area of the Pacific Northwest. It fruits both in the spring and fall, but the fall fruiting is the heavy one. It is frequently found in disturbed areas, for instance, in areas where logs have been handled.

Spores   11–14 x 6–7.5 μm, purple brown in deposit, ellipsoid, smooth, dull yellow brown in KOH.

Observations   *Ambigua* as used here means that its position was intermediate between two genera. There is nothing ambiguous about the concept of the species.

207   Stropharia hornemannii

Identification marks   The cap is distinctly slimy and purplish, purple drab, or purple tinged with olive. In age it is often a dingy tan. The gills are broad and distinctly purple drab when mature. The stalk is long (6–20 cm), nearly cylindric, white, and at first beautifully decorated by the fragments of the white-fibrillose sheath which extends up to the somewhat membranous ring. The taste is disagreeable. The caps are large: 6–20 cm.

Edibility   Not recommended. In Europe it is designated as poisonous by some authors.

When and where   It is a northern species associated with rotting conifer wood, and occurs across the continent in the northern conifer forests. It is frequent at times in the spruce-fir zone of the Rocky Mountains. It fruits during late summer and fall, often during relatively dry seasons, and is seldom found in large numbers.

Spores   11–14 x 5.5–7 μm, dark violet brown in deposit, ovate in face view, slightly inequilateral in profile, yellow brown in KOH, smooth.

Observations   The species was named after its collector.

207 *Stropharia hornemannii* About one-half natural size

Stropharia rugoso-annulata **208**

Identification marks This is a large species with caps 5–15 (20) cm broad, stalks 5–15 cm long and 1–2 cm thick. The caps are glabrous and dark purplish brown to chestnut brown, slowly fading to dull clay color. The thick ring splits radially into segments which at times appear almost clawlike. The odor and taste are mild; the gills are broad and close, whitish at first and dark purplish brown in age.

Edibility Edible and choice. It rates as one of the best with those who have tried it.

When and where It grows in cultivated fields and in particular around plantings of ornamentals where bark has been used as a mulch. In other words, one can look for it very close to home. It is known from both Europe and North America, and fruits in the summer and fall. It was described from Massachusetts.

Spores   10–13 x 6–8 μm, dark purple brown in deposit, smooth, in face view elliptic to ovate, dark purplish in water mounts, dull yellow brown in KOH.

Observations   The specific epithet refers to the uneven surface of the ring, which often finally splits into radial sections.

208   *Stropharia rugoso-annulata*   About one-third natural size

---

209   Psilocybe caerulipes

Identification marks   The cap is 1–3.5 cm broad, convex to obtusely conic becoming broadly convex to flat, with the margin at first decorated with white flecks from the veil. When moist, the cap is dark brown but soon fades to

209   *Psilocybe caerulipes*   About two-thirds natural size

dingy clay color, at which stage obscure greenish stains may show along the edge. The gills are narrow, crowded, and typically adnate. The stalk is 2–3 mm thick and relatively short; its surface is mostly covered with a thin coating of grayish fibrils, but these soon vanish, the base slowly staining blue to greenish.

Edibility   We rate it as dangerous, especially for children in the grazing stage. The poisons are psilocybin and psilocin, which are on the federal list of controlled substances. They are more dangerous to children than to adults.

When and where   *P. caerulipes* is generally found during the summer and early fall on hardwood slash in the area east of the Great Plains.

Spores   7–9 x 4–5 μm, dull purple brown in deposit, smooth, mostly ellipsoid, purple brown in water mounts, dull yellow brown in KOH (under microscope).

Observations   The blue stain on the base of the stalk is often slow to develop. It is this staining reaction that is emphasized in the specific epithet.

Naematoloma fasciculare   210

Identification marks   The yellow gills when the cap is young, the olive to green tones that take over as maturity is reached, the orange yellow to yellow and finally olive cap, and the greenish yellow stalk are distinctive. The raw flesh typically is very bitter, but mild collections have been found. The veil is thin.

Edibility   It is usually rated poisonous, so we cannot recommend even the mild-tasting collections. We have had some reports, however, of people who ate it and suffered no ill effects.

When and where   Its distribution and preference as to substrate are the same as for *N. capnoides*. A small, slender form occurs in the southern states.

Spores   6.5–8 x 3.5–4 μm, purple brown in deposit, ellipsoid to ovoid, smooth, dull yellow brown in KOH, purplish in water mounts.

Observations   *Fasciculare* means growing in bunches, i.e., cespitose.

Naematoloma capnoides   211

Identification marks   The orange brown to dull cinnamon reddish caps are the chief feature by which this species is distinguished from the brick cap (the stalks are also thinner than those of the latter). The gills are pallid and only slowly become clouded with purplish brown. The taste is mild, and the species fruits in large clusters on decaying conifer wood.

Edibility   Edible, and fairly popular as a late season species. Bitter specimens are not often encountered.

When and where   It occurs throughout the conifer forests of North America in the fall or, more rarely, in early spring. It is now abundant in pine plantations in southern Michigan on and around stumps left from thinning operations. In mixed conifer-hardwood stands, one can find collections with colors intermediate between those of the brick cap and those of this species.

Spores   6–7 x 4–4.5 μm, purple brown in deposit, ellipsoid, smooth, dull purplish in water mounts, dull yellow brown in KOH.

Observations   *Capnoides* means smoky (the color of the mature gills).

210 *Naematoloma fasciculare*   About two-thirds natural size

211 *Naematoloma capnoides*   About one-half natural size

212 *Naematoloma sublateritium*   About one-half natural size

Identification marks   The cap is pale to dark brick red, the gills at first are whitish but soon become deep purplish brown to purple drab from the spores, and the veil is thin and leaves only a thin zone of fibrils along the margin of the cap. The taste is usually mild, but bitter specimens are frequently encountered. It is usually found on old hardwood logs and stumps. Typically, it is a late fall species, usually one of the last available to the pothunter.

Edibility   Edible and frequently collected. It is one of the "stump mushrooms."

When and where   It is to be expected over the area covered by hardwood forests in North America, but is apparently absent or at least rare in the Pacific Northwest. It can be harvested by the bushel in the hardwood slashings of the Great Lakes region during a good season.

Spores   6–7.5 x 3.5–4 μm, purple brown in deposit, ellipsoid, smooth, violaceous brown in water mounts, dull yellow brown in KOH.

Observations   Sterile fruiting bodies will be found; these have bright yellow gills. *Sublateritium* means somewhat brick colored.

Bolbitiaceae

These fungi might well be called the suburbanites of the mushroom world, since they appear so regularly in lawns, around plantings, on rubbish and compost piles, in gardens, and in old fields. In the field it is difficult to differentiate between this family and the Strophariaceae, particularly since the two intergrade in the color of the spore deposit. The Bolbitiaceae, however, differ in that the cuticle of the cap is a hymeniform layer or a layer of inflated cells, whereas in the Strophariaceae it is a cutis or ixocutis of appressed to interwoven hyphae. There is no constant difference associated with this feature that will aid in field identifications. In general, however, the Bolbitiaceae have more rusty yellow or tawny spore deposits than the Strophariaceae.

Species of *Conocybe* typically have very slender fragile stalks and bright rusty brown spore deposits (but not as orange as in *Gymnopilus*). The caps typically are conic. The species grow in grassy places, on wood, and on humus in the forest.

Agrocybe, the other genus included here, has stalks more pliant than in *Conocybe*, and duller yellow brown to earth brown (dark brown) spore deposits. The caps are often olive brown when moist but fade to dull clay color or buff. The generic name *Agrocybe* refers to frequent fruitings in a gregarious manner on cultivated soil. *Conocybe* means conic head.

Key to Species

---

213   Conocybe lactea

Identification marks   The cap is 10–15 (25) mm broad at the base when expanded and 10–25 mm high, bluntly conic with a straight margin (not curled in at first). The cap is creamy white or, on the disc, buff to dingy cream color. When faded it is white overall. The flesh is very thin and fragile. The gills are crowded, narrow, and bright ochraceous tawny when mature. The stalk is thin (1.5–2 mm), very fragile, and no veil is present. The fruiting bodies are usually found on lawns and golf courses.

Edibility   Not known, as far as we are aware. *C. lactea* is one of those mushrooms often eaten by toddlers, and it is assumed that it cannot be very poisonous, or we would know more about it.

When and where   Gregarious on lawns, golf courses, and grassy places generally, in spring and early summer after heavy, warm rains. It is to be expected in almost every lawn in suburbia.

Spores   12–16 x 7–9 μm, mostly elliptic in face view, ovate to elliptic in profile, smooth, tawny in KOH.

Observations   *Lactea* refers to the color of milk. The caps are milk white.

---

214   Conocybe filaris

Identification marks   The cap is conic, 6–12 mm broad, soon fading and opaque, pale tawny when moist, and striate. The gills soon become pale tawny and are both broad and close. The stalk is 2–4 cm long and about 1 mm thick. It bears an annulus or ring above the midportion, and the ring is thick and membranous.

Edibility   *C. filaris* contains the toxic cyclopeptides and so must be regarded as POISONOUS—unless it can be proven otherwise.

When and where   On humus and organic debris, on grassy areas, around bushes, etc. The habitat is rather unspecialized. The species is seldom recognized in North America, so we know little of its distribution.

Spores   7–9 x 4–5.5 μm, elliptic to ovate in face view, somewhat inequilateral in profile, smooth, tawny in KOH.

Observations   A number of species in this group look enough alike in the field that we doubt if many people can distinguish them. If a child has been found eating one of them, the doctor on the case will need to expect the worst and proceed accordingly. *Filaris* means of a thread (threadlike).

213 *Conocybe lactea*   About two-thirds natural size

214 *Conocybe filaris*   About natural size

Agrocybe amara   215

Identification marks The cap is 3–8 cm broad, glabrous, pale tan to dull tawny, and the taste of the flesh is decidedly bitter. The stalk is glabrous and pallid. There is no veil.

Edibility Not edible because of the bitter taste. We have no record of any-one trying it.

When and where It was originally collected on dung at the New York Botanical Garden, and the specimens illustrated were photographed at the Matthaei Botanical Gardens of the University of Michigan, where, as shown, it fruited in great abundance on well fertilized soil. As yet, its distribution and fruiting pattern have not been adequately documented.

Spores (9) 10–12 x 5.5–7 μm, ovoid to ellipsoid, smooth, dingy ochraceous as mounted in KOH.

Observations *Amara* means bitter.

215 *Agrocybe amara*   Greatly reduced

---

216   Agrocybe dura

Identification marks Cap 3–12 cm broad, glabrous, slightly viscid and white, becoming dingy buff on the disc. The stalk is white or whitish like the cap, 3–10 mm thick and at first has a thin, somewhat membranous ring near the apex which is soon broken and disappears.

216 *Agrocybe dura*   About one-half natural size

Edibility Edible, and in southern Michigan frequently collected during good seasons; but be sure a white *Amanita* is not collected along with it. The color of the mature gills in the *Agrocybe* will distinguish it.

When and where It grows scattered to gregarious in lawns and pastures after heavy showers in late spring or early summer. It is widely distributed.

Spores 10–14 x 6.5–8 μm, smooth, more or less elliptic in profile, in face view oval, yellow brown in KOH.

Observations The spore size is the best distinction between *A. dura* and *A. praecox*, but the latter is usually found on mulch around plantings rather than in open meadows. Both are edible. *Dura* means hard, and its use for such a soft fruiting body as that of this species is puzzling.

Agrocybe praecox   217

Identification marks The cap is 2–10 cm broad when expanded, glabrous, slightly viscid, pale olive buff young, soon more or less clay color. The stalk is 3–10 mm thick, and the base has white rhizomorphs connecting to it. The ring is located above the midportion of the stalk, is fragile, and is often soon obliterated. The remnants of the veil often decorate the margin of the cap for a time.

Edibility Edible, but see "Observations" below.

When and where It is found clustered to gregarious on mulch around ornamental plantings, in conifer plantations, on accumulations of debris generally, or in rich humus. It fruits in the spring and early summer and is both widely distributed and common.

Spores 8–10 x 5–6 μm, elliptic in profile, more or less ovate in face view, smooth, dull yellow brown in KOH.

Observations There are a number of species with olive umber caps at first which should not be confused with *A. praecox*. One of these caused some "mild" cases of poisoning in Alaska. *Praecox* means early, a reference to its time of fruiting.

217   *Agrocybe praecox*   About one-half natural size

Coprinaceae (Inky Caps)

This family is closely related to the Bolbitiaceae in the anatomy of the fruiting body, but differs in having black to chocolate brown colored spores in deposits and generally much more fragile fruiting bodies. The genus *Coprinus* has evolved the feature emphasized in the common name of the family: inky caps. This is a process of autodigestion, and the process is synchronized with the development of the spores and their subsequent discharge. When the spores have been discharged, enzymes are liberated which liquify the gill tissue that has completed its function. The process of spore maturation generally begins at the gill edge near the cap margin and then progresses toward the disc of the cap. Liquifaction of the "spent" tissue does not interfere with spores still to be discharged, but in this way only one crop of spores is produced by the hymenium. It will be noted that in the large species of *Coprinus*, the young gills are rather closely packed together, thus, in a measure, preventing evaporation which might damage spores still in the first stages of development.

Most of the larger species of *Coprinus* are edible, but for the 400-odd North American species in *Psathyrella* we have only very sketchy information. Both the Bolbitiaceae and the Coprinaceae are scavengers, growing on manure, garden soil, rubbish, wood, and remains of herbaceous plants. They can be collected during the spring, summer, and fall—usually in one's own backyard.

Key to Genera and Species

1. Gills deliquescing .... *Coprinus*
1. Gills not deliquescing 2
    2. Mature gills mottled .... *Panaeolus*
    2. Mature gills evenly colored .... 225. *Psathyrella foenisecii*

Coprinus

The inky caps as a genus are distinguished by the usually blackish brown spores and the pattern of autodigestion of the spore-producing tissue once the spores have been discharged. The species typically are scavengers and frequently inhabit the dung of herbivores. Some of the species have exceedingly small fruiting bodies that develop overnight, shed their spores, and vanish by midmorning. Some of the species produce a peculiar type of intoxication (see p. 18). *Coprinus* is derived from a word meaning dung.

Key to Species

1. Stalk with a nearly basal zone left by a broken veil, beneath it a coating of dark fibrils as a short sheath; cap gray brown (often silvery) and 2–6 cm across the base .... 218. *Coprinus atramentarius*
1. Not as above 2
    2. Cap 4–10 cm high, fibrillose-scaly but with a smooth area at the apex (like a skull-cap) .... 219. *C. comatus*

2. Not as above 3
3. Cap tawny or paler, 2–3 cm broad, at first dusted with faint remnants
   of a granulose veil .... 220. *C. micaceus*
3. Veil fibrillose to submembranous; cap gray (not tawny) 4
   4. Veil heavy and breaking up into pieces (chunks); densely cespi-
      tose-gregarious on rotting wood .... 221. *C. quadrifidus*
   4. Veil of radial white fibrils and soon evanescent; aspect of *C.
      atramentarius* (but with ornamented spores) .... 222. *C. insignis*

Coprinus atramentarius   218
(Inky Cap)

Identification marks   In this, the true inky cap, a layer of brown fibrils
covers the lower part of the stalk and terminates in a distinct though wavy
basal zone. This layer represents the remains of a rudimentary veil. Above
the zone the stalk is white and silky. The cap is dull gray, but may have a
pallid overtone, apparently the remains of a thin veil. In some forms the
center of the cap breaks up into rather distinct scales. The gills are pallid
at first, but as the spores mature they blacken and undergo autodigestion
from the cap margin upward to the apex of the stalk.

Edibility   Edible and moderately popular, but some people experience a
peculiar type of intoxication from eating it and drinking an alcoholic beverage
(see p. 18).

When and where   It is cosmopolitan and fruits from spring to fall during
cool wet weather. It is a "mushroom weed" and lives on buried wood in lawns,
around city dumps, in gardens, in parks, and along city streets. It often occurs
in masses along roads where wood was used as a filler.

Spores   (7) 8–9 x 4.2–5 μm, black in deposit and in KOH, smooth, with an
apical pore, ovoid.

Observations   *Coprinus* refers to dung (stable manure); *atramentarius*
signifies ink.

Coprinus comatus   219
(Shaggy Mane)

Identification marks   The cap when young varies from cylindric to oval.
The stalk is tapered to a point at the base. The cuticle of the cap, which
is continuous in young caps, is soon broken up by expansion of the cap, and
the surface of the latter becomes scaly in various patterns. A small patch
of the original cuticle usually remains over the apex as a kind of skull cap.
Typically, there is a ring on the stalk, but it often breaks and falls off.

Edibility   Edible and popular, but some people consider it tasteless. Use
button stages on which the gills have not darkened. Do not try to keep un-
cooked specimens in the refrigerator overnight.

When and where   This species is the soldier among the mushrooms. It is
not uncommon to see ranks of them in a line along the edge of a blacktopped
road. In one local baseball field in 1962 there must have been a thousand
fruiting bodies; one line extended from first base out into left field clear
across the playing field. It is cosmopolitan and fruits both in the spring and
fall. It prefers hard-packed soil.

Spores   11–14 (15) x 6.3–8 (9) μm, black in deposit, mostly elliptic in face
view, smooth.

218 *Coprinus atramentarius*   About natural size

219 *Coprinus comatus*   About one-half natural size

220 *Coprinus micaceus*   Nearly natural size

Observations The process of autodigestion can be inhibited by immersing the specimens in cold water. Under these conditions they can be kept for several days. *Comatus* means hair, a reference to the shaggy appearance of the cap.

Coprinus micaceus
(Mica Cap)

220

Identification marks The granular or meal-like veil particles, for which the species is named, are often few and not conspicuous. The veil is extremely fragile because its hyphae readily break at the cross walls. The individual cells (or small groups of them) are the mealy particles already mentioned. The color of the cap is ochraceous brown to pale tan or, when faded, nearly white. It fruits in large clusters in the spring and again in the fall, and is our most common "urban" mushroom.

Edibility Edible. Though small, one usually finds enough fruiting bodies for a meal. Considerable water is produced when they are fried, so cook only a small number at a time. Many people find it rather tasteless.

When and where It occurs throughout North America. The fruiting bodies arise from buried wood, especially old stumps that have been covered with dirt in the process of making a lawn. It is one of the first to be found by the beginner—and the one eaten more frequently than any other by toddlers.

Spores 7–9 x 4–5 μm, somewhat ovoid, smooth, dark brown under the microscope.

Observations The specific epithet refers to the glistening particles of the veil remnants on the cap.

Coprinus quadrifidus

221

Identification marks The cap is medium sized for the genus and at first is covered by a heavy veil which breaks up into pieces, as shown in the photograph. In dense shade the veil remnants are often white, but in more exposed

221 *Coprinus quadrifidus*   About two-thirds natural size

situations the outer surface of the "wart" or piece of the veil is brownish. The fruiting bodies occur in dense clusters on remains of hardwoods in wet areas in late June and early July. The fruiting period is rather short.

Edibility   Not poisonous, but those who have tried it found it too bitter to be enjoyed. Not recommended.

When and where   It is abundant in some areas east of the Great Plains, and possibly along rivers in the Plains area. The hardwood swamps of southeastern Michigan produce it in great quantity during the first hot, humid weather of the season.

Spores   7–9 x 4–5 μm, blackish in deposit, ovate in face view, wall smooth.

Observations   The mass of rhizomorphs at the base of a cluster and permeating the substratum is termed an *ozonium*, and is also a significant taxonomic feature of this species. The specific epithet means split into four parts.

---

222   Coprinus insignis

Identification marks   The general aspect of this species is that of *Coprinus atramentarius* with the exception that, when young, a fibrillose white veil more or less covers the cap. It soon disappears. The mature cap is more rimose-striate than in *C. atramentarius*, and we have never seen *C. insignis* growing in the characteristically large clusters of the latter.

Edibility   POISONOUS; at least material collected in Europe produced a case of poisoning. The situation hinges on whether *C. alopecia* is the same as *C. insignis*—both have the same type of ornamented spore. We badly need a chemical analysis of American specimens.

When and where   It is found solitary or in small clusters around wood of hardwoods and often at the base of living maple trees with advanced heart rot, in summer and early fall east of the Great Plains. Not common.

Spores   10–13 x 6–7.5 μm, black in deposit, rugulose-wrinkled, nearly black under the microscope in KOH.

Observations   *Insignis* means distinctive: in the above species the type of veil and the large ornamented spores are unusual in the genus.

222   *Coprinus insignis*   Nearly natural size

Panaeolus

The species of *Panaeolus* have black spore deposits. Since the spores mature in small patches more or less simultaneously, the mature gills are obscurely mottled with lighter and darker areas. The paler areas are the ones from which spores have been discharged or on which they have not yet become pigmented. Appropriately, *Panaeolus* means variegated. (A few species of *Psathyrella* also have mottled gills.) Species of *Panaeolus* are also scavengers; one of the poisonous species (*P. subbalteatus*) is common in well-manured gardens.

Key to Species

1. Stalk with a thin ring; cap thinly viscid at first, pallid when mature or old .... 223. *Panaeolus semiovatus*
1. Stalk lacking a ring; cap about chestnut brown when moist, not viscid, when faded usually retaining a moist marginal zone of the darker color .... 224. *P. subbalteatus*

Panaeolus semiovatus   223

Identification marks   The cap is 3–6 (9) cm broad and 2–6 cm high, obtusely conic or finally more expanded, glabrous, slightly viscid, pale leather color gradually becoming whitish; when the spores have matured the cap may be grayish. The gills are pallid becoming mottled with dark (black) areas. The stalk often bears a thin ring, or the veil remnants are left hanging on the cap margin when the veil breaks.

Edibility   Edible and good, but not recommended. The genus contains a number of species causing poisonings described under the psilocybin and psilocin type. Small fruiting bodies of *P. semiovatus* might easily be confused

223   *Panaeolus semiovatus*   About two-thirds natural size

with some of these. Children in particular react adversely to the above hallucinogenic compounds.

When and where This species typically is found on the dung of horses early in the spring, or high in the mountains in the summer where it is cool. The species is cosmopolitan in distribution.

Spores (15) 17–22 x 8–11 μm, black in deposit, ellipsoid, smooth, often obscurely angular in face view.

Observations The specific epithet means somewhat ovate (egg-shaped).

---

224 Panaeolus subbalteatus

Identification marks The cap is 2–5 cm broad, obtusely conic to expanded-umbonate, glabrous, dark reddish brown when moist, and usually remains moist in a band along the margin. The odor and taste are mild. The cap margin is not appendiculate at first. The gills are broad, close and mottled at maturity. The stalk is 4–9 cm long and 2–6 mm thick, and brown beneath a gray pruina.

Edibility POISONOUS. Murrill named it *P. venenosus* because it was responsible for a case of poisoning in which five people nearly died. *P. subbalteatus* contains psilocybin and is hallucinogenic.

When and where It is especially abundant in well-manured gardens, on spent mushroom compost, and on manure piles. It is common and widely distributed, and fruits during the spring and early summer as a rule. It can often be collected in quantity in gardens and under plantings mulched with manure.

Spores 11–14 x 7–9 μm, blackish in fresh deposit, smooth, ovate in profile view, somewhat angular-elliptic in face view, very dark brown in KOH.

Observations Unlike many of the fungi containing psilocybin and psilocin, this species has fruiting bodies that do not stain blue. *Subbalteatus* means somewhat belted.

---

225 Psathyrella foenisecii
(Haymaker's Mushroom)

Identification marks The stalk is very slender and fragile, the cap is 1–3 cm broad and very fragile, and the gills are dark cocoa brown to grayish brown when mature. There is no veil. The species fruits on lawns, golf courses, and similar habitats during the hot humid summer weather.

Edibility It is reported as edible by some authors, but we do not recommend it. Some populations may contain psilocybin and psilocin. It is one of the "lawn species" that toddlers find and eat when they are in the grazing stage. It can be identified from stomach contents by the size, shape and ornamentation pattern of the spores. The danger to the child lies in the fact that we have 400-plus species of this genus in North America, and we know little of their chemistry. At least one case of serious poisoning in a child has been linked to this or a closely related species.

When and where It is cosmopolitan and abundant on grassy areas across the continent.

Spores 12–15 (18) x 7–9 μm, chocolate brown in deposit and under the microscope, somewhat elliptic in face view, ornamented by a pattern of areolate (flat) patches representing remains of an outer wall.

Observations The cap is very dark when moist and nearly white when faded. The danger for toddlers is that the parents may not be sure which species the child ate, since many lawn fungi fruit along with the *Psathyrella*. This species is placed in *Panaeolus* by some authors and *Paneolina* by others. *Foenisecii* pertains to the hay harvest (cutting and drying).

224   *Panaeolus subbalteatus*   Nearly natural size

225   *Psathyrella foenisecii*   Nearly natural size

Russulaceae (Milk Mushrooms and Their Allies)

These mushrooms all have thick fragile stalks which may be quite hard in some species. The caps are broad and fragile, the spore deposits are white to yellow or orange yellow, they all have a characteristic squatty appearance, and (in North American species) no veils are present. Those with a milky juice (latex) belong in *Lactarius*, and if no latex is present, in *Russula*, but be sure to check this on young, fresh specimens, because in old ones the latex does not always show when the gills are injured. To test for the latex take a razor blade or sharp knife and cut across the gills or into the apex of the stalk. If a latex is present, a drop or two will show at the cut. The brittleness of the fruiting body, which the collector soon notices, is caused by many large inflated cells in clusters or groups scattered through the flesh of the cap and stalk. These are in a matrix of filamentous hyphae which give the cap the firmness it has.

The species nearly all grow on soil or humus and possibly form mycorrhiza with many forest trees, although if this is true, they are not as specific in host relationships as many of the boletes, for instance. The fruiting of *Russula* and *Lactarius* marks the beginning of what is often called the summer mushroom season in the Great Lakes region, southward, and eastward. In Michigan this season starts around the fourth of July.

Key to Genera

1. Latex present . . . . *Lactarius*
1. Latex absent . . . . *Russula*

Lactarius (Milk Mushrooms)

The milk fungi are often sought out for food, and some of the species are rather popular, though their generally coarse consistency often gives them a low rating. However, the ones we have tried remained firm after cooking and were entirely satisfactory. When the latex is copious it may make the species unsuitable for pan frying. Poisoning from *Lactarius*, when it does occur, is seldom if ever fatal, and there is some question whether the genus has ever caused more than acute indigestion. The literature is full of contradictory statements about their edibility. The statement that not a single species retains its acrid taste after cooking has been found incorrect by a number of our acquaintances who decided to experiment with the genus. When conflicting statements are rife, we suspect that some of the differences noted are inherent in the people and not in the mushrooms—and some, no doubt, are the result of misidentifications. For those who desire to collect mushrooms in July and August in the area east of the Great Plains, this genus deserves careful attention, which is why we have emphasized it here. Spore sizes given here are exclusive of ornamentation.

Noteworthy microscopic features of this genus include the spore ornamentation, which becomes blue to gray or violet in iodine (is amyloid), and the clusters or columns of inflated cells in the flesh (with the exception of two or three species) which account for the granular texture of cooked specimens.

The name is derived from a word for milk or juice.

Key to Species

226   Lactarius controversus

Identification marks   The cap is white at first but may develop dull rose to dull lavender stains in age. The surface is slightly sticky to slippery when moist, and the margin is sharp and practically naked rather than cottony or

226   *Lactarius controversus*   About natural size

hairy. The gills develop a pink to salmon flush as they mature, and the latex is white and unchanging. The taste of the raw flesh is very acrid.

Edibility   Edible, but not recommended. This is a coarse mushroom said to be of poor flavor. We have no data of our own, and, of course, reports are not always accurate. An acquaintance found that the acrid taste did not disappear after prolonged parboiling followed by frying.

When and where   This mushroom fruits during the summer and is often very abundant. It occurs under aspen and other species of *Populus*, and is common on the cutover lands of the Great Lakes region and in the aspen zone of the Rocky Mountains. The best fruiting encountered to date, however, was under a stand of old cottonwood trees at the south end of Priest Lake in northern Idaho.

Spores   6–7.5 x 4.5–5 μm, cream color in deposit, ellipsoid, ornamented with a broken to partial reticulum.

Observations   The specific epithet means turned against or turned in the opposite direction.

Lactarius deceptivus   227

Identification marks   This is a large species with caps up to 25 cm broad or more. When young the cap is white in all parts, but the depressed disc soon becomes more or less pale crust color and breaks up into scales. The margin is characterized by a cottony roll of tissue which collapses as the cap expands. The gills are close, whitish, and often forked. The latex is milk colored and unchanging; the taste of the raw flesh is acrid and the consistency is coarse. The base of the stalk, and often the entire surface, is velvety. The cottony marginal roll of tissue and the velvety stalk are the critical field characters.

Edibility   Edible, but not recommended. It is coarse, and apparently there is difficulty in getting rid of the acrid taste, though Peck, who considered it fair, mentioned that the acrid taste disappeared with cooking.

When and where   It is common during late summer and fall in the Great Lakes region under hemlock and hardwoods, along the edges of bogs, near

227   *Lactarius deceptivus*   About two-thirds natural size

the edge of woodland pools in hardwood forests, and in oak stands where there is an understory of blueberry bushes (*Vaccinium* sp.). It is one of the common August-September mushrooms east of the Great Plains.

Spores 9–12 (13) x 7.5–9 μm, white or nearly so in deposit, broadly ellipsoid, ornamented with distinct isolated warts and spines.

Observations The caps are finally clay color in age. The specific epithet means deceiving.

---

228 Lactarius subvellereus var. subdistans

Identification marks This large, coarse, white mushroom—with its cream colored latex and dry velvety cap and stalk—has a very acrid taste and subdistant to distant gills. In age or after injury, brown discolorations frequently develop on the cap. The margin of the young cap is sharp, in contrast to that of *L. deceptivus*, which is of soft cottony material.

Edibility Edible, but not recommended. Some people cannot tolerate it.

When and where It fruits during warm, wet weather in July and August in deciduous or mixed woods, particularly those with oak, east of the Great Plains. It is often abundant along roads through oak-aspen forests in the upper Great Lakes area.

Spores 7.5–9 x 5–6.5 (7) μm, white in deposit, ellipsoid to broadly ellipsoid, ornamented with low, isolated warts.

Observations This species was treated under the name *L. vellereus* in previous issues of the *Guide*—following Kauffman's treatment in *The Agaricaceae of Michigan*. Since then, in Europe, a large-spored species has come to be known as *L. vellereus*. It is very rare in North America. In variety *subvellereus* the gills are close. *Subdistans* means somewhat distant (of the gills); *subvellereus* means somewhat fleecy.

---

229 Lactarius piperatus

Identification marks The most important character of this large, white milk fungus is the extremely crowded gills—so crowded that when viewed fresh or in a photograph, individual gills frequently cannot be distinguished. In addition, the cap is dry, the gills narrow, neither the cap nor the stalk are velvety, and the white latex dries white (or may stain the gills yellowish) and is very acrid.

Edibility Poisonous? Definitely not recommended, since a variety of this species (var. *glaucescens*) has been implicated in a case of poisoning.

When and where Common in the summer in hardwood and mixed forests east of the Great Plains.

Spores (4.5) 5–7 x 5–5.4 μm, white in deposit, ellipsoid, ornamentation of low lines and warts, not reticulate.

Observations This is the central species in the group of large, white, coarse, acrid, milk fungi. Although mushrooms called *L. piperatus* are eaten in some areas, it is usually not clear which of the species are involved. It is simply another case of a marginal species. Some people have used it after parboiling it, and some have pickled it, but again we are not sure which varieties were used. *Piperatus* means peppery (acrid).

228 *Lactarius subvellereus* var. *subdistans*   About natural size

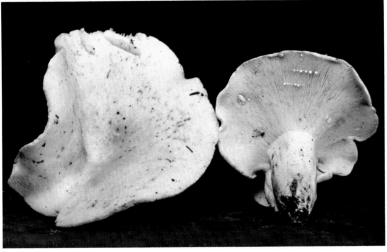

229 *Lactarius piperatus*   About two-thirds natural size

Lactarius neuhoffii   **230**

Identification marks Among the large white species of *Lactarius*, this one is distinguished by having a glabrous (not velvety) cap and stalk, close gills which are tinted cream color to pale ochraceous at maturity, and a firm rather than cottony margin. The cap is not viscid. The latex is white and dries cream color to pale yellow; both the latex and the raw flesh taste very acrid.

Edibility We have no reliable data on it, but do not recommend trying it. It was described only recently. Previously, it was confused with other large, white, acrid species here in North America.

When and where It fruits in midsummer in the hardwood and mixed forests east of the Great Plains. It seems to favor oak. It often fruits in large numbers, and the fruiting bodies are relatively long-lived.

Spores 7.5–9.5 x 6.5–8 μm, white in deposit, broadly ellipsoid, orna-mented with low warts connected by fine lines and forming at most a broken reticulum, the elements mostly under 0.2 µm high (too small to measure accurately).

Observations This species has been confused with *L. piperatus* for many years, and in most North American reports on the edibility of *L. piperatus* it is generally impossible to tell which species was actually eaten. (Compare *L. deceptivus*, *L. piperatus*, and *L. subvellereus* with *L. neuhoffii*.) Dr. Walther Neuhoff, for whom the species was named, was a prominent German mycologist.

230 *Lactarius neuhoffii*   About one-half natural size

231   Lactarius indigo var. indigo

Identification marks This is about the easiest of all milk fungi to identify, since the cap, gills, stalk, and latex are all blue in young specimens. Wounds soon stain green, however, as they do in several species with colored latices.

231 *Lactarius indigo*   About two-thirds natural size

The cap is thinly slimy at first, but soon becomes merely slightly sticky, and in age the color fades considerably. The taste of the raw flesh is bitterish in some collections, but this apparently disappears in cooking.

Edibility   Edible, but there are not many reports as to its quality. One report states merely that it was coarse but good.

When and where   This is a species of mixed pine and hardwood forests east of the Great Plains. It is most abundant in the Southeast and the area bordering the Gulf of Mexico. It has been found as far north as the south shore of Lake Superior. It fruits during the summer and fall.

Spores   7–9 x 5.5–7.5 μm, cream color in deposit, broadly ellipsoid to subglobose, ornamented with a broken to nearly complete reticulum.

Observations   The specific epithet refers to the color of the fruiting bodies. Variety *diminutivus* is known from the Gulf Coast in Texas. It has smaller, more slender fruiting bodies with more distant and decurrent gills and possibly brighter blue flesh.

Lactarius subpurpureus   232

Identification marks   This colorful mushroom has a dull rosy purple cap which often has a grayish lustre in age; persistently reddish purple, subdistant gills; a deep purplish red latex; and a mild to faintly peppery taste. Green stains develop in age or on injured areas.

Edibility   Edible. We have no evidence that any of the species in the group with brightly colored latices (when first exposed) cause severe poisoning.

When and where   This species is characteristic of coniferous and mixed woods that include hemlock and pine. It fruits in the summer and fall in the region east of the Great Plains, typically in a solitary or scattered manner.

Spores   8–11 x 6.5–8 μm, cream color in deposit, ellipsoid, ornamentation a partial reticulum.

Observations   This species is seldom slimy to the touch, but may feel slightly greasy. *L. paradoxus* has a latex about the same color, but the gills are close and the cap is silvery to grayish blue. It is primarily a Gulf Coast species. *Subpurpureus* means somewhat purple.

Lactarius thyinos   233

Identification marks   The cap is thinly slimy when fresh, and more or less carrot color. The gills and stalk are similarly colored. The latex is near saffron color to orange, and wounds on the gills or other parts slowly stain deep purple but do not become green. Like a perfectly fresh cap, the stalk is thinly sticky to slimy.

Edibility   Edible, similar to *L. deliciosus*. The brilliant orange colors persist after cooking and make this an attractive species to serve.

When and where   This mushroom is fairly abundant in the Great Lakes region and the eastern United States and Canada, but is not known west of the Great Plains. Its typical habitat is a cold springy cedar swamp or similar situation.

Spores   9–12 x 7.5–9 μm, pale yellow in deposit, subglobose to broadly ellipsoid, ornamented with a partial to broken reticulum.

Observations   This species often fruits in the same area as *L. deliciosus*, and mixed collections are all too easy to make. Contrary to the statement

232　*Lactarius subpurpureus*　　　　　About two-thirds natural size

233　*Lactarius thyinos*　　　　　About two-thirds natural size

made in the previous edition of this *Guide*, *L. thyinos* does not stain green (we think we were the victims of a mixed collection). *Thyinos* means of the cedars.

234　Lactarius deliciosus

Identification marks　The cap is carrot color to more orange when young and fresh, but often fades to dull tan in age or becomes stained with green. The latex is carrot orange from the beginning and in some varieties slowly becomes purple. In all varieties wounds, and at times the entire mushroom, stain green. The cap surface is only slightly sticky at first. The stalk is not at all slippery; at first it is usually covered by a faint bloom.

Edibility Edible and choice, but it is best when cooked slowly. Some varieties are better than others.

When and where It is common on moist but well-drained humus in the Rocky Mountains and Great Lakes region, as well as eastern North America. It fruits during the summer and fall. In the fall it is also abundant along the Pacific Coast.

Spores 7–9 x 6–7 μm, pale buff to cream color in deposit, with minute warts and bands forming a partial reticulum.

Observations The specific epithet means delicious. *L. deliciosus* differs from *L. thyinos* in having close gills, a dry stalk, and in staining green. In var. *areolatus*, which is common in the Rocky Mountains, the cap is often areolate-cracked in age.

234 *Lactarius deliciosus*   About natural size

Lactarius aquifluus   235

Identification marks The strong, fragrant odor which becomes even more pronounced if the specimens are dried; the clear colorless latex; the medium to large size; the cap that is smooth at first but often breaks up into patches in age; the hollow, fragile stalk; and the mild to very slightly acrid taste are the important field characters.

Edibility Edible. Peck, who described the species, also tested and reported on its edibility. In North America it has been confused with *L. helvus* which is reported by European investigators as poisonous.

When and where This is a species of the peat bogs of the North, and of mixed or conifer forests on low ground. It often appears in untold quantities during wet weather in late summer and early fall. It is often the most abundant mushroom on peaty soil from the Great Lakes eastward.

Spores (6) 7–9 x (5.5) 6–7.5 μm; ellipsoid; ornamented with lines and warts joined to form an irregular, partial to nearly complete reticulum.

Observations This is the species treated in previous editions of the *Guide* as *L. helvus*. *L. helvus* was described by Fries as a mushroom with an acrid taste and white (not watery) latex. *L. aquifluus* has a basically mild taste and watery latex. *Aquifluus* refers to the waterlike latex.

235 *Lactarius aquifluus*   About natural size

236   Lactarius subserifluus

Identification marks This reddish orange milk fungus has a mild, un-changing, colorless (watery) latex; a hard, firm stalk with a tuft of more or less rust colored (orange cinnamon) hairs at the base; and gills which typically darken in age. The odor is not distinctive.

Edibility We have no information on its edibility.

When and where It is found scattered to gregarious under hardwoods, especially oak-hickory stands, during the summer and early fall. It is common in southern Michigan during wet seasons and occurs south to the Gulf Coast region.

Spores 6–7.5 x 6–7 μm, pinkish buff in deposit, globose to subglobose, ornamented with a partial reticulum.

236 *Lactarius subserifluus*   About natural size

Observations This is one of the species which for years was confused with *L. subdulcis* (see also *L. thejogalus*). To date we are not convinced that the true *L. subdulcis* occurs in North America. *Serifluus* is derived from *serum* (lymph) and *fluus* (flowing); the prefix *sub* means somewhat.

Lactarius gerardii var. subrubescens 237

Identification marks The combination of a deep yellowish brown velvety cap, a medium sized stature, distant and somewhat decurrent gills, and a white spore deposit characterize this species. In this variety the latex is white but stains injured areas pink. In var. *gerardii* the latex does not stain injured areas.

Edibility We have no information on its edibility.

When and where It generally fruits from July to September in hardwood and conifer forests east of the Great Plains.

Spores 7–10 x 6.5–8 μm, white in deposit, broadly ellipsoid to globose, ornamented with a complete to nearly complete reticulum.

Observations Of the milk fungi with velvety brown to blackish caps, this is one of the easiest to identify on field characters—the distant decurrent gills and stubby stature are characteristic. The species was named for W. R. Gerard of New York who first collected it. *Subrubescens* means becoming somewhat reddish.

237 *Lactarius gerardii var. subrubescens*   About two-thirds natural size

---

Lactarius fumosus 238

Identification marks A dry smoky brown cap which varies to pale dingy yellow brown or whitish, a taste which is peppery to acrid to some degree, crowded gills, and a white latex which stains injured areas reddish form a distinctive package.

Edibility We have not obtained any information on its edibility, but do not recommend it. There are some questionable species in the subgenus, and the group itself has only recently been monographed.

When and where This is a characteristic summer to fall mushroom found in various types of woods east of the Great Plains. It is encountered almost every season in the region of the Great Lakes, but seems to be less frequent southward.

Spores 6–8 μm, pinkish buff in deposit, globose to subglobose, ornamented with a broken reticulum.

Observations *Fumosus* refers to the smoky color of the fruiting body.

238   *Lactarius fumosus*   About natural size

239   Lactarius corrugis

Identification marks This sister species to *L. volemus* is distinguished by its very dark reddish brown velvety cap which near the margin is usually very wrinkled, and by the darker, somewhat yellowish cinnamon gills. The

239   *Lactarius corrugis*   About two-thirds natural size

gills are often quite dark in young specimens. The latex is copious in both species and, where exposed to the air, soon stains the gills brown. This is also true for a number of other species related to *L. volemus*.

Edibility   Edible. It is as good or better than *L. volemus*.

When and where   It fruits at about the same time and in the same habitats as *L. volemus*: mid to late summer or early fall. It is, apparently, more abundant in the Southeast than it is in the Great Lakes region. Its area is that generally east of the Great Plains.

Spores   9–12 x (8.5) 9–11 (12) μm, white in deposit, subglobose to globose, ornamented with a nearly complete reticulum.

Observations   One is likely to find intermediates between this and *L. volemus* in the Southeast. *Corrugis* means very wrinkled or folded.

Lactarius volemus   240

Identification marks   This mushroom is easy to recognize by the golden tawny to brownish orange dry cap and the copious milk white latex which turns brown and/or stains the gills brown on exposure to air. Typically, the taste is mild and the gills close. In the southeast a yellow variety (var. *flavus*) is quite common.

Edibility   Edible and choice. Cook it slowly, or it is apt to come out rather hard and granular. It is excellent in a casserole with bacon. The copious latex may interfere with pan frying. After being picked, the specimens slowly develop a disagreeable fishy odor, but this in no way affects the taste.

When and where   This is the outstanding midsummer edible mushroom in the hardwood forests of the area east of the Great Plains. It is often abundant in grassy oak woods at about the time *Boletus variipes* appears. It can also be found in beech-maple forests. It also is frequent in the region around the Gulf of Mexico.

Spores   7.5–9 (10) x 7.5–8.5 (9) μm, white in deposit, subglobose to globose, ornamented with a regular, complete to nearly complete reticulum.

Observations   The specific epithet refers to a kind of large pear.

Lactarius subpalustris   241

Identification marks   These are: a dingy mushroom that has a pale dull buff (not pure white) latex that stains injured areas lilac to purple; a mild taste; and a spotted (scrobiculate) stalk, which is sticky at first but soon becomes dry.

Edibility   We have no data on it, but recommend not eating it: all milk fungi that develop purple stains are under suspicion.

When and where   It is found scattered in hardwood forests, on wet but not soggy ground, in summer and early fall. Its distribution is poorly known at present, but we expect it occurs over much of the eastern United States and Canada (east of the Great Plains). Until recently it was confused with *Lactarius maculatus*—an acrid, zonate species.

Spores   8–11 x 7–8 (9) μm, pinkish buff in deposit, subglobose to broadly ellipsoid, ornamentation not forming a reticulum but in the form of warts and irregular ridges mostly not connected to any great degree.

240 *Lactarius volemus*   About two-thirds natural size

241 *Lactarius subpalustris*   About two-thirds natural size

Observations We predict that this will be found to be a southern species with its range extending up to the Great Lakes. *Palustris* means swampy or marshy; *subpalustris* applies to low wet ground, often near a swamp.

242   Lactarius repraesentaneus

Identification marks The cap finally becomes rather large, (up to 18 cm) wide, the whole fruiting body is more or less yellow to pale straw color, and the cap is decidedly hairy along the margin and for some distance toward the disc. The latex is milk white but quickly stains wounds dull lilac to violaceous. The stalk is scrobiculate and at first slightly sticky. The taste is mild to slightly acrid.

Edibility   Poisonous? Do not eat any *Lactarius* in which the wounds stain lilac to violaceous.

When and where   This is a species of the northern conifer forests and, in the western area, of the spruce-fir zone in the mountains. It is very abundant in late August after heavy rains, particularly in areas where the forest borders a mountain meadow. We have collected it by the bushel in the border zone at Squaw Meadows above Upper Payette Lakes in Idaho.

Spores   9–11 x 6.5–8 μm, yellowish in deposit in most American collections, broadly ellipsoid to ellipsoid, ornamented with warts and ridges which do not produce a reticulum.

Observations   This European species was originally described as having a white spore deposit, but the current concept in Europe is of a species with a yellowish deposit. We have both in North America, but so far the white-spored one is known only from Colorado. The specific epithet, as we interpret it, means the showy one.

242   *Lactarius repraesentaneus*   About one-third natural size

---

Lactarius torminosus   **243**

Identification marks   The cap is a delicate pink over the disc, and the margin is pallid. The depressed center (disc) is typically glabrous and slightly sticky when fresh; the arched margin is coarsely fibrillose, and the edge is distinctly fringed (bearded) in young specimens. The gills may also develop a strong pinkish tint. The taste is very acrid, and the latex is white and unchanging, or, in var. *nordmanensis*, stains the gills dingy ochraceous.

Edibility   In the Soviet Union it is preserved with oil and vinegar and considered a delicacy. Generally in the western world it is considered poisonous. In North America it can be easily confused with other species whose edibility has not been determined.

When and where   It apparently forms mycorrhiza with several species of birch. It fruits during the late summer and fall and is a common and abundant species. In cities where birch is planted extensively, such as Seattle and Portland in the Pacific Northwest, it often occurs in parks and lawns (and is more abundant in these cities than in the surrounding areas, since birch is not commonly native there).

Spores 7.5–9 (10) x 6–7.5 μm, white to cream color in deposit, ellipsoid, ornamented with a broken to partial reticulum.

Observations The specific epithet means gripping.

243 *Lactarius torminosus*   About natural size

244   Lactarius sordidus

Identification marks As the name implies, this is a dirty to muddy mushroom in appearance. It has a dull yellowish brown to brownish yellow cap that is toned olive over the center, a white unchanging latex which stains injured areas a gray brown to dark olive brown, an acrid taste, and a hard scrobiculate stalk. The stalk is colored about like the cap. When KOH or ammonia is dropped on the surface of the cap, the spot of contact instantly turns magenta.

244 *Lactarius sordidus*   About two-thirds natural size

Edibility We have no data on its edibility, but recommend avoiding acrid species in general.

When and where Late summer to fall, often in large patches, under spruce and balsam-fir as well as other conifers. It is most abundant from the northern Great Lakes region eastward, but has been found as far south as the Tennessee mountains and west to northern Idaho and Alaska.

Spores 5.5–7 x 5–6 μm, white in deposit, ellipsoid, ornamented with a more or less broken reticulum.

Observations This is one of three North American species which have been confused with *L. necator* of Europe: *L. olivaceo-umbrinus* is western and has spores 7–9 x 6–8 μm; *L. atroviridis* occurs primarily under oak and is dark green. *Sordidus* means dingy or dirty; *necator* means a murderer; *olivaceo-umbrinus* means olive-umber; and *atroviridis* means blackish green.

Lactarius argillaceifolius   245

Identification marks The dull brownish gray cap is slimy when moist but appears varnished when the slime has dried. In age the cap becomes paler and is often more or less dull pinkish brown or, at the margin, buff color. The off-white to cream color latex causes broken places slowly to stain gray to olivaceous. The stalk is dingy cream color to pallid. The taste of the flesh is typically acrid in young material; it may be nearly mild in old specimens. The gills are whitish at first, but become dingy ochraceous tan (near clay color) in age (hence the specific epithet).

Edibility Not established. For years the species was confused with *L. trivialis*, which has been reported as poisonous, but we are not sure now which species was actually eaten.

When and where It occurs under oak, often on sandy soil, east of the Great Plains. In the Great Lakes region the appearance of this species marks the beginning of the summer mushroom flora. It first appears around July 4 and continues to fruit into September.

Spores 8–10 (11) x 7–8 μm, pinkish buff in deposit, subglobose to broadly ellipsoid, ornamented with isolated warts and ridges which form at most a broken reticulum.

245 *Lactarius argillaceifolius*   About one-half natural size

Observations The specific epithet means clay colored gills. The name *L. trivialis* was used for this species in previous issues of the *Guide*. Variety *megacarpus*, with gigantic fruiting bodies, occurs under oak in the Pacific Coast states.

246 Lactarius subflammeus

Identification marks This brightly colored mushroom has a scarlet cap when young that soon fades to brilliant orange, and is slimy when fresh. The stalk is also bright orange, but the gills are whitish. The latex is white, and neither changes color nor stains injured parts. The taste is slowly acrid.

Edibility We have no data on its edibility, but do not recommend it because of the acrid taste.

When and where It is common in the fall under conifers in the Pacific Northwest south into northern California.

Spores 7.5–9 x 6.5–7.5 μm, white in deposit, ellipsoid, ornamented with ridges and warts not united into a reticulum.

Observations This mushroom was called *L. aurantiacus* in a previous edition, but *L. aurantiacus* should occur under hardwoods. From the Pacific Coast to the Rocky Mountains there are several species with bright red to orange fruiting bodies which show differences in taste, latex color and color changes, and microscopic features. These were all lumped under *L. aurantiacus* at some point. Such confusion is brought about, usually, by a lack of a type specimen for the European species. *Subflammeus* means almost flame color.

247 Lactarius thejogalus

Identification marks Among the apparent myriad of small reddish species of *Lactarius*, this one can be identified because it typically grows near birch trees, and when fresh and young the fruiting bodies have an acrid taste and a white latex that slowly turns yellow or stains white paper yellow. It has an evenly colored cap often with a small umbo, and has no distinctive odor. The cap is moist but not sticky or slimy. In age, the taste may be less acrid to mild, and the latex is less likely to change to yellow.

Edibility Reported as edible, but of mediocre quality. We do not recommend it.

When and where On damp soil and humus typically near birch, often in large numbers. It fruits in the summer and fall in the northern and montane areas of North America. In Michigan it is the common late summer and fall small reddish *Lactarius* around the margins of bogs and swamps, on hummocks in swamps, or in low woods where birch occurs.

Spores 7–9 x 6–7.5 μm, pale yellowish in a thick deposit, white in a thin one, ellipsoid, ornamented with isolated warts and a few short ridges not connected into a reticulum.

Observations This is one of about a dozen relatively small, dull red to orange red species which have been included under the name *L. subdulcis* in North America. We are not convinced that *L. subdulcis* occurs over here. *Thejogalus* is derived from Greek words meaning brimstone and milk.

246　*Lactarius subflammeus*　　　　　　　　　　Nearly natural size

247　*Lactarius thejogalus*　　　　　　　About three-fourths natural size

Lactarius rufus 248

Identification marks　The fruiting body has a dark red cap and stalk and pallid gills when young (which stain reddish or become flushed reddish in age). The cap is dry, and the latex is white and unchanging. The taste is mild at first, but if you chew the material for a few minutes, it becomes excruciatingly acrid. This delayed action is one of the best means of identifying the species. Some variants of the species, however, are rather promptly acrid.

Edibility　Usually rated poisonous in the literature, but in Finland, we are told, it is one of the most popular species. *Lactarius boughtoni* is placed in synonymy with *L. rufus*; Boughton, who collected it, ate it and pronounced it good. This should mean that *L. rufus* is edible, but we refuse to recommend it on the basis of logic alone.

When and where In sphagnum bogs it is often abundant under spruce. In upland forests it also occurs under pine and in southern Michigan has become common in pine plantations where the trees are 10–15 inches in diameter. In the west, it is also present under pine and spruce. It is a late summer and early fall species of northern and montane regions.

Spores 8.5–11 x 6–8 μm, pale yellow in deposit, broadly ellipsoid, ornamented with a partial reticulum.

Observations *Rufus* means red.

248 *Lactarius rufus*   About two-thirds natural size

249   Lactarius chrysorheus

Identification marks This medium-sized mushroom has a glabrous cap which is merely sticky to moist when fresh and is typically marked with more or less diffuse, concentric bands of dull ochraceous to pale yellowish cinnamon on a paler yellowish ochraceous to buff background. The latex is white at first, but quickly becomes sulphur yellow on exposure to air. The taste slowly becomes rather strongly acrid.

Edibility Suspected. Avoid all species in which the latex is white at first and turns yellow on exposure to air.

When and where It occurs in hardwood and mixed forests, typically with oak, east of the Great Plains and along the Pacific Coast. While it seldom fruits in abundance, it appears every year in many localities.

Spores 6–8 (9) x 5.5–6.5 μm, pale yellow in deposit, broadly ellipsoid, ornamented with warts and ridges at times forming a broken reticulum.

Observations In the Great Lakes region and eastward, *L. vinaceorufescens* is often confused with *L. chrysorheus*. However, the former species has flesh pink tones in the cap and stalk, and the entire fruiting body discolors in age to a dull vinaceous red to dingy reddish brown. Its latex is white quickly changing to yellow on exposure. *Chrysorheus* means exuding a golden liquid.

264

249 *Lactarius chrysorheus*   About natural size

Lactarius affinis   **250**

Identification marks   This rather large mushroom has a slimy to sticky cap which is more or less evenly light pinkish tan to pale ochraceous, an acrid taste, white latex, and an unspotted stalk which is about the same color as the cap and is likely to be thinly slimy at first. *L. trivialis* is very close to this species, but is lead gray at first and only in age fades (or changes) to the color of *L. affinis*.

Edibility   We have no information on its edibility, but do not recommend it because of the danger of confusion with *L. trivialis*.

When and where   This is a characteristic mushroom of the mixed conifer and hardwood forests east of the Great Plains. It usually fruits in the late summer and fall.

250 *Lactarius affinis*   About one-half natural size

Spores 9–10.5 x 7–8 μm, yellowish in heavy deposit, ellipsoid, ornamentation as ridges and warts connected to form at most an incomplete reticulum.

Observations A variety in which the latex is white but dries dull olive is called var. *viridilactis*. It is encountered about as frequently as the type variety and in the same general habitats. *Affinis* means related (in this instance related to *L. trivialis*).

Russula

These species have essentially the same features as *Lactarius*, but a latex is not present, though in some species the gill edges may be beaded with hyaline droplets. Considerable consumption of *Russula* species by pot-hunters over the last fifteen years has resulted in the conclusion that the genus is no more dangerous than *Lactarius*, *Pholiota*, or *Agaricus*. It is true beyond any dispute that casual collectors gather and eat great quantities of *Russula* species without knowing which species they are eating. Once again, it seems the best policy is to place the responsibility for the welfare of the collector on the collector (which is where it rests anyhow), and simply give him or her as much help as possible in making the "right" decisions. It is in this vein that we have increased materially the number of species treated in this revision of the *Guide*. We caution the public against eating any of the species with white fruiting bodies which stain black when injured, but we cannot promise that anyone who does eat them will be poisoned. Most of the North American species are edible, but poisonings have been attributed to this group in recent times. In our opinion most species in this group are coarse and unattractive as a food item, and it would not be unusual if cases of indigestion were encountered. The *R. foetens* group in general has species with such a disagreeable taste when cooked or raw that no one is likely to try them more than once. We *do not* recommend experimenting with them. Even the old rule of thumb about not eating any of the acrid species has been found invalid by repeated experiments reported in the literature. The spore ornamentation is amyloid. The ornamentation is included in our measurements unless otherwise stated. *Russula* means reddish.

Key to Species

Russula virescens   251

Identification marks   The spore deposit is white, the taste is mild, and the
surface of the cap is dry and unpolished to velvety and soon breaks up into
patches. The margin is not appreciably furrowed (sulcate-striate). The color
of the cap is grayish green to dull blue green, but the gills and the stalk are
white.

Edibility   Edible, and highly recommended by some authorities. It also has
the advantage that it can be readily recognized in the field.

When and where   East of the Great Plains it is common and abundant in
open hardwood forests after heavy rains in July, August, and early September. In poor seasons it is usually solitary.

Spores   6.5–8.5 (10) x 5–6.5 (7) μm, white in deposit, mostly ellipsoid,
ornamentation variable—some with mostly isolated warts, most spores with
warts some of which are connected by fine lines, and some with a weak
partial reticulum.

Observations   There are a number of species of *Russula* with green caps,
so check for the presence of the patches formed by the breaking up of the
cap cuticle, i.e., examine mature caps. *Virescens* means becoming green.

Russula crustosa   252

Identification marks   The cuticle of the cap is continuous at first and is near
pinkish buff in color. It soon breaks up into a pattern (shown in the photograph) revealing the pale context beneath. The margin is pallid or with a faint
tinge of greenish blue but not a true green as in *R. virescens*, the most closely
related species. The spores are white in deposit. The taste is mild.

Edibility Edible, according to Kauffman, who knew it well.

When and where It is common and often abundant east of the Great Plains, especially in the Great Lakes region, summer and early fall, in woods of hardwoods, especially oak and hickory.

Spores 7–9 x 5.5–7 μm, white in deposit, ellipsoid to subglobose, ornamentation as warts 0.2–0.3 μm high and with some fine connecting lines.

Observations Specimens will be found which appear to be intermediate between *R. virescens* and this species, but this does not mean that *R. crustosa* and *R. virescens* should be regarded as a single species. *Crustosa* means with a rind; in this mushroom it is a thin cuticle that breaks up in patches.

251 *Russula virescens*   About natural size

252 *Russula crustosa*   About two-thirds natural size

Russula variata 253

Identification marks   The color of the cap is of various shades of green often splashed with purple to dull red or, at times, dull lilac on the margin. The surface is viscid and shiny, but soon dry. The gills are white to off-white and *many of them* branch (fork) at least once some distance from the stalk. The taste is mild to tardily acrid, and the spore deposit white.

Edibility   Edible and choice. Peck, who co-authored the species, stated that it was edible and good.

When and where   It is one of the conspicuous and abundant midsummer mushrooms in the aspen-birch-maple forests on the cutover pine lands of the Great Lakes area and eastward, but occurs in other associations of deciduous woody plants also. In southern Michigan its appearance marks the beginning of the summer mushroom season.

Spores   7–10 (11) x 6–8 (9.5) μm, white in deposit, ornamentation of warts 0.3–0.9 μm high (usually isolated, but some fine lines connect some of them).

Observations   The specific epithet means variable. Some investigators regard *R. variata* to be a variety of *R. cyanoxantha*, a European species.

253   *Russula variata*   About two-thirds natural size

Russula aeruginea 254

Identification marks   The glabrous, thinly slimy, dull green cap; mild or practically mild taste; and yellow spore deposit along with the gills spotting brownish in age distinguish this species. The pellicle (skin) of the cap is separable for about halfway to the disc. The habitat under aspen is also significant to the collector looking for a meal, since it is under aspen that he is likely to find it in large numbers.

Edibility   Edible and popular.

When and where The best fruitings we have seen were west of the Great Plains under aspen and in mixed stands of aspen and lodgepole pine. It is also abundant in the Great Lakes region and eastward, but there the habitat it prefers is not as clearly defined.

Spores 6–9 (10) x 5–7 μm, pale yellow in deposit, broadly ellipsoid, ornamentation of warts and some fine radiating lines but no reticulum formed, prominences up to 0.5 μm high.

Observations The specific epithet means verdigris (dull greenish).

254   *Russula aeruginea*   About two-thirds natural size

255   Russula paludosa

Identification marks The cap is large (to 15 cm or more) and rather firm. The color is usually a deep dull red, but orange to yellow tones develop, and the flesh is white but tends to become ash color where injured or in age. The

255   *Russula paludosa*   About one-half natural size

taste is variable: more or less acrid to bitter or merely faintly unpleasant. The stalk is much more robust than that of *R. emetica*, and more frequently is tinged pink to red. The spore deposit is pale yellow.

Edibility   Reported as edible in the literature, but we have no data of our own on it.

When and where   During the summer and early fall it is usually solitary to scattered in wet situations under conifers, such as mossy areas under black spruce, boggy areas, etc. It is to be expected in the region of the Great Lakes during August and September.

Spores   7.5–11.5 x 7–10 (10.5) μm; pale yellow in deposit; broadly ellipsoid; ornamentation of short ridges and warts, the prominences 0.7–1.2 (2) μm high, the warts isolated or some connected by lines.

Observations   *Paludosa* means of the swamps.

Russula emetica   256

Identification marks   The deep to pale scarlet, fragile cap; the very acrid taste; the white stalk; and the white spore deposit allow this species to be readily recognized—but be sure your specimen has all of these features. It is a very common species in bogs and conifer forests generally.

Edibility   Edible and Poisonous—depending on which authority one consults. In the older literature it was frequently reported as poisonous, but in recent years more reports indicating it is edible if properly cooked have appeared. We regard it as a "marginal" species as to edibility and do not recommend it.

When and where   It fruits in the summer in the Rocky Mountains, in the fall or late summer in the area east of the Great Plains, and in the fall in the Pacific Northwest, always under conifers.

Spores   9–12 x 7.5–9.5 μm, broadly ellipsoid to subglobose, ornamentation amyloid, elements 0.5–1 μm high, pattern a weak broken reticulum.

Observations   This is a variable species, but also one frequently misidentified because collectors do not pay attention to the field characters given above. *Emetica* means provoking sickness.

256   *Russula emetica*   About one-half natural size

257 Russula foetens (a collective species)

Identification marks The odor which is somewhat of almonds at first but very disagreeable in old specimens, the caps colored a dark to pale yellow brown with sulcate and tuberculate-striate margins, and a very disagreeable taste identify this group. When young the gills are often beaded with drops of a colorless liquid, but this is not considered to be a latex. In some of the segregates of this collective species, the bases of the stalks develop cinnabar red stains.

Edibility Inedible because of the flavor, and, since we are using the name in a collective sense, we urge that readers not experiment with this species. The technical literature must be consulted to identify the species and varieties included here.

When and where In one or more of its variants it is found in the wooded areas of North America during the summer and fall, often in large numbers.

Spores Data on spores are omitted here since the species is a collective one.

Observations The specific epithet means with a fetid odor.

257   *Russula foetens*   About two-thirds natural size

258 Russula compacta

Identification marks The cap is large (up to 18 cm) and firm, and becomes somewhat areolate on the disc in age. The disc is depressed; it soon becomes tan to reddish cinnamon, and this color slowly spreads to the margin, or the latter often remains white to pallid. The taste is slightly bitter, and the odor is somewhat fishy at first but becomes offensive in old specimens or when the specimens are dried. It persists for years in the dried material. The spore deposit is white.

Edibility   Listed as edible, but not likely to be very appealing due to the odor and taste.

When and where   It is a northern species in mixed conifer and deciduous forests. We have found it in pure stands of either type, but most abundantly around patches of sphagnum (but not in floating bogs). It occurs as far south as Florida.

Spores   7.5–10 x 6.3–8.5 μm, white in deposit, mostly broadly ellipsoid to subglobose, ornamentation of warts 0.7–1.2 μm high, either isolated or connected by lines to form somewhat of a reticulum.

Observations   The specific epithet means solid or compact.

258   *Russula compacta*   About one-half natural size

Russula cascadensis   259

Identification marks   The entire fruiting body is white, and the cap scarcely changes. The taste is intensely acrid. The gills are close to crowded, and stain dingy yellow to pale tan. The spore deposit is a pale creamy yellow. It is a small to medium-sized mushroom related to *R. delica*.

Edibility   Its powerfully acrid taste raw should discourage sampling it. We have no data on it that we trust, though some people who were made ill said this was the species they ate.

When and where   It is frequently collected in the conifer forests of the Pacific Northwest in the fall.

Spores   6.5–8.5 x 4.5–6.7 μm (excluding ornamentation), pale creamy yellow in deposit, mostly ellipsoid, ornamentation 0.2–0.7 μm high, of isolated warts (some spores in addition show fine to heavy lines forming with the warts a more or less complete to broken reticulum).

Observations   The white species more or less similar to *R. delica* form a "collective" group much as those related to *R. foetens*. *Cascadensis* means of the Cascades, a mountain range in the western United States.

259 *Russula cascadensis*   About two-thirds natural size

260   Russula brevipes

Identification marks The fruiting body is white overall but by old age shows brown stains around larval tunnels (worm holes), and ochraceous to clay color stains often show on cap and stalk. Rarely is the cap brownish overall. The gills are white (as indicated) but slowly become tinged yellow to olive buff and are close (not distant, as in *R. delica*). The taste raw for flesh of the cap or gills is mild to slightly acrid.

Edibility Edible, but requires special preparation. It is popular with a number of collectors in northern Idaho.

260 *Russula brevipes*   About two-thirds natural size

When and where It is common and abundant across the continent in conifer as well as hardwoods, summer and fall.

Spores 8–10 x 6.5–8.5 (10) μm (excluding ornamentation), white to pale
cream in deposit, broadly ellipsoid to subglobose, ornamentation 0.7–1.7
μm high (mostly of isolated warts but with some fine and heavy connecting
lines present).

Observations The species is variable, and a very acrid western variety
(var. *acrior*) is known. One often finds the fruiting bodies by spotting a hump
in the moss or duff of the forest floor. *Brevipes* means short-stalked (short-
footed if translated literally).

Russula dissimulans   261

Identification marks As in the fruiting bodies of *R. albonigra*, those of this
species are white at first but by maturity have usually become black or at
least a dark fuscous brown. *R. dissimulans* differs from *R. nigricans* in that
the former has close instead of distant gills, but stains red and then black
like the latter. The spore deposit is white.

Edibility Probably edible: Kauffman listed *R. nigricans* as edible, and we
believe the two species have been confused in the past and both used for
food. We do not recommend it, however, since this group contains some
poisonous species, even though none of these have as yet been found in
North America.

When and where Solitary to gregarious in coniferous and mixed forests
across the continent, late summer and fall, abundant at times.

Spores 7.7–10.8 x 6.5–9 μm; white in deposit, mostly broadly ellipsoid to
subglobose; ornamentation amyloid, elements 0.1–0.5 μm high (estimated),
in the form of warts and lines in an incomplete reticulum or warts not connected.

Observations *Dissimulans* means the one which is disguised.

Russula albonigra   262

Identification marks The cap, gills, and stalk are dull white at first but soon
darken and in age are black. This color change is direct; no red or yellow
stage intervenes. The taste is both bitter and acrid. The gills are crowded,
and the spore deposit is white.

Edibility We do not recommend trying any of the *Russulae* which blacken
on bruising or in age. A species of this group has caused fatal poisoning in
the Orient. *R. albonigra* (under the name *Russula sordida*) has been reported as edible.

When and where It is very abundant some seasons in the Pacific Northwest, where the caps at times reach 25 cm broad. In the eastern half of the
continent, "*R. sordida*" appears to take its place as a variant of *R. albonigra*.
It fruits in the late summer and fall.

Spores 7–10.5 x 6–8.5 μm; mostly broadly ellipsoid to subglobose; ornamentation amyloid and prominences about 0.1 μm high, warts connected by
fine lines to form a mostly broken reticulum.

Observations *Albonigra* means white and black.

261   *Russula dissimulans*   About natural size

262   *Russula albonigra*   About one-fourth natural size

Gasteromycetes

The members of this group of Basidiomycetes do not forcibly discharge their basidiospores from the basidia. It is a heterogeneous group. Some species closely resemble members of the Agaricales and are often placed in that order; others, such as the true puffballs, are distinctive in their own right. The Key to Major Groups of Fungi Illustrated (p. 23) shows how to distinguish the Secotiaceae and Phallales from the rest of the Gasteromycetes.

Secotiaceae

Members of this family are often dismissed as misshapen or aborted fruiting bodies of a bolete or gilled mushroom, but they will not produce spore deposits—the spores are not discharged from the basidia. Like the members of the Agaricales, these fruiting bodies have a stalk and cap, but in place of gills there is a wrinkled and anastomosing mass of tissue (the gleba) where the spores are produced. This group is seldom illustrated in field guides, with the result that the casual collector passes them by, assuming that they are abnormal fruiting bodies of true mushrooms. We take pleasure in including five of these species. Each of these fungi has the basic anatomical features of a different family of mushrooms: Bolbitiaceae for *Gastrocybe*, Cortinariaceae for *Thaxterogaster*, Russulaceae for *Macowanites*, and Boletaceae for *Gastroboletus*. As suggested in part by these five examples, it is thought that one reason the Gasteromycetes show such diversity in form is that they evolved from many different "lines" of Basidiomycetes.

Key to Species

1. Stalk 1.5–2.5 mm thick, long and slender; cap narrowly conic and soon drooping . . . . .263. *Gastrocybe lateritia*
1. Not as above 2
    2. Stalk with a thin slime veil and tinged violet near the base; gleba yellow brown at maturity . . . . .267. *Thaxterogaster pingue*
    2. Not as above 3
3. Gleba of intricately folded and anastomosing white, pallid, or yellowish "gills"; aspect of fruiting body that of a small *Russula* . . . .
    . . . . .264. *Macowanites americanus*
3. Gleba of tubes as in a bolete, aspect of fruiting body that of a bolete 4
    4. Tubes staining blue when injured . . . .266. *Gastroboletus turbinatus*
    4. Tubes not staining when injured . . . . .265. *Gastroboletus scabrosus*

Gastrocybe lateritia   263

Identification marks   The pattern of development of the fruiting body is peculiar. It starts out with the appearance of a young specimen of a *Conocybe*: a conic cap upright at the end of a straight stalk. As the head or cap matures, the stalk seems to weaken and the cap bends downward, first to a more or less horizontal position and finally inverted (with the "bottom up"). The spores are then mature or nearly so, but because of the position of the cap, if discharged from the basidia in the usual manner for an agaric, there is no way for them to fall free of the cap. Actually the spores are not discharged. The cap simply gelatinizes into a slimy mass containing the spores and falls to the ground as the stalk collapses. The features of the spores, however, relate the fungus to the Bolbitiaceae of the Agaricales.

Edibility   Of no practical value.

When and where   Sometimes abundant on lawns in the Great Lakes area after heavy rains in June or early July.

Spores   (9.5) 10.5–12 (14) x (6) 7–8 µm, smooth, apical pore present, wall yellow brown in KOH.

Observations   *Gastrocybe* means stomach cap; *lateritia* pertains to bricks, in this case meaning somewhat brick colored.

263   *Gastrocybe lateritia*   About two-thirds natural size

264   Macowanites americanus

Identification marks   The "cap" is 1–5 cm broad, very fragile, with a cuticle continuous át first but soon cracking irregularly exposing the white context. The cap edge is at first connected to the stalk or at least touching it; later the cap partly expands and the gill chamber (gleba) is visible to a greater or lesser extent. The "gills" are more or less fused in places to produce an irregular tissue partly lamellate and partly poroid. The stalk often projects slightly or, at first, is enclosed by the margin of the cap (practically enclosing the base). Odor and taste are mild. The color of the cap is variously pink, lilac, purple red, or yellow to olivaceous (some caps are unicolorous with one of the above colors).

Edibility   Apparently edible; at least one rancher in the Sawtooth Mountains of Idaho informed us he had been collecting it in his horse corral and eating it for the past six or seven years. Lodgepole pine was nearby.

When and where   It is a common species in the mountains of central Idaho in the summertime. We have not seen it in Colorado. The largest fruitings noted to date were under spruce and fir.

Spores 9–13 x 8.5–11 μm, ornamentation strongly amyloid, as warts and ridges at times forming a partial reticulum.

Observations The fruiting bodies of this genus resemble an aborted *Russula* fruiting body, but they never expand completely, and no spore deposit can be obtained. The genus is named after MacOwan, a collector in South Africa during the latter part of the last century. The specific epithet means the American species.

264　*Macowanites americanus*　　　　　　　　　　　　About natural size

Gastroboletus scabrosus　　　　　　　　　　265

Identification marks This genus differs from other bolete-like genera in having the tubes curved and distorted in such a way that the spores, if discharged from the basidia, could not fall freely into the air currents as do

265　*Gastroboletus scabrosus*　　　　　　　　　　Nearly natural size

the spores in a true bolete. In this species the cap is dingy yellow brown, dry, and unpolished. When exposed to air the flesh becomes dull pinkish buff mottled with olive gray. The stalk develops blackish brown stains when bruised and is roughened with small yellow brown squamules. The taste is mild, and the odor is not distinctive.

Edibility   To our knowledge it has not been tested.

When and where   On sandy soil in oak-hickory forests, southern Michigan, late summer to early fall.

Spores   15–18.5 x 4–5 μm, subfusiform, smooth, pale brown in KOH.

Observations   This and the following species resemble imperfect or aborted specimens of boletes, but are classified as Gasteromycetes because the spores are not discharged from the basidia. As these fungi become better known, their range no doubt will be extended. *Scabrosus* means rough.

266   Gastroboletus turbinatus

Identification marks   This fungus has a fruiting body that is usually mistaken for an aborted bolete, but, as mentioned for the previous species, the spores are not discharged from the basidia, and the tubes do not become arranged in a truly vertical position. It stains blue, as do many species of *Boletus*, and the tubes are yellow. The cap varies greatly in color, from dark brown to mostly red.

Edibility   Apparently not known, and we have no data of our own on it.

When and where   It is a feature of the bolete flora of the conifer forests of the Pacific Northwest and extends east into the Rocky Mountains in the spruce-fir zone. It can be found nearly every season, but is hardly to be regarded as common. Often it barely breaks through the duff. We find it mostly during the summer.

Spores   (9.5) 13.5–18 (20) x (5.5) 6.5–9.5 μm, in face view oblong to ovate, in profile somewhat inequilateral, ochraceous tinged brown in KOH, inamyloid.

Observations   *Turbinatus* means a spinning top, such as a child's toy.

266   *Gastroboletus turbinatus*   About natural size

Identification marks The globose to obtuse cap often becomes depressed in age. It is viscid at first and is pale to dark date brown. By maturity the cap margin pulls away from the stalk enough to expose some of the dull brown gleba. In dry weather the stalk may not project from the combined cap and gleba (it then forms a more or less globose fruiting body). In wet weather the stalk elongates to 1–4.5 cm long. It is usually viscid near the base and tinged weakly with violet. As can be seen from the illustration, the stalk extends through the gleba to the apex of the cap and is really a "stipe-columella."

Edibility We have no data on it.

When and where This species is very widely distributed in the conifer forests west of the Great Plains, but many of the fruiting bodies are hypogeous. In the Cascade Mountains they are more often stipitate and become epigeous by maturity. Fruiting occurs in the summer in the Rocky Mountains and in the fall in the Pacific Northwest.

Spores (12) 14–17 (20) x (6.5) 8–9.5 (11) μm, more or less ellipsoid, verrucose with rusty brown small warts.

Observations The generic name means Thaxter's stomach, but we translate it as Thaxter's Gasteromycete. *Pingue* refers to grease; the cap has a lubricous feel or is actually subviscid.

267 *Thaxterogaster pingue*   About natural size

Selected Gasteromycetes

In this group we illustrate a variety of different types of fruiting bodies; an effort has also been made to include the best edible kinds. The group is a safe one for the beginner because no poisonous species are known, but this does not mean that all are good. There is always the chance of poisonous species turning up.

It must be remembered that it is the immature stages that are edible—the stages too young to be identified by the regular procedures. This contrasts with the other edible fungi we discuss, in which freshly matured specimens are as good as the younger ones. Puffballs in which the interior has become powdery or slimy or colored are not good to eat. Only specimens that are homogeneous and white clear through when cut in half should be considered for consumption. This rule eliminates some species in which the gleba becomes colored very early in its development, but these species are second rate at best, and some do cause gastrointestinal upsets in some people. Stinkhorn eggs will be eliminated because they are not homogeneous as viewed in section. There is a layer of gel under the surface, and the outline of the spore-producing tissue and cap, if present, can also be distinguished. The greatest danger in eating puffballs is that one may collect a button stage of a poisonous *Amanita*. When a specimen is cut in half longitudinally, the outline of the stalk, gills, and cap will be evident if the "puffball" is an *Amanita* button. In the Rocky Mountains where *Amanita* buttons frequently develop slowly because of dry weather, puffballs and *Amanita* buttons may be very similar superficially, and people have confused the two with nearly fatal consequences.

Key to Genera and Species

1. Fruiting body resembling a small bird's nest ..... 279. *Crucibulum laeve*
1. Not as above 2
   2. Fruiting body resembling a small potato, typically growing underground; interior (gleba) neither powdery nor black at maturity .... 280. *Rhizopogon idahoensis*
   2. Not as above 3
3. Spore case opening by a pore or apical hole 3–5 mm wide 4
3. Spore case opening in an irregular manner 5
   4. Outer wall of fruiting body splitting into persistent rays ....
      .... 274. *Geastrum coronatum* & 275. *Astreus pteridis*
   4. Outer wall in the form of powder or small warts, often easily rubbed off .... *Lycoperdon*
5. Interior of fruiting body of pea-shaped pockets of tissue containing the spores; fruiting body releasing an inky juice when sectioned ...
   .... 276. *Pisolithus tinctorius*
5. Not as above 6
   6. Fruiting body wall (at least that part enclosing the gleba) breaking up into soft, papery pieces that fall away by maturity .... *Calvatia*
   6. Not as above 7
7. Fruiting body white when young, becoming brown by maturity; wall hard by maturity; gleba white at first and long remaining so, then becoming dull yellow to olive brown before maturity ....
   .... 273. *Mycenastrum corium*
7. Fruiting body dull yellow (ochraceous) when young, becoming duller by maturity but not changing markedly; wall thick and tough; gleba white soon becoming purplish black before maturity ...... *Scleroderma*

Calvatia

This is the genus of the giant puffballs, all of which are edible if obtained before the gleba has started to change color. Both species illustrated are common east of the Rocky Mountains. The species most interesting to the specialist, however, are found in our western plains area and in the western mountains. The largest one we have seen is *Calvatia booniana*, which, of all things, grows in the sagebrush country of the north central Rocky Mountains. *Calvatia* means bald or becoming bald.

Key to Species

1. Fruiting body lacking a sterile base . . . . 268. *Calvatia gigantea*
1. Fruiting body with a well-developed sterile base . . . . . 269. *C. craniformis*

Calvatia gigantea   268
(Giant Puffball)

Identification marks   It is best recognized in its young stages by the kid-glove-like smooth exterior and its relatively large size. It is white at first and attached to the ground by a cordlike rhizomorph. It ranges in size from a baseball to that of a bushel basket. The gleba is yellow brown at maturity. The wall of the fruiting body simply breaks into pieces which fall to the ground leaving the gleba exposed.

Edibility   Edible and popular. It is often sold at farmer's markets.

When and where   It is to be expected in the area east of the Rocky Mountains on low, rich, wet humus or soil, often under brush near woodland pools, along ditches, and along old roads. In Michigan it fruits from mid-August on into October. The giant puffballs of the western mushroom province need further critical study. *Calvatia booniana* is a feature of the sagebrush areas.

Spores   3.3–5.5 μm, globose, weakly ornamented, yellowish to tawny in Melzer's solution.

268   *Calvatia gigantea*   About one-fourth natural size

Observations Small specimens are not necessarily young; they may simply be arrested in their development. Section specimens lengthwise and look for pin-holes, indicating presence of worms, and for any signs of a yellowing of the gleba, indicating that is too old for human consumption. The generic name *Langermannia*, instead of *Calvatia*, is sometimes used for this puffball. The specific epithet means very large.

269 Calvatia craniformis

Identification marks The fruiting body is 6–15 cm or more at widest dimension, up to 20 cm high, narrowly to broadly pedicellate, the "stalk" sterile (often referred to as a "sterile base"). The wall of the fruiting body breaks up, finally, into flakes which fall away, exposing the yellowish brown spore mass (the gleba). The gleba is white at first but changes to brownish olive as the spores mature.

Edibility Edible, but not rated highly. Some people experience gastrointestinal disturbances from ingesting it.

When and where It occurs chiefly east of the Rocky Mountains in the fall and is abundant during seasons with heavy September rainfall. In Michigan it is one of the few fleshy fungi found in quantity in locust plantations.

Spores 2.5–3.5 μm, faintly ornamented, pedicel short to lacking, dingy ochraceous in KOH, inamyloid.

Observations *Craniformis* means shaped like a skull.

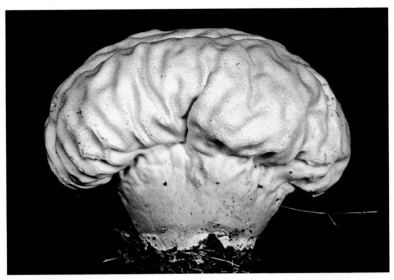

269 *Calvatia craniformis*   About one-half natural size

Lycoperdon

In contrast to *Calvatia*, these fungi have a fruiting body that opens by an apical pore to effect release of the spores. A sterile base may or may not be present. The species are terrestrial or lignicolous and are often found in abundance.

Key to Species

1. Outer wall separating from spore sac in flakes, flakes consisting of a number of warts adhering to each other ....
....................................270. *Lycoperdon marginatum*
1. Not as above 2
   2. Spines on young fruiting body cone-shaped, falling away individually, resulting scars outlined with small scurfy particles ...
.... 271. *L. perlatum*
   2. Young fruiting body lacking spines, surface smooth or obscurely patterned .... 272. *L. pyriforme*

Lycoperdon marginatum 270

Identification marks The fruiting bodies are 1–3 (4) cm broad, subglobose and soon more or less flattened so that at maturity they are broader than tall. Usually they are plicate on the underside. The outer layer is a thick, white, soft covering soon blocked out into pointed warts; this layer separates from the inner layer and sloughs off in pieces made up of few to many warts. The gleba is olive to grayish brown at maturity. A distinct sterile base is present but not conspicuous.

Edibility Edible, but it takes a lot of work to collect enough for a meal.

When and where On sandy soil generally, and in waste places such as fire lanes and thin pastures. It fruits mostly during the summer months north of the Ohio River. It is to be expected in the area east of the Rocky Mountains in the habitats described. Ordinarily it does not occur in large numbers.

Spores 3.5–5.5 μm, globose, nearly smooth, olive to olive brown in KOH, minutely ornamented, dextrinoid.

Observations *Marginatum* means with a distinct margin; its application to this species is unclear.

Lycoperdon perlatum 271

Identification marks The cone-shaped spines over the enlarged fertile portion are distinctive, along with the spotlike scars left when they fall off. The narrowed basal portion is made up of empty chambers. The mature gleba is olive brown or darker in color.

Edibility Edible, and one of the best small puffballs. Beware of any tinge of yellow in the interior; one overage specimen can spoil the dish.

When and where It is a very common and widely distributed collective species (with many variations) found on humus as well as on wood in late summer and fall.

Spores 3.5–4.5 μm, globose, lacking a pedicel, olive brown in KOH, minutely ornamented, inamyloid to dextrinoid (in one and the same mount).

Observations *Perlatum* relates to enduring, a reference to the persistence of the fruiting bodies.

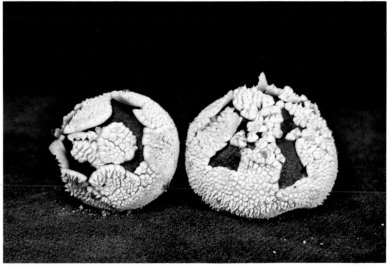

270　*Lycoperdon marginatum*　　　　　　　　　　　　　　Natural size

271　*Lycoperdon perlatum*　　　　　　　　　　　　　　Natural size

272　Lycoperdon pyriforme

Identification marks　The color is white, becoming more or less tan to rusty brown depending on the degree of exposure to light. The sterile base varies greatly in length depending on the location of the specimens. The fertile enlarged part may be smooth, ornamented with small tufts of material, or the latter are present as broad flattened patches. The fertile part is 1–4 cm broad and opens by a hole at the apex which is frequently termed a "pore" but is often about 5 mm across. The gleba is olive brown at maturity. Coarse white strands of mycelium extend out from the base into the substrate.

Edibility   Edible if white throughout the interior. To make collecting it practical, one should look for large fruitings, perhaps around old sawdust piles.

When and where   It fruits during the summer and fall on woody debris, and is common as well as very widely distributed.

Spores   2.8–3.5 μm, globose, appearing smooth or almost so (under light microscope), olive brown in KOH, dextrinoid.

Observations   Old overwintered spore cases are white to pallid and persist on into the following summer in many instances. *Pyriforme* means pear-shaped.

272   *Lycoperdon pyriforme*   About one-half natural size

Mycenastrum corium   273

Identification marks   The fruiting body is up to 20 cm in diameter, and globose to subglobose. It is covered at first by a thick outer layer of floccose to felted material which becomes pulled apart into patches as the fruiting body enlarges. In addition, the tissue of the outer layer shrinks during this period so that finally the hard, thick inner shell is most evident. The latter is about 2 mm thick and dark dull brown. It finally opens by splitting irregularly. The spore mass is white at first, then yellow to olive, and finally olive brown to purple brown at maturity.

Edibility   Not recommended. No doubt it has been collected and eaten (in the immature stages), but was mistaken for a species of *Calvatia*. We have not had reports of testing on authentically identified specimens.

When and where   It is found in pastures and near where livestock have been bedded in spring, summer, and fall. Originally considered to be a western species in North America, it has now been found east of the Rocky Mountains on numerous occasions.

Spores   8–12 μm, globose, reticulate, dark brown in KOH.

Observations   *Mycenastrum* apparently means fungous star. *Corium* refers to the leathery peridium of the fruiting bodies.

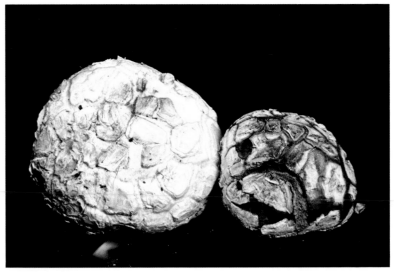

273 *Mycenastrum corium*   About one-half natural size

---

274   Geastrum coronatum

Identification marks   This earthstar has a bluish drab spore sac, a mouth (pore) area outlined by a distinct groove, and the edge of the pore bordered with fine fibrils or teeth. The gleba is purplish brown to chocolate color by maturity, and the spore sac is pedicellate and has a basal collar. At maturity the outer layer splits into segments (rays) which bend backward to the extent that the spore sac is finally elevated; the fruiting body is often found "standing" on the points of the rays.

Edibility   Not edible.

When and where   It is widely distributed in the northern hemisphere. We find it most frequently on sandy soil under pine late in the season.

274 *Geastrum coronatum*   About one-half natural size

Spores 4.5–6 μm, globose, dark yellow brown in KOH, ornamented with small warts, inamyloid.

Observations *Geastrum* means earthstar; the specific epithet means crowned.

Astreus pteridis   275

Identification marks This is our largest earthstar; the fruiting bodies often measure 15 cm across when the rays are expanded. The spore sac opens by a small pore which gradually enlarges, and in age the top of the sac is often weathered away. The upper (inner) surface of the rays soon develop the pattern of checking shown in the photograph. The surface of the spore sac is at first fibrillose-reticulate, but this soon wears away. The outer shell is 3–6 mm thick, woody when dry, and dingy brown.

275a *Astreus pteridis*   About one-half natural size

275b *Astreus hygrometricus*   About one-half natural size

Edibility   Not edible because of the consistency.

When and where   It is found in small groups or solitary on soil and humus in the fall, often on old logging roads in stands of Douglas fir but not limited to this tree. Apparently it is most abundant in the Pacific Northwest, but it has also been found in Iowa. Its fruiting period appears to be late summer and fall. It is not common.

Spores   8–12 μm, globose, obscurely roughened, inamyloid.

Observations   *Astreus hygrometricus*, the other species of *Astreus* in North America, is one of our commonest and most widely distributed species on sand or sandy soil. The spore mass (gleba) is cocoa colored (paler than in *A. pteridis*). As one can readily see at a glance, the two are easily distinguished. *Astreus* means a star. *Pteridis* refers to ferns.

276   Pisolithus tinctorius

Identification marks   The pockets, or pealike structures visible in the interior when specimens are sectioned longitudinally, are diagnostic, along with the honeylike odor of fresh material and the inky juice which stains everything it touches. The size of the fruiting bodies varies greatly.

Edibility   Not recommended. Apparently it has been used medicinally in China in times past.

When and where   It is found during late summer and fall in various habitats. The senior author's first encounter with the species was a collection from the late Professor F. K. Sparrow's potato patch during victory garden days. The next was along a road bank in the Mt. Hood National Forest on Wawpanitia Summit in a dense montane forest of conifers. We now know that the fungus forms mycorrhiza with a great variety of plants, and is receiving considerable attention from those studying growth rates in trees. Apparently it is very widely distributed, but is more frequently encountered in the South and West than in the Great Lakes region.

Spores   8–12 μm, globose, cinnamon in mass, verrucose, the warts blunt.

Observations   *Pisolithus* refers to the pockets about the size of a pea in the immature gleba. *Tinctorius* means usable in dyeing processes.

276   *Pisolithus tinctorius*   About natural size

Scleroderma

These are the "hard-skinned" puffballs, as the name implies, in which the gleba very soon becomes dull lilac to violaceous umber. They are very common at least east of the Great Plains, but the habitat varies with the species, as one would expect. While some fruit in dry sandy soil, others fruit in wet areas, such as in and along bogs. Species in this genus frequently cause gastrointestinal disturbances and should not be consumed in quantity.

Key to Species

1. Fruiting bodies usually on wet humus in deciduous woods, along or in bogs, etc.; opening variously . . . . 277. *Scleroderma citrinum*
1. Fruiting bodies almost buried in sand and splitting radially to expose the spore mass . . . . 278. *S. flavidum*

Scleroderma citrinum   277

Identification marks   The color is dingy ochraceous to brownish yellow or pale leather color, but not (or only rarely) the true yellow its name implies. The interior becomes dark violaceous to purplish before the fruiting body is half grown—a feature of a number of species of this genus. The pattern of the warts or scales over the surface is an important field character in its general aspects. The fruiting body is 2.5–9 cm broad or thick.

Edibility   Not recommended. It is edible for some people but not for others, and is low-grade at best.

When and where   It is the most common of all the hard-skinned puffballs. It is found during the summer and fall at or near the edges of bogs, on rotten logs in conifer and hardwood forests, and along old roads. It is widely distributed in the forested areas of North America.

Spores   9–12 (13) μm, including the ornamentation, globose, verrucose-reticulate, dark brown.

277   *Scleroderma citrinum*   About natural size

Observations In the previous edition of this *Guide* the name *S. aurantium* was used. It is now considered a synonym of *S. citrinum*. *Citrinum* means lemon yellow.

278   Scleroderma flavidum

Identification marks The upper surface of the fruiting body is more or less smooth, and the whole structure is at first buried in the sand. The base is a mass of fibers (mycelium) binding sand to the extent of forming a stalklike structure. The top of the fruiting body opens up to form raylike segments somewhat like the rays in a *Geastrum*.

Edibility Not recommended.

When and where East of the Great Plains it is found in sandy areas during late summer and fall. It is common in its habitat but overlooked by many collectors because most of the time a hump in the sand is the only indication of its presence. Overwintered specimens are commonly encountered in the spring.

Spores 9–14 μm including the spines which are 1–1.5 μm long, globose, dark violaceous in mass.

Observations *Flavidum* means yellowish.

278   *Scleroderma flavidum*   About two-thirds natural size

279   Crucibulum laeve
(Bird's Nest Fungus)

Identification marks The common name is actually applied to a group of fungi in which the fruiting body, with its packages of spores, in some measure resembles a bird's nest with eggs in it. The "eggs" are the packages of spores (peridioles) and are dispersed as a unit. In *C. laeve* a thin layer of tissue covers the "nest" at first, and the peridioles are lens-shaped. The outer surface of the "nest" is velvety to fibrillose, and the color varies from tawny yellow to cinnamon brown.

Edibility   Inedible, but probably not poisonous.

When and where   It occurs gregarious to scattered on woody debris such as elderberry branches, old berry canes, fallen branches of willow trees, and old sawdust piles. It is common and widely distributed, and usually fruits during the late summer and fall.

Spores   (4) 7–10 x 4–6 μm, hyaline, and thick-walled.

Observations   *Crucibulum* means a crucible, and *laeve* means smooth.

279   *Crucibulum laeve*   About two-thirds natural size

Rhizopogon idahoensis   **280**

Identification marks   This is a whitish, large *Rhizopogon* with conspicuous strands (rhizomorphs) of hyphae over the surface. The fruiting bodies slowly become wood brown (grayish brown) as they mature; they tend to stain grayish lilac where injured. KOH on a fresh surface stains it bluish black.

280a   *Rhizopogon idahoensis*   Natural size

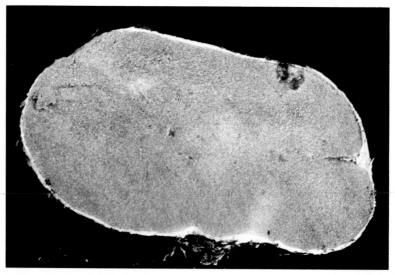

280b *Rhizopogon idahoensis*   Natural size

The spores are amyloid, an unusual character for species of this genus. The fruiting bodies are large, some being 6–7 cm thick.

Edibility   We have no data on it.

When and where   It fruits during late summer to fall under conifers in the Rocky Mountains. It fruits prolifically after heavy late summer and early fall rains.

Spores   (6.5) 7–9 x 2.3–3 μm, oblong in face view, hyaline in KOH, smooth, amyloid.

Observations   It is named for the state of Idaho, the area in which so many unusual species of *Rhizopogon* have been found.

Phallales

The members of this order are commonly called stinkhorns because the minute spores are mixed with a slime to form a foul-smelling mass on the fruiting body. The smell attracts insects, which carry the spores away on their feet. The cap, when one is present, is more like a thimble than the spreading caps of many gilled mushrooms.

Key to Species

1.   Stalk with a cap at apex on which the slimy gleba is borne . . . .
. . . . 282. *Phallus ravenelii*
1.   Stalk without a cap, the slimy gleba simply plastered on its surface
near the apex . . . . 281. *Mutinus caninus*

---

281   Mutinus caninus

Identification marks   The expanded fruiting body consists of a volva, which represents the remains of the egg, and a pointed column, which near the apex is smeared with a gelatinous mass of slime and spores. The spore mass is lifted up by the elongation of the column and is exposed where flies and other winged insects can find it readily. The insects are attracted by the foul odor, come and wallow in the slime, and go away carrying numerous spores on or in their bodies.

Edibility   The eggs are reported to be non-poisonous—but who cares?

When and where   It fruits solitary to gregarious on grassy ground, around rotten wood, compost piles, etc., in the summer and fall. It is widely distributed east of the Rocky Mountains, but, like other phalloids, it is much more abundant southward.

Spores   4–7 x 2–2.5 μm.

Observations   A white variety has been found both in Oregon and in Michigan.

281   *Mutinus caninus*   About natural size

Phallus ravenelii   **282**

Identification marks   The odor of decaying flesh is a striking feature of this and other stinkhorns, as they are commonly called. *P. ravenelii* has a cap with a granulose surface at the apex of the column or stalk. The granulose nature of the surface is best seen when the slime has been dissipated. There is no skirt or veil hanging down from the underside of the cap, and, as a rule, the eggs have a lilac pink tone.

Edibility   As far as we know not poisonous, but we doubt that it will ever be popular.

When and where   It is common around old sawdust piles, around decaying wood in the forest, and where wood has been used as a fill. It fruits during late summer and fall east of the Great Plains, where it is not uncommon.

Spores   2–3.5 x 1.5 μm.

Observations   The small size of the spores of most phalloids is considered to be the result of evolution to favor dispersal of the species by insect vectors. This species was named in honor of H. W. Ravenel (1814–87), an early American mycologist who collected mainly in South Carolina.

282   *Phallus ravenelii*   Slightly reduced

Hints for the Mushroom Collector

Where to Find Selected Mushrooms
(According to Season)

LATE WINTER AND SPRING

Agaricus bitorquis (formerly *A. rodmani*)—On hard-packed soil along city streets, in school yards, and similar places.

Clavicorona pyxidata—On wood of poplar (aspen), but not restricted to one genus of hardwoods.

Coprinus atramentarius—On lawns (but coming from buried wood), or obviously on or near a dead tree or stump.

Coprinus micaceus—Same as for *C. atramentarius*.

Flammulina velutipes—On dead or dying elm trees, also on poplar.

Galerina autumnalis—On wood of both hardwoods and conifers; it fruits both during the spring and fall, and is poisonous.

Gyromitra gigas (formerly *Helvella gigas*)—Near melting snow banks in conifer forests in the mountains, and, in early to late April, in northern areas generally.

Marasmius oreades—On lawns, in pastures and on grassy places generally.

Morchella angusticeps—In conifer forests, but common under aspen and less frequent under other hardwoods.

Morchella crassipes and *M. esculenta*—Around dying elms, but in various types of habitat in addition.

Mycena overholtsii—On rotting conifer logs in mountain forests of the western states; no data on edibility but to be regarded as dangerous.

Pleurotus ostreatus—The whitish variant, mostly on poplar.

LATE SPRING AND EARLY SUMMER

Boletus variipes—In sandy oak woods.

Cantharellus cibarius and *C. cinnabarinus*—Open oak woods, beech-maple stands, and in brushy places, often along old roads in the woods.

Dentinum repandum—In moist places in deciduous and conifer forests.

Grifola umbellata (formerly *Polypilus*)—Under hardwood trees, especially oak and beech.

Lactarius volemus—Under hardwoods, especially oak and beech.

Leccinum insigne and *L. aurantiacum* (formerly *Boletus*)—The former is very abundant under poplar, the latter under conifers or, less frequently, under hardwoods.

Suillus pictus (formerly *Boletinus*)—Under white pine.

LATE SUMMER AND FALL INTO EARLY WINTER

This is the time when mushrooms fruit in great abundance and variety. No listing is given for this period. Consult the list of better edible mushroom species.

Edible Mushrooms for Beginners

Agaricus campestris

Boletus edulis

Boletus mirabilis

Calvatia gigantea

Cantharellus cibarius

Clavicorona pyxidata

Coprinus comatus

Coprinus micaceus

Craterellus fallax

Dentinum repandum

Grifola frondosa

Hericium, all species

Lactarius deliciosus

Lactarius indigo

Lactarius volemus

Lycoperdon perlatum

Morchella angusticeps

Morchella esculenta

Pleurotus ostreatus

Sparassis radicata

Suillus granulatus

Suillus luteus

Mushrooms Associated
with Certain Trees

Tree	Mushroom
Aspen (poplar)	*Flammulina velutipes* (wood decay)
	Lactarius controversus (mycorrhiza)
	Leccinum insigne (mycorrhiza)
	Pholiota squarrosa (wood decay)
	Pleurotus ostreatus (wood decay)
Birch	*Lactarius torminosus* (mycorrhiza)
	Leccinum atrostipitatum (mycorrhiza)
	Leccinum scabrum (mycorrhiza)
Larch	*Fuscoboletinus spectabilis* (mycorrhiza)
	Suillus cavipes (mycorrhiza)
Pine	*Armillaria ponderosa* (mycorrhiza)
	Armillaria zelleri (mycorrhiza)
	Chroogomphus vinicolor (mycorrhiza)
	Suillus granulatus (mycorrhiza)
	Suillus luteus (mycorrhiza)
	Suillus pictus (mycorrhiza)

Better Edible Mushroom Species

Agaricus augustus
Agaricus bitorquis
Agaricus campestris
Agaricus pattersonae
Armillaria ponderosa
Armillariella mellea
   (do not eat it raw)
Boletus edulis
Boletus mirabilis
Boletus zelleri
Calvatia gigantea
Cantharellus cibarius
Cantharellus subalbidus
Clavicorona pyxidata
Clitocybe nuda
Coprinus comatus
Craterellus fallax
Dentinum repandum
Fistulina hepatica
Grifola frondosa
Gyromitra gigas
Gyroporus castaneus
Gyroporus cyanescens

Hericium (all species)
Lactarius corrugis
Lactarius deliciosus
Lactarius volemus
Lepiota procera
Lepiota rhacodes
Marasmius oreades
Morchella angusticeps
Morchella crassipes
Morchella esculenta
Pholiota squarrosoides
Phylloporus rhodoxanthus
Pleurotus ostreatus
Pluteus cervinus
   and *P. magnus*
Polyozellus multiplex
Rozites caperata
Russula variata
Russula virescens
Sparassis radicata
Suillus brevipes
Suillus granulatus
Suillus luteus

Microscopic Characters

These figures illustrate a few of the characters basic to the study of mushroom spores.

Figure 1 represents the basidium in the Tremellales. The young stage (probasidium) is a single cell, but as it matures two walls form which are roughly parallel to the long axis of the cell, thus producing a 4-celled apparatus (shown to the right in cross section). From the apex of each of these cells an elongated tube extends through the jellylike fruiting body to the surface, and the basidiospores are formed at the tips.

Figure 2 represents the basidium of the Auriculariales. It is essentially a septate hypha in which each cell produces a spore. It is a basidium because the spores are those of the sexual stage of the fungus.

Figure 3 illustrates the most common type of basidium, a single cell cut off from the parent hypha by a cross wall at the base. The shape does not vary much in the thousands of species with this type of basidium. The left spore is shown in profile view, the right spore in face view.

Figure 4 represents an inoperculate ascus containing ascospores. The spores in this type of ascus would be squirted out through the pore at the apex.

Figure 5 illustrates an empty operculate ascus with the lid (operculum) open —an indication that the spores have been discharged.

Figure 6 illustrates an ellipsoid spore in profile view with ornamentation in the form of isolated warts. Based on *Lactarius deceptivus*.

Figure 7 represents a globose spore with ornamentation in the form of a complete reticulum. Based on *Lactarius volemus*.

Figure 8 represents a spore with ornamentation as a partial to incomplete reticulum. Based on *Lactarius thyinos*.

Figure 9 represents two spores of *Galerina autumnalis* showing the wrinkled surface of the spore and the lack of ornamentation in the region above the apiculus. This region is often termed the plage or suprahilar depression.

Figure 10 illustrates a spore of *Psathyrella foenisecii* ornamented with irregular platelike areas.

Figure 11 illustrates a sausage-shaped spore. Based on *Phyllotopsis nidulans*.

Figure 12 illustrates a profile (left) and face view (right) of a spore with an apical or germ pore. Based on *Stropharia rugoso-annulata*.

Figure 13 shows a square to angular spore. Based on *Entoloma salmoneum*.

Figure 14 shows a profile view of an inequilateral spore; this type of spore is common in the boletes. Based on *Leccinum scabrum*.

Figure 15 illustrates a boat-shaped spore in face view. Based on *Boletus frostii*.

Figure 16 represents a *Clitopilus* spore in face view and from the apex. Note that these spores have shallow grooves going the length of the spore.

Figure 17 represents two spores of *Mitrula elegans*; one spore is 2-celled.

Figure 18 represents two views of a spore of *Boletellus russellii*; one view is from the apex of the spore, the other a side view showing the striate condition of the spores.

Figure 19 represents a *Discina* spore with apical projections and the surface minutely wrinkled.

Figure 20 represents a spore of *Helvella crispa* showing oil droplets in the spore.

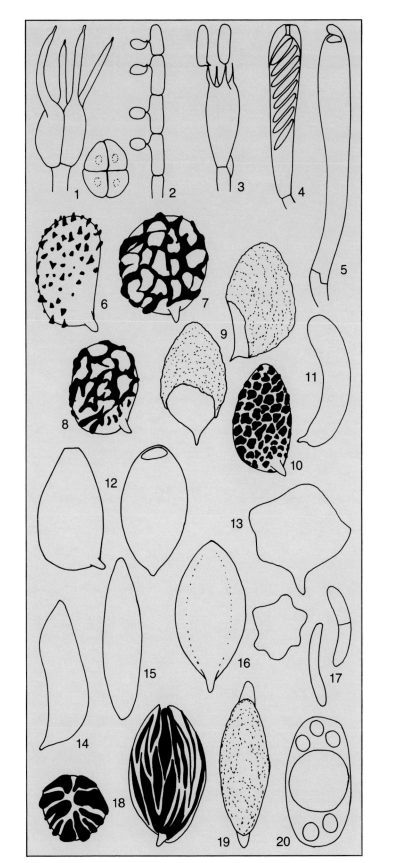

Glossary

ABNORMAL (of a specimen): not properly developed. Used to describe a difference which is very pronounced but not inherited, such as the development of gills on top of a cap in a gilled mushroom.

ABRUPT: terminating suddenly or sharply differentiated. Used to describe the base of a stalk or apex of a bulb.

ACRID (taste of a raw mushroom): causing a biting or prickling sensation on the tip of the tongue.

ACUTE: pointed; (of gills) sharp-edged.

ADNATE: (of gills) bluntly attached to the stalk; (of the pellicle on the cap) not separable.

AGARIC: a fruiting body of a gilled mushroom (used as a short term for a member of the Agaricales).

ALVEOLATE (of a surface): with shallow broad pits.

AMYLOID (of spores or tissues): bluish to violet when treated with iodine.

ANASTOMOSING (of gills, ridges, wrinkles, etc.): connecting crosswise to form angular areas or pits bounded by connecting lines.

ANNULUS: the ring of tissue left on the stalk from the breaking of the partial veil.

APEX (pl. apices): the tip of the part described.

APICAL PORE: *see* germ pore.

APOTHECIUM: the generally cuplike or saucerlike fruiting body of Discomycetes.

APPENDICULATE (of the cap margin): with pieces of the veil hanging along the margin.

APPRESSED (of fibrils or hairs on a cap or stalk): lying flat against the surface.

AREOLATE: cracked into more or less hexagonal areas, much like a dried-out mud flat.

ASCOSPORE: a spore produced in an ascus.

ASCUS (pl. asci): a cell *in* which spores are formed following fusion of two nuclei and division of the resulting fusion nucleus.

AVELLANEOUS (a color): pale gray tinged with pink.

AZONATE (of the surface of a cap): lacking concentric bands of a different appearance than the remainder of the cap.

BASIDIOCARP: a fruiting body which bears its spores on basidia.

BASIDIUM (pl. basidia): a structure *on* which spores are formed following fusion and division of the nucleus; usually a single cell in most mushrooms.

BEADED (of gills): the condition in which the gill edges have droplets of a clear liquid on them.

BROAD (of gills): a relative term used to describe the depth of the gills. It is contrasted with *moderately broad* and *narrow*.

BUFF (a color): pale yellow toned with gray, i.e., a dingy pale yellow.

BULBOUS (of a stalk): having an oval to abrupt enlargement (bulb) at the base.

CAMPANULATE (of a cap): bell-shaped.

CANESCENT: having a bloom or appearing as if coated with a light hoarfrost.

CAP: the umbrellalike expansion on the apex of the stalk in a mushroom. It bears the gills, teeth, or pores on the underside. *Pileus* is the technical term for it.

CAPILLITIUM: the threadlike elements mixed in with the spores in a ripe puffball.

CAPITATE: provided with a cap or head.

CARPOPHOROIDS: fleshy masses of fungous tissue of irregular size and shape and lacking a true hymenium.

CAULOCYSTIDIA: sterile cells occurring on the surface of the stalk.

CAUSTIC POTASH: see KOH.

CELLS (of fungi): the living protoplasmic units into which the hyphae are divided.

CELLULAR: made up of cells.

CESPITOSE (or caespitose): growing in clusters with the bases attached to each other.

CLAVATE: club-shaped; as applied to the stalk it means thickened evenly to the base.

CLAVATE-BULBOUS (of a stalk): with a more abrupt thickening at the base than is indicated by just clavate.

CLOSE (of gills): a relative term to indicate the spacing of gills—*see* crowded.

COLLAR: a close-fitting roll of universal veil tissue around the apex of the bulb in an *Amanita*.

COLUMELLA: a column or vein of sterile tissue extending into or through the spore-bearing tissue; mostly in the Secotiaceae where the upper part of the stalk is termed the columella or the whole a "stipe-columella."

CONFLUENT (of stalk and cap): continuous with each other; merging with no perceptible differentiation.

CONTEXT: the flesh of the cap and stalk (regardless of whether the consistency is soft, tough, or woody).

CONVEX (of a cap): rounded like an inverted bowl.

CONVOLUTED: wrinkled into large folds.

CORTINA: a cobwebby partial veil made up of loosely arranged silky fibrils.

CROWDED (of gills): spaced very close together. *Crowded*, *close*, *subdistant*, and *distant* are the four relative terms used to describe gill spacing.

CUTICLE (of a cap): the differentiated surface zone. Not all species have such a layer.

CUTIS: a type of cuticle on a cap or stalk composed of dry interwoven hyphae.

CYSTIDIUM (pl. cystidia): a sterile cell with some special feature such as size, thickened wall, content, or shape. Cystidia are common in the hymenium of many species but may appear on other parts of Basidiomycete mushrooms as well.

DECURRENT (of gills): extending downward on the stalk.

DEPRESSED (of a cap): having the central part sunken slightly below the margin.

DEXTRINOID: taking on a reddish brown to vinaceous red color in Melzer's solution or other iodine-containing solutions.

DISC (of a cap): the central part of the surface of the cap extending roughly halfway to the cap margin.

DISCOMYCETE: those Ascomycetes with fleshy fruiting bodies that are generally cup-shaped or saucer-shaped.

DISTANT (of gills): spaced far apart. *See also* crowded.

ECCENTRIC: to one side of center, off center.

EGG (of a fungous fruiting body): the somewhat egg-shaped button stage enclosed by a universal veil, as in a stinkhorn or *Amanita*.

ELEVATED (of a cap margin): raised slightly so it is above the disc of the cap.

ELLIPSOID: a three dimensional object with an elliptic outline.

ELLIPTIC: shaped like a compressed circle with curving sides. Contrasts with oblong, where the sides are parallel.

ENTIRE (of gill edges): even, the edge not cut into small projections or teeth.

EVEN (of cap surface): with no depressions or elevations.

FAIRY RING: a naturally occurring circle of fruiting bodies of any mushroom.

FALSE VEIL: a tissue that grows out from the margin of the cap but does not become intergrown with the stalk, though the remains of the veil may form a ring around the stalk. Found principally in the Boletaceae.

FARINACEOUS (of odor or taste): like that of fresh meal.

FeSO$_4$: the chemical abbreviation for an iron salt. The usual concentration used for spot tests is about ten percent ferrous sulphate in water. A positive reaction on the tissue of the fruiting body is green to olive, olive gray, or, in some fungi, pinkish. A strong reaction is olive black. In age the solution will become rusty orange and have a precipitate, but is still useful.

FETID (of odor): disagreeable, repulsive, resembling rotting meat.

FIBRILLOSE: covered with appressed hairs or threads (fibrils) more or less evenly disposed.

FIBROUS (of stalk): composed of tough stringy tissue.

FILIFORM: threadlike.

FLESH (of a mushroom): the tissue of the fruiting body; also called context.

FLESH COLOR: the color of caucasian skin.

FLESHY: soft in consistency and decaying readily; contrasts with woody and membranaceous.

FLOCCOSE-SCALY (of a cap): provided with tufts of a woolly nature, usually remains of the universal veil.

FLORA: the species of plants occurring naturally in a region. The flora of a region includes all the plants. However, we often speak of the agaric flora, the moss flora, the fern flora, etc. Students of the seed plants often misuse the term by saying the flora of such and such a place when they mean only the vascular-plant flora.

FREE (of gills): not attached to the stalk at any time during their development.

FRUITING BODY: the part of the fungous plant which produces and liberates the spores. We use the term *mushroom* to mean the same thing in this book.

FURFURACEOUS: roughened with branlike particles.

FUSCOUS (a color): the color of a storm cloud varying to a dark smoky brown, with variable amounts of violet present.

GELATINOUS: jellylike in consistency.

GENUS (pl. genera): the first major grouping above the rank of species in plant classification, e.g., *Cortinarius*, *Helvella*. Genera are composed of species having certain characteristics in common, or they may consist of single unique species.

GERMINATE (of a spore): to begin vegetative growth by sending out a hypha.

GERM PORE: in some species of fungi (particularly those with thick-walled spores), a specialized area through which germination occurs; often seen as a lighter area at or near the apex of the spore.

GILLED FUNGI: mushrooms with gills.

GILLS: the knifeblade-like, radially arranged plates of tissue on the underside of gilled mushroom caps. The technical term for these is *lamellae* (sing. *lamella*).

GLABROUS: bald, without hair. The term *smooth* is not necessarily an equivalent.

GLANDULAR DOTS (on stalks of some boletes): slightly sticky spots of a darker color (usually) than the rest of the stalk.

GLEBA (of puffballs): the mass of spores plus some filaments of sterile tissue (capillitium) which make up the main volume of most puffballs. In fungi related to puffballs, the mass of spore-bearing tissue which is usually enclosed during part or all of its development.

GLOBOSE: globular, spherical.

GLUTINOUS: covered with a slimy or sticky layer.

GRANULOSE: covered with granules, either free or attached.

GREGARIOUS: growing in groups but with the specimens separate at the base; a relative term describing a condition between *scattered* and *cespitose*.

HABIT: manner of growth, i.e., solitary, scattered, gregarious, or cespitose.

HABITAT: the type of place in which a plant naturally grows.

HYALINE: transparent or translucent.

HYGROPHANOUS (of a cap): changing color markedly on fading.

HYMENIFORM: with the cells arranged in a palisade, as in a hymenium.

HYMENIUM: the spore-bearing layer of tissue on the surface of gills, teeth, tubes, etc., the spore-bearing cells being arranged in a palisade.

HYMENOPHORE: the part of the fruiting body that bears the hymenium.

HYPHAE (sing. hypha): the collection of individual threads of the vegetative part of the fungous plant and the fruiting bodies.

IMBRICATE (of scales): overlapping one another like shingles on a roof.

INAMYLOID: neither dextrinoid nor amyloid in Melzer's solution. The material remains uncolored to light rusty orange (the color of the solution itself).

INEQUILATERAL (of spores): a subfusiform spore in which the two halves, as seen in profile view, are not of the same configuration.

INFERIOR: below another part.

INNATE (of fibrils or scales): attached, not readily removable.

INOPERCULATE (of Ascomycetes): the situation in which the asci lack a lid or operculum; they may open by a pore to release the spores.

INTERVENOSE (of gills): with conspicuous veins between the gills.

IRON SALTS: *see* FeSO₄.

IXO-: prefix meaning slimy.

KOH: Potassium hydroxide. We use a 2.5 percent to 3 percent aqueous solution. It can be applied directly to the fruiting body to ascertain color changes, or used as a mounting medium to revive dried material. It is also used to ascertain color changes of spores, hyphal walls, and pigment deposits.

LACUNOSE: with broad pits or holes.

LAMELLAE: technical term for the gills of a mushroom.

LARVAE: immature wormlike stages of insects such as flies; often found in mushrooms. They make small tunnels or holes in the flesh.

LATERAL: attached by one side.

LATEX: a juice, often milky but sometimes colored, which is extruded when the fruiting body is injured (at least when young and fresh).

LIGNICOLOUS: wood-loving, growing on wood.

LUBRICOUS: having a buttery feel.

MARGIN: the edge, i.e., the outermost part of the cap near the edge and including it; the free edge of a cap, or the free edge of a gill.

MELZER'S SOLUTION (reagent): an iodine solution used to test spores and tissue. Composed of 1.5 gms potassium iodide (KI), 0.5 gm iodine, 22 gms chloral hydrate, and 20 gms water.

MILD (of taste): lacking a distinct taste, bland.

MUSHROOM: the somewhat umbrellalike fruiting body of fleshy fungi, or, as used here, any fleshy fungus fruiting body. The term (in North America) applies to both edible and poisonous species. Poisonous species elsewhere are sometimes called toadstools.

MYCELIOID: moldy in texture, as if covered with mycelium.

MYCELIUM: the collective term for all the threads making up the vegetative part of an individual fungous plant.

NAKED (of a cap or stalk): devoid of any type of covering; glabrous.

NARROW (of gills): a relative term, the opposite of broad, indicating the depth of gills.

NON-AMYLOID: not amyloid, i.e., not becoming bluish to violet in iodine.

OBTUSE: blunt, not pointed.

OPERCULATE (of an ascus): having the opening or mouth covered by a lid.

ORNAMENTATION (of spores): the material and its distribution over the spore surface, such as dots, lines, and various patterns.

PALLID (a color): very pale; when used alone it means an off-white.

PARASITIC: the condition of one organism (the parasite) living on and getting nourishment from another (the host) to the detriment of the host.

PARTIAL VEIL: the inner veil which extends from the margin of the cap and at first covers the gills or pores. Contrasted to the universal veil.

PEDICEL: a narrow base or stalk.

PELLICLE: a thin gelatinous skin over the cap of some mushrooms.

PENDANT: hanging down.

PERIDIOLE (in bird's nest fungi): the small pill-like structures in the "nest" consisting of a group of spores with a wall around them.

PERIDIUM (of puffballs): the wall, often layered, of the spore sack.

PERITHECIA (sing. perithecium): in Ascomycetes, the flask-shaped structures, opening by a pore at the apex of a neck, in which asci develop. The spores from the asci are ultimately forced through the neck and out through the pore.

PILEUS: the technical term for the cap of a mushroom.

PITTED: covered with distinct depressions.

PLIANT: flexible.

PLICATE: folded, pleated like a fan.

PORES: the minute to distinct holes in the layer of tissue on the underside of the cap, lined with hymenium. They contrast with gills and spines.

POROID: having pores.

POTASSIUM HYDROXIDE: *see* KOH.

PRUINOSE: appearing as if frosted lightly by minute particles.

PSEUDORHIZA: a rootlike process which often extends deep into the ground (in actuality it grows up to the surface; the fruiting body then forms on top of it).

RAPHANOID (of taste): radishlike.

RHIZOMORPH: a stringlike or thin ropelike aggregation of hyphae; part of the spawn of the mushroom plant.

RING: same as an annulus.

RIVULOSE: having fine wavy grooves or cracks.

RUGOSE: wrinkled.

SAPROPHYTIC: the condition of an organism living on and being nourished by dead organic matter. Contrast with parasitic.

SCALES (of cap or stalk): torn portions of cuticle or veil.

SCATTERED (of habit): fruiting bodies growing scattered over a relatively wide area, not grouped together.

SCROBICULATE: having large, shiny, depressed spots or areas, as on the stalk of some species of *Lactarius*.

SECOTIOID: a fruiting body resembling an unexpanded agaric or bolete fruiting body but not forcibly discharging its spores; resembling the fruiting body of a species of *Secotium*.

SESSILE: lacking a stalk.

SERRATE: notched or toothed on the edge.

SHEATH: boot, usually referring to veil remnants on the lower part of the stalk. When such a covering is present, the stalk is said to be peronate.

SHELVING (of fruiting bodies): arranged in an overlapping fashion like shelves.

SIMPLE (of fruiting bodies): unbranched.

SMOOTH (of a surface): even, lacking wrinkles or projections.

SORDID: dirty or dingy in appearance.

SPAWN: same as mycelium.

SPECIES: populations of individual organisms representing a single kind; that is, having certain characters in common which distinguish those populations from all other organisms.

SPINES: pointed conelike teeth.

SPONGY (of flesh): soft and tending to be water-soaked.

SPORE DEPOSIT: a mass of spores deposited naturally (or from a mushroom so set up that it will shed spores), which is visible to the naked eye.

SPORES: the reproductive bodies of fungi and other lower plants. They perform the same reproductive function as seeds but are completely different structurally.

SQUAMULES: small scales.

STALK: the stemlike portion of a mushroom; if a stalk is present, it supports the cap. The technical term is *stipe*.

STERIGMATA (sing. sterigma): the prongs of the basidium on the apex of which the spores are formed.

STERILE BASE: the basal region of some puffballs which does not produce spores; it is often chambered.

STIPE: technical term for stalk.

STIPITATE: having a stipe or stalk.

STRIAE: radiating lines or furrows on a mushroom cap, or the longitudinal lines on a stalk.

STRIATE: having striae.

STRIGOSE: having long, coarse hairs.

STUFFED (of a stalk): having the center filled with a distinct pith which may break down leaving a hollow.

SUB-: a prefix meaning almost, somewhat, or under.

SULCATE: rather deeply grooved but not plicate.

SUPERFICIAL: merely resting on the surface, not attached.

SUPERIOR (ring or annulus): attached above the middle of the stalk.

TAWNY (a color): about the color of a lion.

TERRESTRIAL: growing on the ground, contrasts with lignicolous.

TOADSTOOL: a name commonly applied to mushrooms; toadstools may be either edible or poisonous according to American usage.

TOMENTUM: a covering of soft hair.

TRAMA: internal tissues, as of the cap, stalk, or hymenophore; the technical term used for such regions when discussing the anatomy of a fruiting body.

TUBE MOUTH: the tissue around the opening of a tube on the underside of the cap of pore fungi.

TUBERCLE: a wartlike or knoblike outgrowth.

UMBER (a color): tobacco brown or darker.

UMBO (of a cap): a raised conic or convex area at the center of the cap.

UMBONATE: furnished with an umbo.

UNEQUAL (of gills): of different lengths—some reach the stalk, others do not.

UNIVERSAL VEIL: the veil which envelops the young fruiting body in some mushrooms; it is an outer layer of tissue which is distinct from the cap and stalk.

VARIANT: an unofficial designation for a collection differing slightly from the type but for which the user of the term does not want to use a formal designation. One may speak of variants of a species or of a variety.

VEIL: a layer of tissue—see partial veil and universal veil.

VENTRICOSE: swollen at the middle.

VERRUCOSE: warty.

VINACEOUS (a color): the color of a red wine or a paler red.

VIRGATE: streaked.

VISCID: sticky to the touch.

VOLVA: the remains of the universal veil left around the base of the mushroom after the veil has broken.

WARTS (on a cap or stipe): small squatty or pyramidal chunks of the universal veil tissue.

ZONATE: marked with concentric bands (zones) of a different appearance from the remainder of the surface.

Selected Books on Mushrooms and Related Fungi

Mushroom Terminology and Nomenclature
MILLER, O. K., AND DAVID F. FARR (1975)
An Index to the Common Fungi of North America (Synonymy and Common Names).
Vaduz, Liechtenstein: Bibliotheca Mycologica 44. Pp. 1–206.
SNELL, WALTER H., AND ESTHER A. DICK (1957)
A Glossary of Mycology.
Cambridge, Mass.: Harvard University Press. Pp. 1–171.

Mushroom Growing
CHANG, S. T., AND W. A. HAYES (EDITORS) (1979)
The Biology and Cultivation of Edible Mushrooms.
New York: Academic Press. Pp. i–xxii plus 1–891: with figs.
HARRIS, BOB (1976)
Growing Wild Mushrooms.
Berkeley, Calif.: Wingbow Press. Pp. 1–87; 16 color pls.
SINGER, ROLF (1961)
Mushrooms and Truffles: Botany, Cultivation and Utilization.
New York: Interscience Publishers, Inc. Pp. 1–272. This is an excellent book on the background of mushroom growing.

Technical Literature
(Only fairly modern studies in English are included)
COKER, W. C., AND ALMA HOLLAND BEERS (1943)
The Boletaceae of North Carolina.
Chapel Hill, N.C.: The University of North Carolina Press. Pp. 1–96; 65 figs.
CORNER, E. J. H. (1950)
A Monograph of Clavaria and Allied Genera.
London: Oxford University Press. Pp. 1–740; 16 pls.
CORNER, E. J. H. (1970)
Supplement to "A Monograph of Clavaria and Allied Genera."
Lehre, Germany: J. Cramer. Pp. 1–297; 3 pls.
DENNIS, R. W. G. (1978)
British Ascomycetes.
Vaduz, Liechtenstein: J. Cramer. Pp. 1–585; 44 color pls.; 31 figs.
GRUND, D. W., AND K. A. HARRISON (1976)
Nova Scotian Boletes.
Vaduz, Liechtenstein: J. Cramer. Pp. 1–283; 68 pls.; 79 figs.
HARRISON, K. A. (1961)
The Stipitate Hydnums of Nova Scotia.
Ottawa: Canada Department of Agriculture. Publication 1099. Pp. 1–60; 3 pls.
HESLER, L. R., AND ALEXANDER H. SMITH (1963)
North American Species of Hygrophorus.
Knoxville, Tenn.: The University of Tennessee Press. Pp. 1–416; 126 figs.
HESLER, L. R., AND ALEXANDER H. SMITH (1979)
The North American Species of Lactarius.
Ann Arbor, Mich.: The University of Michigan Press. Pp. 1–814; 154 pls.; 249 figs; 147 spore pls.
LARGENT, DAVID L. (1977)
The Genus Leptonia on the Pacific Coast of the United States.
Vaduz, Liechtenstein: J. Cramer. Pp. 1–286; 94 figs.
MARR, CURRIE D., AND DANIEL E. STUNTZ (1973)
Ramaria of Western Washington.
Lehre, Germany: J. Cramer. Pp. 1–232; 109 pls.
MCKENNY, MARGARET, AND DANIEL E. STUNTZ (1971)
The Savory Wild Mushroom (Revised edition).
Seattle, Wash.: The University of Washington Press. Pp. 1–242; 32 color pls.; 156 figs.

OVERHOLTS, L. O. (1953)
The Polyporaceae of the United States, Alaska and Canada.
   Ann Arbor, Mich.: The University of Michigan Press. Pp. 1–466; 132 pls.
SHAFFER, ROBERT L. (1968)
Keys to Genera of Higher Fungi (2nd edition).
   Ann Arbor, Mich.: University of Michigan Biological Station. Pp. 1–131.
SINGER, ROLF (1975)
The Agaricales in Modern Taxonomy.
   Vaduz, Liechtenstein: J. Cramer. Pp. 1–912; 80 pls.
SMITH, ALEXANDER H. (1947)
North American Species of Mycena.
   Ann Arbor, Mich.: The University of Michigan Press. Pp. 1–521; 99 pls.;
   55 figs.
SMITH, ALEXANDER H. (1951)
Puffballs and Their Allies in Michigan.
   Ann Arbor, Mich.: The University of Michigan Press. Pp. 1–131; 43 pls.
SMITH, ALEXANDER H. (1972)
The North American Species of Psathyrella.
   New York: Memoirs New York Botanical Garden 24. Pp. 1–633; 95 pls.;
   867 figs.
SMITH, ALEXANDER H., AND L. R. HESLER (1968)
The North American Species of Pholiota.
   Monticello, N.Y.: Lubrecht & Cramer. Pp. 1–402; 90 pls; 519 figs.
SMITH, ALEXANDER H., AND ROLF SINGER (1964)
A Monograph on the Genus Galerina Earle.
   New York: Hafner Publishing Co. Pp. 1–384; 20 pls.; 289 figs.
SMITH, ALEXANDER H., HELEN V. SMITH, AND NANCY S. WEBER (1979)
How to Know the Gilled Mushrooms.
   Dubuque, Iowa: Wm. C. Brown Co., Publishers. Pp. 1–334, 453 figs.
SMITH, ALEXANDER H., AND HARRY D. THIERS (1971)
The Boletes of Michigan.
   Ann Arbor, Mich.: The University of Michigan Press. Pp. 1–428; 157 pls.;
   133 figs.
SMITH, HELEN V., AND ALEXANDER H. SMITH (1973)
How to Know the Non-Gilled Fleshy Fungi.
   Dubuque, Iowa: Wm. C. Brown Co., Publishers. Pp. 1–401; 355 figs.
THIERS, HARRY D. (1975)
California Mushrooms: A Field Guide to the Boletes.
   New York: Hafner Press (a subsidiary of Macmillan Publishing Co.).
   Pp. 1–261; microfiche 1–54.

Mushroom Cookery
GRIGSON, JANE (1975)
The Mushroom Feast.
   New York: Alfred A. Knopf, Inc. Pp. i–xx plus 1–300.
MYCOLOGICAL SOCIETY OF SAN FRANCISCO, INC. (1963)
Kitchen Magic with Mushrooms.
   Berkeley, Calif.: Mycological Society of San Francisco, Inc. Pp. 1–95.
PUGET SOUND MYCOLOGICAL SOCIETY (P. SHIOSAKI, EDITOR) (1969)
Oft Told Mushroom Recipes.
   Seattle, Wash.: Puget Sound Mycological Society. Pp. 1–178.
   This volume has been republished by Pacific Search of Seattle, Wash., as
   Wild Mushroom Recipes.
TRACY, MARIAN (1968)
The Mushroom Cookbook.
   Garden City, N.Y.: Doubleday & Company, Inc. Pp. 1–99.

Mushroom Poisoning
LINCOFF, GARY, AND D. H. MITCHEL, M.D. (1977)
Toxic and Hallucinogenic Mushroom Poisoning.
   New York: Van Nostrand Reinhold Co. Pp. 1–267; 28 color figs.
RUMACK, BARRY H., AND EMANUEL SALZMAN (1978)
Mushroom Poisoning: Diagnosis and Treatment.
   West Palm Beach, Fla.: CRC Press Inc. Pp. 1–262; 51 color illus.

Index

Numbers in boldface are species numbers; those in italics indicate pages on which descriptions can be found.

Alexander H. Smith was Professor and Professor Emeritus of Botany at the University of Michigan. He studied mushrooms for nearly six decades until his death in 1986. He was well known for his enthusiasm and interest for mushrooms and mushroomers as well as for his many publications.

Nancy Smith Weber was an adjunct research investigator at the University of Michigan Herbarium for many years where she worked with her father. Since 1990 she has continued to study morels and related mushrooms in western North America as a member of the faculty of the Department of Forest Science at Oregon State University.